UNPACKING FRACTIONS

Includes 7 free web apps!

The fraction apps referenced in this book relate to the
chapter topics and are offered free of charge at
www.apps4math.com.
The apps are designed to enhance teaching and
facilitate learning while making both more enjoyable!

UNPACKING FRACTIONS

Classroom-Tested Strategies to Build Students' Mathematical Understanding

MONICA NEAGOY

ASCD
Alexandria, Virginia USA

NATIONAL COUNCIL OF
TEACHERS OF MATHEMATICS

1703 N. Beauregard St. • Alexandria, VA 22311 1714 USA
Phone: 800-933-2723 or 703-578-9600 • Fax: 703-575-5400
Website: www.ascd.org • E-mail: member@ascd.org
Author guidelines: www.ascd.org/write

NATIONAL COUNCIL OF
TEACHERS OF MATHEMATICS
www.nctm.org
publications@nctm.org

Deborah S. Delisle, *Executive Director,* Robert D. Clouse, *Managing Director, Digital Content & Publications;* Stefani Roth, *Publisher;* Genny Ostertag, *Director, Content Acquisitions;* Carol Collins, *Senior Acquisitions Editor;* Julie Houtz, *Director, Book Editing & Production;* Jamie Greene, *Associate Editor;* Thomas Lytle, *Senior Graphic Designer;* Mike Kalyan, *Director, Production Services;* Andrea Hoffman, *Senior Production Specialist;* Absolute Services, Typesetter

Published simultaneously by ASCD, 1703 North Beauregard Street, Alexandria, Virginia 22311, and the National Council of Teachers of Mathematics, 1906 Association Drive, Reston, VA 20191-1502.

PAPERBACK ISBN: 978-1-4166-2123-2   ASCD product #115071   n03/17
PDF E-BOOK ISBN: 978-1-4166-2125-6; see Books in Print for other formats.
NCTM stock #15368
Quantity discounts: 10–49, 10%; 50+, 15%; 1,000+, special discounts (e-mail programteam@ascd.org or call 800-933-2723, ext. 5773, or 703-575-5773). For desk copies, go to www.ascd.org/deskcopy.

Library of Congress Cataloging-in-Publication Data

Names: Neagoy, Monica.
Title: Unpacking fractions : classroom-tested strategies to build students' mathematical understanding / Monica Neagoy.
Description: Alexandria, Virginia : ASCD/National Council of Teachers of Mathematics, [2017] | Includes bibliographical references and index. | Description based on print version record and CIP data provided by publisher; resource not viewed.
Identifiers: LCCN 2017000276 (print) | LCCN 2016054420 (ebook) | ISBN 9781416621256 (PDF) | ISBN 9781416621232 (pbk.)
Subjects: LCSH: Fractions—Study and teaching (Elementary) | Fractions—Study and teaching (Middle school) | Fractions—Study and teaching (Secondary)
Classification: LCC QA137 (print) | LCC QA137 .N43 2017 (ebook) | DDC 372.7/2—dc23
LC record available at https://lccn.loc.gov/2017000276

26 25 24 23 22 21 20 19 18 17   1 2 3 4 5 6 7 8 9 10 11 12

UNPACKING FRACTIONS

Classroom-Tested Strategies to Build Students'
Mathematical Understanding

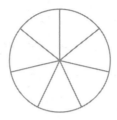

Foreword

by Gail Burrill, Past President of the National Council of
Teachers of Mathematics

Researchers have investigated the teaching and learning of fractions, ratios, and proportions for years. Despite this widespread and longstanding work, the average percent of correct responses, internationally, on PISA and TIMSS items related to fractions and ratios is typically between 30–50 percent. This is a signal that students in countries around the world struggle with these concepts. Although students in some countries do extremely well, scores in the United States are usually below average.

Early work on fractions suggested that part-whole partitioning was the overarching construct for thinking about fractions and ratios. *Unpacking Fractions* carefully considers the misconceptions and misunderstandings students bring to fractions from this approach and advocates that a fraction should be considered a number. Monica Neagoy also uses number lines as a central representational tool in teaching fraction concepts. These approaches are consistent with the Common Core State Standards for Mathematics and reinforced by research. Neagoy also emphasizes the role of the unit in thinking about fractions and considers the fundamental role of equivalence in analyzing the relationship between two fractions—a mathematical concept often ignored.

Perhaps the most critical message in this book is the importance of taking time to build conceptual understanding rather than rushing to teach algorithms to mastery. Neagoy explores how the notions of multiplicative and additive thinking relate to working with fractions and stresses the need for careful use of language in order to avoid constructing flawed mental images of fractions. In addition to developing a coherent picture of fractions, *Unpacking Fractions* includes valuable teaching tips and bridges to algebra that make the book a must-read resource for teachers—and one that will help them make a difference in how their students understand fractions and develop fractional thinking.

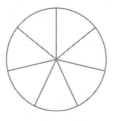

Introduction

The Challenge of Fractions

The losses that occur because of the gaps in conceptual understanding about fractions, ratios, and related topics are incalculable. The consequences of doing, rather than understanding, directly or indirectly affect a person's attitudes toward mathematics, enjoyment and motivation in learning, course selection in mathematics and science, achievement, career flexibility, and even the ability to fully appreciate some of the simplest phenomena in everyday life.

Susan J. Lamon (2012, p. xi)

The need for better teaching and learning of fractions is one of the few topics in the curriculum with which mathematics educators at every grade level would agree. At conference after conference, teachers bemoan students' resistance to fractions, the trouble they have making sense of them, and their ineptitude at solving problems involving fractions. I offer three fundamental reasons we must take a closer look at how we teach fractions in the United States:

1. *Fractions play a key role in students' feelings about mathematics.* For many students, fractions present a first mathematical

stumbling block. Students begin disliking mathematics when they must surrender their sense making and yield to sense-*less* memorization.

2. *Fractions are fundamental to school math and daily life.* Although fractions underpin many complex mathematical topics, including ratios, rates, percents, proportions, proportionality, linearity, and slope, their importance is not limited to mathematical study. As the quote on the previous page indicates, fluency with fractions is also required for many activities of daily life: following recipes, calculating discounts, comparing rates, converting measuring units, reading maps, investing money, and more.

3. *Fractions are foundational to success in algebra.* In its final report, *Foundations for Success*, the National Mathematics Advisory Panel (2008) concluded that (1) algebra is the gateway to success in high school and college, and (2) the main reason for U.S. students' failure in algebra is their poor proficiency with fractions. The worthy goal of "algebra for all" is not possible unless "fractions for all" is a reality. And in our present educational system, a solid grounding in algebra is foundational to a STEM career.

The selection of topics in this book, though by no means exhaustive, was made on the basis of research studies that address the teaching and learning of fractions, evidence from teacher practice, and my own work over the past 25 years with teachers, students, and parents (in both the United States and abroad) from which I have preserved recordings, questions, answers, insights, and samples of student work. It is my hope that readers will find that this book enhances their knowledge of fractions, deepens their appreciation of the complexity involved in teaching them, and perhaps even challenges some long-held beliefs.

Appreciate the Fraction Challenge

No area of elementary mathematics is as mathematically rich, cognitively complicated, and difficult to teach as fractions, ratios, and proportionality.
John P. Smith III (2002, p. 3)

In this section, I introduce the principal reasons fractions are so difficult for students. In Chapters 1 through 7, we'll look at ways to help students move past these difficulties, using strategies and problems that foster understanding of underlying concepts.

From Natural Numbers to Real Numbers

In order to tackle students' greatest challenges with fractions and to feel confident in trying new pedagogical moves, it is important for professionals who work with teachers or students in any grade to know how the number system builds from natural numbers to real numbers (Figure 0.1).

Natural numbers. During early childhood and up to about age 8, children engage with counting numbers, or *natural numbers*—also called *positive whole numbers*. Natural numbers are denoted in mathematics by the symbol $\mathbb{N}$. In set notation, we write $\mathbb{N} = \{1, 2, 3, 4...\}$. In the United

FIGURE 0.1
Grade-by-Grade Progression from Natural to Real Numbers

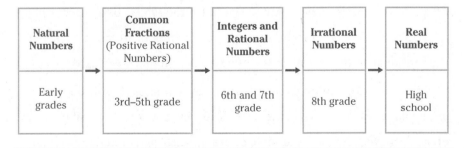

Natural Numbers	Common Fractions (Positive Rational Numbers)	Integers and Rational Numbers	Irrational Numbers	Real Numbers
Early grades	3rd–5th grade	6th and 7th grade	8th grade	High school

States, 0 is not considered a natural number, but the exclusion of 0 from the set of natural numbers is not universal.

Integers. The next important set of numbers is generated by appending to $\mathbb{N}$ zero and all the "opposites" or "negatives" (*additive inverses*) of the natural numbers. These numbers are called *integers*, denoted by the symbol $\mathbb{Z}$, and are typically introduced to students in the middle grades. In set notation, we write $\mathbb{Z} = \{ \ldots -4, -3, -2, -1, 0, 1, 2, 3, 4 \ldots \}$. Since the natural numbers are a subset of the integers, *every natural number is an integer*.

Rational numbers. The common fractions introduced in the upper elementary school grades, such as $\frac{1}{2}, \frac{3}{4}$, and $\frac{2}{3}$, are a subset of the *rational numbers*. Rational numbers, denoted by the symbol $\mathbb{Q}$, are numbers that can be expressed in the form $\frac{a}{b}$, where a and b are integers, provided $b \neq 0$. In set notation, we write $\mathbb{Q} = \left\{ \frac{a}{b} \text{, where } a \text{ and } b \text{ are members of } \mathbb{Z}, \text{ but } b \neq 0 \right\}$. Every rational number has an equivalent decimal form—for instance, $\frac{1}{2} = 0.5$. Thinking of the symbol $\frac{a}{b}$ as a *quotient* of two integers helps students remember the symbol $\mathbb{Q}$.

Notice that any integer can be written in the form $\frac{a}{b}$ in many ways. For example, –5 can be written as $\frac{-5}{1}$ or $-\frac{10}{2}$, and +7 can be written as $\frac{+7}{1}$ or $\frac{21}{3}$. Therefore, *every integer is a rational number*.

Irrational numbers. In 7th or 8th grade, students learn about a whole new set of numbers, such as π or $\sqrt{2}$, which cannot be written as quotients of two integers. These are known as *irrational numbers*, because they didn't make sense to the ancient Greeks who discovered them. Irrational numbers do not have a universally accepted symbol, although *I* is often used. Unlike the two preceding relationships, the rational numbers are not a subset of the irrational numbers; rather, the two sets are mutually exclusive.

Real numbers. Rational and irrational numbers together form the set of *real numbers*, denoted by the letter $\mathbb{R}$. By high school, the universe of numbers within which students operate has grown to include all real numbers as shown in Figure 0.2 on the next page.

FIGURE 0.2
The Real Number System

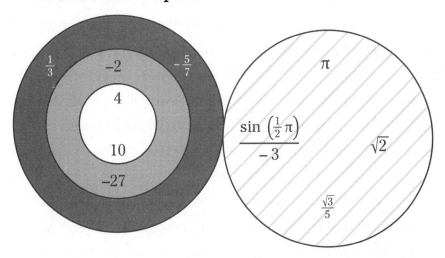

Note: The real number system contains $\mathbb{N}$, the natural numbers symbolized by the white set; $\mathbb{Z}$, the integers symbolized by the light gray set; $\mathbb{Q}$, the rational numbers symbolized by the dark gray set; and I, the irrational numbers (whose symbol is not universal), symbolized by the hatched set.

At this point, you may be wondering, "Aren't rational numbers a *middle school mathematics topic*?" Yes, but not exclusively. The higher expectations of the K–12 Common Core State Standards for Mathematics (CCSSM) require a more profound exposure to rational numbers before the middle grades. In fact, the CCSSM formally introduce fractions in 3rd grade, building on students' prior informal experiences, such as cutting apples into equal halves or sharing a chocolate bar fairly among four people. A recent National Council of Teachers of Mathematics (NCTM) publication for teachers explicitly states, "Rational numbers compose a major area of school mathematics that is crucial for students to learn but challenging for teachers to teach. Students in grades 3–5 need to understand rational numbers well if they are to succeed in these grades and in their subsequent mathematics experiences" (Barnett-Clarke, Fisher, Marks, & Ross, 2010, p. 1).

A Word on the Word *Fraction*

Unlike the term *rational number*, *fraction* does not have a universal mathematical definition. In elementary school mathematics, fractions refer to positive rational numbers, such as $\frac{2}{3}$ or $\frac{9}{7}$. They are grouped into *proper* and *improper* fractions, depending on whether they are less than or greater than 1. By middle school, though, symbolic expressions such as $\frac{\sqrt{5}}{2}$ and $\frac{\pi}{4}$ are also called fractions, as they represent quotients of two quantities—albeit non-integer quantities—written in fraction form. If a fraction is defined as a symbolic expression of the form $\frac{N}{D}$, where numerator N and denominator D can be any non-zero quantity, then *any rational number can be written as a fraction*, but *not every fraction is a rational number* (Figure 0.3).

FIGURE 0.3
Fractions That Are and Are Not Rational Numbers

Rational Numbers				*Not* Rational Numbers			
$\frac{7}{13}$	$\frac{3}{2}$	$\frac{-5}{11}$	$-\frac{4}{1}$	$\frac{\pi}{2}$	$\frac{\sqrt{2}}{3}$	$\frac{\sin\left(\frac{\pi}{6}\right)}{4}$	$\frac{-5}{\sqrt[3]{7}}$

That said, for the rest of this book, whose main focus is mathematics as taught in grades 2–6, a fraction will designate a *non-negative rational number*, meaning one that is positive or zero. And, since most elementary school teachers use the term *whole numbers* instead of *natural numbers* with their students, I will use *whole number* and *natural number* interchangeably. In the United States, whole numbers usually include zero.

Two other forms: decimals and percents. Every rational number can be expressed in three forms: as a fraction, as a decimal, and as a percent. Although elementary school students begin to explore decimals, and middle school students are introduced to percents, this book focuses primarily on the conceptual development of fractions, only a little on decimals, and not at all on percents. This is partly due to limited space but also because, as Collins and Dacey (2010) note, "One of the greatest errors fifth- and sixth-grade teachers typically make is introducing conversion of fractions to decimals *before* students have developed mastery with fractions on a conceptual level" (p. 16).

Cognitive Shifts to Consider

Multiplicative thinking, a new big idea students encounter in Grade 3, is the foundation for an entire network of interconnected concepts including multiplication, division, fractions, ratios, rational numbers, proportional relationships, and linear functions—all of which are central to algebra.

Monica Neagoy (2014, p. 7)

The advent of fractions engenders important shifts in students' ways of thinking about these new numbers that we must be aware of and sensitive to in our pedagogy. I would like to address two major ones: the shift from additive to multiplicative thinking, and the shift from whole numbers to rational numbers.

From additive to multiplicative thinking. From their earliest notions of numbers through roughly age 8, children live in an additive world. They experience situations that involve adding to (joining together or composing) and subtracting from (taking apart or decomposing; taking away or removing). Counting itself is an additive process; we add 1 to each number to obtain the next number. Even when solving comparison problems—*How much more? How much less? How much longer? How much shorter? How much older? How much younger?*—students think additively. The very way that questions are formulated leads students down the additive path. For instance, "How much taller is Dante than Ashley?" invites a student to reason, "How many inches [or other units] must I add to Ashley's height to get Dante's height?" or "How many inches do I get if I subtract Ashley's height from Dante's?" Either way, this is additive thinking.

Consider another comparison problem: Plant A went from a height of 2 feet to a height of 8 feet in one year. Plant B went from 6 feet to 12 feet in the same year. If you ask your students which plant grew more, they will probably answer that both grew the same amount—namely, 6 feet. But that's looking at the problem additively and considering the *absolute* growth: 8 – 2 = 6 and 12 – 6 = 6.

Let's now examine the *relative* growth and ask, "How many times its original height is each plant at the end of the year?" Plant A quadrupled in height, whereas Plant B only doubled in height. Therefore, Plant A grew more, *relative to its original height*. An equivalent but more sophisticated way of saying this is "Plant A grew three times its original height, whereas Plant B grew once its original height."

Most real-world numbers aren't always so nice and neat, with whole-number multiples. If, say, Plant A grew from 2 to 3 feet, and Plant B grew from 6 to 8 feet, then we would say that Plant A grew $\frac{1}{2}$ of its original height, whereas Plant B only grew $\frac{1}{3}$ of its original height. Such reasoning exemplifies *multiplicative thinking* and necessarily involves rational numbers.

Consider a final example. If you ask a rising 6th grader to compare $\frac{13}{15}$ and $\frac{14}{16}$, chances are that the student will say they are equal, because in both cases the numerator and denominator differ by 2. The student's explanation might be, "I add the same number, 2, to the top number to get the bottom number, so they're the same." This is a testimony to ingrained additive thinking. Despite learning the equivalent fraction algorithm, most students leave elementary school unaware of the double multiplicative nature of equivalent fractions. Why? Because we don't take the time to unpack it for them and then revisit it in multiple contexts!

Figure 0.4 illustrates both the *between* (or *across*) *ratio* of 1 to 5 and the *within* (or *downward*) *ratio* of 1 to 4 in two equivalent fractions. If this multiplicative nature of fractions were cultivated during the last three years of elementary school, then students wouldn't think of comparing $\frac{13}{15}$ and $\frac{14}{16}$ additively. Multiplicative thinking underpins fractions, which in turn underpin the mathematics of ratios, rates, percents, proportions, linearity, and rational functions.

FIGURE 0.4

The Double Multiplicative Nature of Fraction or Ratio Equivalence

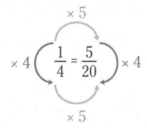

From whole numbers to rational numbers. The shift from whole numbers to rational numbers follows the shift from work with *discrete quantities* to work with *continuous quantities*. Simplistically put, discrete quantities are things we can *count*, such as blocks, cell phones, or people; continuous quantities are things we can *measure*, such as length, area, or time.

The action of measuring is a multiplicative process par excellence, but it almost never results in an exact whole number of units. Students begin to work with measurement in 3rd grade; hence, the need for an understanding of rational numbers. But in this shift toward rational numbers, students unfortunately continue to apply their familiar whole-number thinking. Their reasoning often goes like this:

- $\frac{1}{4}$ is greater than $\frac{1}{3}$, because 4 is greater than 3.
- 0.157 is greater than 0.63, because 157 is greater than 63.
- $\frac{2}{3} + \frac{1}{2} = \frac{3}{5}$, because 2 + 1 = 3 and 3 + 2 = 5.
- 4 + 0.3 = 7 or 0.7, because 4 + 3 = 7 and 0.4 + 0.3 = 0.7.
- $\frac{2}{3} \times 9$ can't be 6 because "multiplication makes numbers bigger."
- $4 \div \frac{1}{2}$ can't be 8 because "division makes numbers smaller."

The chapters that follow address these and other misconceptions, each of which is subtle and deserves attention. The key is to emphasize for students the deeper aspects of whole-number reasoning that remain unchanged (such as the meanings of operations) while simultaneously pointing out new mathematical ways of thinking ushered in by rational numbers—such as the multiplicative comparison of two quantities.

The Rush to Algorithms

Set building number sense for fractions among elementary school–aged students as the goal as opposed to building procedural skill with adding, subtracting, and multiplying fractions.

Kathleen Cramer and Stephanie Whitney (2010, p. 21)

The teaching and learning of fractions is notoriously associated with memorizing computational algorithms or procedures. A case in point is the ubiquitous rhyme "Ours is not to reason why, just invert and multiply," which gives the algorithm for dividing fractions. It is this lack of sense making, so pervasive in traditional mathematics instruction, that leads to frustration, surrender, and even failure.

For decades—if not centuries—"knowing" fractions has been synony-mous with knowing how to perform fraction operations, and "knowing" ratios and proportions has meant knowing how to solve proportional equations, such as $\frac{3}{7} = \frac{10}{x}$. Traditional instruction of rational numbers has commonly been rule based. Consider these six rules:

- To add or subtract fractions, first find common denominators and then add or subtract numerators accordingly.
- To multiply fractions, just multiply across—both numerators and denominators.
- To divide two fractions, invert the second fraction and then multiply the fractions.
- To multiply or divide a decimal by a multiple of 10, move the decimal point to the right (for multiplication) or left (for division) as many digits as there are zeroes in the multiple of 10.
- You *cannot* have zero as the denominator.
- To solve a proportion $\left(\text{e.g., } \frac{3}{7} = \frac{10}{x} \right)$, cross-multiply and then divide by the coefficient of x.

Human brains enjoy reasoning logically, finding meaning, discovering patterns, and making connections. Deprived of these actions, the natu-rally curious mind instead surrenders to passivity and accepts math as merely a set of meaningless numerical procedures (which—in the world of algebra—become a set of meaningless symbolic procedures). If I asked you "Why?" after each of the six rules, would you be able to explain? Could you illustrate each rule for your students with a real-world context?

Don't feel bad if you cannot. Traditionally, teachers were not expected to unpack the whys—our focus was more on the how-tos. But in our technological world, with machines computing faster and more accurately than humans can and with the CCSSM setting higher expectations, the bar has been raised for teachers and students alike. We are now expected to reason, understand, evaluate, explain, justify, and prove—in short, we're expected to use higher-order thinking skills!

What Can You Expect from This Book?

The following chapters address seven big ideas in the teaching and learning of fractions. Each chapter begins with a vignette from a real classroom. The chapters then explore students' most common misconceptions regarding the topic in question, based on my research and practice, followed by a thorough unpacking of productive mathematical thinking. Each chapter ends with seven challenging multistep and thought-provoking problems for teachers to explore with their students.

Featured in every chapter are four additional resources:

Bridges to Algebra establish an important connection between the fraction concept at hand and an algebraic notion to be encountered in later years.

Mathematical Practices illustrate one of the eight Common Core State Standards for Mathematical Practice using an aspect of fraction instruction.

Teaching Tips highlight a practice you are encouraged to adopt that could enhance your fraction teaching.

Fraction Apps relate to the chapter topics and are offered free of charge at www.apps4math.com. The apps are designed to enhance teaching and facilitate learning while making both more enjoyable!

Chapter 1 discusses the dense web of meanings that surround the concept of fractions. We begin with students' own mental images and ideas about fractions and show how we can help them construct new knowledge by building on their existing informal knowledge of fractions through careful observation and focused conversations.

Chapter 2 describes multiple uses of visual and tactile models in fraction instruction. We address questions such as the following: *Which models are effective? Are all models equivalent? What limitations might they present? Should we use one or many models?*

Chapter 3 examines common student misconceptions related to the concept of the *whole* or *unit* and consider the importance of the unit in developing foundational fraction concepts.

Chapter 4 takes on one of our greatest pedagogical challenges in teaching fractions: helping students both see with their eyes and understand with their minds that equivalence between two fractions can be maintained, despite numeric or symbolic transformation. It shows how we can build on students' intuitive methods and understandings of equivalence to address their principal stumbling blocks.

Chapter 5 focuses on building number sense. In order to compare two quantities or numbers judiciously, we must first have good number sense—and an important part of number sense is recognizing the relative magnitude of numbers. When it comes to fractions, however, this ability is direly lacking; many students don't or can't compare or order fractions without resorting to a memorized algorithm.

Chapter 6 explores how students' computation patterns can emerge organically in well-designed tasks with a teacher's guidance. A premature focus on the memorization of algorithms reinforces the erroneous but prevalent belief that mathematics is more about memorizing procedures than about reasoning about powerful ideas. We emphasize the importance of giving students time to develop good fraction and operation sense before rushing to teach computation algorithms.

Chapter 7 unpacks the whole number–decimal connection, the fraction-decimal connection, common student misconceptions, and recommendations for overcoming them.

The concluding chapter summarizes seven habits of mind that foster good fraction sense, recalls the dangers of the long-standing rule-based approach to teaching fractions, and looks ahead to ratios and proportions.

It is my sincere hope that *Unpacking Fractions* will inspire educators to help students shift from fear to enjoyment and from meaningless memorization to deep understanding. It seems reasonable that the shift from failure with fractions to success with fractions will follow naturally.

CHAPTER 1

Convey the Many Meanings of $\frac{a}{b}$

Elementary and middle school programs must provide students with adequate time and experiences to develop a deep conceptual understanding of this important area of the curriculum.

John A. Van de Walle, Karen S. Karp, and Jennifer M. Bay-Williams (2010, p. 286)

The ways in which students understand the meaning and concept of fractions have important implications for what they will understand and be able to do later on when faced with new ideas that build on this concept—including quotients, decimals, percents, ratios, rates, proportions, proportionality, and linearity. In high school or college calculus, some students will encounter even more advanced mathematical ideas, such as the notion of derivative as the ratio of differentials $\frac{dx}{dy}$.

By the *meaning* of a fraction $\frac{a}{b}$, I mean the many possible concepts the symbol can represent. And by *understanding*, I mean what results from a student's interpretations of words, symbols, actions, and discussions pertaining to fraction contexts and situations. Students assign meaning according to a web of connections that they build over time, through interactions with their own interpretations of fractions and through interactions with other students as they, too, struggle to construct new understandings.

This makes the teacher's role in fraction knowledge building all the more crucial: teachers must offer students rich and varied experiences if they are to develop a dense web of meanings around the concept of *fraction*—meanings they can fall back on when they become confused, forget a memorized procedure, or learn a new fraction-related concept (such as ratio). Building a robust *fraction sense* is not simple. It is much more than correctly naming a fraction's components, accurately shading a given fraction of a region, or successfully carrying out a computational algorithm. It is even more than knowing the procedural rules for trans-forming, say, a fraction to a decimal or a percent to a fraction. The key to a well-grounded fraction sense is *time*. Mathematical knowledge building takes time—and by time, I mean *years*.

A good place to start is with students' own mental images and ideas about fractions. Teachers of course cannot read the minds of their students to see these internal representations. Rather, they must access them indirectly by making inferences from students' discourse about fractions, the outer representations they construct, and their ongoing interactions with fractions through drawing, gesturing, and writing. Through careful observation and conversation, we can detect misconceptions, help students make connections between their existing informal knowledge and the new mathematical constructs we hope to teach them, and help them use their intuition to construct new knowledge.

Roberto's Story

Roberto taught middle school for several years and then left to take a better-paying job in industry. But after a while he found that the good money alone was not fulfilling; he missed teaching, and he especially missed the kids, so he decided to return to the classroom. He had hoped to go back to his middle school, but there were no openings, so he took a position teaching 5th grade instead. What follows are some key moments I observed during Roberto's introductory lesson on fractions during his first year of teaching 5th grade.

Roberto wrote "$\frac{3}{4}$" on the board and asked his students to write down or draw whatever came to mind when they saw this fraction. After some reflection time, students shared their ideas; Roberto asked two students to record all of the answers on the board.

Many students offered part-whole interpretations of the fraction, represented by the shading of $\frac{3}{4}$ of a square, rectangle, or circle, accompanied by explanations such as Tatiana's: "I have a cookie and eat a quarter of it, so three-fourths is left. I see the picture of the circle with a quarter of it missing."

Another student, Kaleb, used his class instead of a region to explain his idea of $\frac{3}{4}$:

Kaleb: 21 students in our class!

Roberto: How is 21 students an interpretation of $\frac{3}{4}$?

Kaleb: We're 28 students in this class. I split the class in four groups of seven students. Three groups is 21 people, so that's three-fourths of our class.

Roberto: Ah! Now I see. Can anyone explain in what way Tatiana's $\frac{3}{4}$ of a cookie and Kaleb's $\frac{3}{4}$ of you 5th graders are different and in what way they're the same?

After an insightful discussion about the difference between *discrete* quantities (such as students, tables, and marbles) and *continuous* quantities (such as time, money, length, and area), Roberto identified for students their most popular interpretation of $\frac{3}{4}$ as the "part-whole" meaning of a fraction: "When we partition the whole or set into four equal parts and take three parts, then $\frac{3}{4}$ is one part, $\frac{1}{4}$ is the other part, and $\frac{4}{4}$ is the whole." Here are some other meanings students shared about $\frac{3}{4}$:

- 0.75 (3 students)

- 45 minutes (2 students)

- 75¢ (1 student)

- $\frac{3}{4}$ of a mile (1 student)

- 75% (1 student)

Only about a quarter of the class expressed an idea other than the part of a region or set.

Roberto posed another question to the class:

Roberto: Suppose I decided to group 75¢, $\frac{3}{4}$ of a mile, and 45 minutes into one category of ideas you all came up with. What might be my criterion behind that grouping? Serena?

Serena: They're all real.

Roberto: They're all real-world examples—is that what you mean, Serena?

Serena: Yes.

Roberto: What do those examples tell us about the real world?

Another enlightening discussion ensued about measuring quantities in the real world, such as money (75¢), distance $\left(\frac{3}{4}\text{ of a mile}\right)$, and time (45 minutes), and how when we measure real-life quantities, we often get non-integer measures, which are called *fractional measures*. Roberto's more subtle goal for this discussion was to make explicit to students the implicit nature of the unit they took for granted in all three interpretations: $1.00 (or 100 cents), 1 mile, and 1 hour (or 60 minutes), respectively.

Roberto ended this discussion on fractions by drawing four squares on the board and shading three.

He said, "First I asked you what images the symbol 3 over 4 conjured up in your mind. Now I'm asking what this set of four squares, with three of them shaded, illustrates to you." In quasi-unison, the class answered, "Three-fourths." Roberto waited a moment and then inquired, "Anything else?"

Finally, one student in the back row shyly asked, "Could it also be a fourth?"

"Explain your thinking," Roberto prompted.

"One white square out of four."

"Absolutely!" He paused. "Anything else?" This question was greeted with silence.

Roberto concluded with a homework assignment: "For tomorrow, think about whether the illustration could represent $\frac{1}{3}$ or $\frac{4}{3}$, in addition to $\frac{1}{4}$ or $\frac{3}{4}$."

This experienced teacher, though new to the elementary school grades, benefited from the perspective on rational numbers expounded in the middle grades. His ability to align students' developing ideas with the new ideas he wanted to teach—not by merely stating definitions or rules but through effective classroom math talk—was evident. He regularly made students' ideas more explicit, for their own benefit as well as others'. He drew powerful connections among the different solutions provided as ways to guide his students to new mathematical territory: the distinction between *discrete* versus *continuous* quantities, which he differentiated as "quantities we can *count*" versus "quantities we can *measure*." Instead of lamenting the high number of part-whole interpretations, he used them to review the notion of part-to-whole and the importance of the *unit* in measuring.

Teaching Tip: Revoicing During Whole-Group Discussions

Given the noise and confusion that can occur in a classroom of 20–30 students, there has been a growing interest in the notion of *revoicing* in classroom discourse. Enyedy and colleagues (2008) describe revoicing as a discursive teaching practice that promotes deeper conceptual understanding: teachers position students in relation to one another, which facilitates classroom debate and fosters mathematical argumentation. While that sounds like a sophisticated practice, it's something that teachers do daily. Nevertheless, we can become more effective at revoicing by being more mindful. For example,

- We can respond neutrally. When we revoice a correct answer, is our restatement accompanied by a smile of approval or an affirming tone of voice? Conversely, is our restatement of an incorrect answer tainted by a frown or an interrogative tone of voice? Rather than result in further classroom participation, such revoicing ironically cuts it short. If we add too much of our own thinking to our students' utterances, we discourage them from reasoning further, both on their own thinking and on the contributions of others (O'Connor & Michaels, 1996).

- We can improve the effect of rebroadcasting students' ideas by adding a verification right after a neutral reformulation, such as "Is that what I heard?" or "Is that what you just said?" If the restatement is for the purpose of clarity, try asking, "Is that what you mean?" or "Is that what you're trying to say?" The ball is then back in the student's court, and the discussion progresses.

- We can invite a student to do the revoicing, which ensures neutrality. Asking, "Did everyone hear what Sandra said?" in tones of interest or excitement is one way of drawing attention to an answer or statement, whether correct or incorrect, that you wish to highlight or use as a teaching tool.

CCSS.Math.Practice.MP3 states that students will "construct viable arguments and critique the reasoning of others" (Common Core State Standards Initiative, 2010). If this is not yet an established mathematical practice in your classroom, then many students may answer that they did not hear Sandra's response—*but there's always at least one student who did.* Ask that student to revoice for the benefit of the whole class: "Can you please restate what you heard Sandra say?'

Recognizing Misconceptions

Beneath the fraction symbol $\frac{3}{4}$ in particular, or the fraction symbol $\frac{a}{b}$ in general, lies a multitude of meanings and interpretations that students develop and come to know over time through a variety of out-of-school experiences and instructional tasks involving thinking, talking, gesturing, doing, operating, and solving. Traditionally, though, elementary school students' experiences with fractions have been restricted to the part-whole interpretation. More recently, mathematics educators and researchers have realized that this limited view of fractions has left students with an impoverished foundation for the complex system of rational numbers and operations. Consequently, teachers such as Roberto are making conscious attempts to discuss and explore all of the meanings of fraction symbols described in this chapter.

Limited Ideas About the Meaning of a Fraction

Rather than having misconceptions about the meaning of fractions, what we observed in Roberto's classroom is what research verifies: students' ideas associated with fractions are limited. About three-fourths of the 5th graders (20 out of 28) in the vignette gravitated toward the part-whole interpretation of $\frac{3}{4}$ and only one student thought of a fractional part of a *set* or *collection* rather than a fractional part of a *region*. Despite standards and curricula that claim to stress the measure, number, quotient, operator, and ratio meanings of fractions alongside the part-whole metaphor, the latter is most commonly used to introduce fractions to young students because it builds on their grounded understanding of partitioning for equal sharing. However, for students acquainted with only the part-whole construct of $\frac{3}{4}$ ("three parts out of four equal parts"), the fraction $\frac{5}{4}$ will seem senseless: How can we take five parts out of only four equal parts? Further down the line, when studying division with fractions, dividing a whole number by a fraction will seem meaningless as well: The expression $5 \div \frac{2}{3}$, or $\frac{5}{2/3}$ or $\frac{5}{\frac{2}{3}}$ will be interpreted as "5 parts out of $\frac{2}{3}$ parts" or even "5 parts out of (2 parts out of 3 equal parts)," which is even harder for students to grasp than "5 parts out of 4."

Difficulty Conceptualizing a Fraction as a Single Number

The CCSSM introductory standard in the grade 3 category "Number and Operations—Fractions" clearly states, "Develop understanding of fractions as numbers" (Common Core State Standards Initiative, 2010). However, the composite nature of fractions creates a serious obstacle. How is the meaning of 3 combined with the meaning of 4 supposed to give meaning to the numeral $\frac{3}{4}$? Moreover, when students try to represent $\frac{3}{4}$ as a point on the number line, knowing the location of the points representing 3 and 4 on the number line doesn't really serve them. Conceptualizing a fraction as a single entity is expressed in the upper elementary school grades by representing a fraction as a single point on the number line. The fact that not one of Roberto's students mentioned the idea that $\frac{3}{4}$ could be a number, or drew a point on the number line to show their thinking, confirms the research on children's primary difficulty when beginning their journey into fractions: thinking of a fraction as a single number.

Unpacking the Mathematical Thinking

Deeply understanding fractions involves knowing what the word *fraction* and the symbol $\frac{a}{b}$ mean, appreciating the different mathematical concepts associated with fractions, and knowing how these fit together in a web of related meanings. Two factors infuse a mathematical construct with meaning: the mathematical *theory* behind the construct and the mathematical *applications* of the construct. Kieren (1976), Vergnaud (1979), and Freudenthal (1983) independently suggested that a fully developed rational number construct implies a rich set of integrated *subconstructs*, including part-whole, measure, quotient, ratio, and multiplicative operator. Since understanding fractions in grades 3–5 is a precursor to understanding rational numbers later on, it is essential that we begin in 3rd grade to introduce these related meanings of fractions, and their associated processes, by exposing students to multiple applications. We begin with the part-whole meaning of fraction.

The Part-Whole Meaning of $\frac{a}{b}$

While students have limited out-of-school contexts in which they can construct meaning for fractions, they do have extensive experience partitioning, mostly with the goal of forming equal shares. Young children have a good understanding of constructing fractional parts of a whole, such as 2 *one-halves* of a square sandwich, 3 *one-thirds* of a rectangular chocolate bar, or 4 *one-fourths* of a circular birthday cake. The *parts* are what result when the *whole* is partitioned into equal-size portions or fair shares.

Students are less comfortable with *parts of a set*, as we will see in later chapters. Roberto's three shaded squares is an example of a part of a set of four squares.

The CCSS Math Content.3.NF.A.1 states that students should interpret a fraction $\frac{a}{b}$ as the quantity formed by a parts of size $\frac{1}{b}$ (Common Core State Standards Initiative, 2010) and does not use the traditional phrase heard in classrooms everywhere: "$\frac{a}{b}$ is a parts out of b equal parts." What is behind this subtle linguistic distinction? Namely, it guards students against inferring four ideas that don't serve them as they move through the grades and construct more complex ideas associated with the symbol $\frac{a}{b}$:

- **Inclusion.** When $\frac{a}{b}$ is stated as "a parts out of b equal parts," there is a sense that the a parts are a subset of the b parts. From this, students conclude that the whole and the parts must be *of the same nature*. Consequently, the question "What fraction of the children in the school choir are girls?" makes sense to them because girls *are* children—but when later tackling ratios, questions like "What fraction of the number of boys in the choir is the number of girls?" will confuse them because girls *are not* boys.

  Note: An analogy with a continuous quantity is "What fraction of the salad dressing is oil [part to whole → *fraction*]?" versus "What fraction of the oil volume is the vinegar volume [part to part → *ratio*]?"

- **Size.** Interpreting $\frac{a}{b}$ solely as a parts out of b equal parts infers that a must be smaller than b, since we take the a parts out of the b parts. Thus, fractions $\frac{2}{3}$ and $\frac{4}{5}$ make sense to students, but $\frac{7}{5}$ and $\frac{10}{13}$ do not— how can we take 7 parts out of 5 parts? This language consequently favors "proper" fractions (i.e., those that are less than 1).

  Note: In my opinion, we should gradually do away with the terms *proper* or *improper* to characterize fractions. The non-mathematical meaning of the adjective *improper* only exacerbates students' discomfort with fractions greater than 1. Once students understand the concept of a fraction, and the procedure for constructing it, placing $\frac{5}{3}$ on a number line is no more difficult for them than placing $\frac{2}{3}$. Treating *all* fractions equally, whether they are less than or greater than 1, will make for a more seamless transition to rational numbers.

- **Separate numbers.** The restricted "*a* parts out of *b* equal parts" interpretation has a delaying effect on the progression toward viewing a fraction as *a single number*. If, when seeing $\frac{3}{5}$, a student thinks exclusively of the actions "I cut the whole into 5 parts and then take 3 parts," then the student is mentally manipulating two different numbers or quantities: 5 parts on the one hand, and 3 parts on the other. This delays the more mature understanding of $\frac{3}{5}$ as a single number, with a representation as a unique point on the number line.

- **Additive thinking.** Perhaps the greatest limitation of the "*a* out of *b*" language is the obstacle it presents to multiplicative thinking, an important precursor to proportional thinking. Consider Roberto's fraction $\frac{3}{4}$. Thinking of it in terms of "the parts I shade or take" and "the parts I don't shade or don't take" is thinking *additively*, because $\frac{3}{4} + \frac{1}{4} = \frac{4}{4}$.

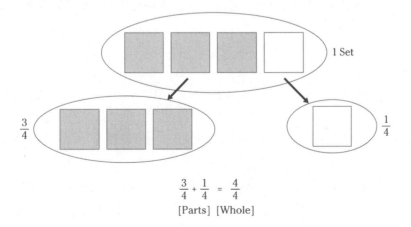

$$\frac{3}{4} + \frac{1}{4} = \frac{4}{4}$$
[Parts] [Whole]

On the other hand, interpreting $\frac{3}{4}$ as "3 parts of size $\frac{1}{4}$" is thinking *multiplicatively*: I first consider the fractional unit $\frac{1}{4}$ of the set (represented by one square), then I count three copies (or iterations) of $\frac{1}{4}$—or better yet, "I multiply 3 times the fractional unit $\frac{1}{4}$ to get $\frac{3}{4}$."

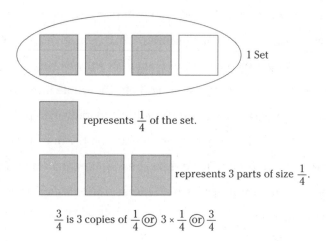

$\frac{3}{4}$ is 3 copies of $\frac{1}{4}$ (or) $3 \times \frac{1}{4}$ (or) $\frac{3}{4}$

With this multiplicative mindset, the fraction $\frac{5}{4}$ is conceptualized no differently: "I first identify the fractional unit $\frac{1}{4}$, then I think of $\frac{5}{4}$ as '5 iterations of $\frac{1}{4}$' or '5 times $\frac{1}{4}$.'"

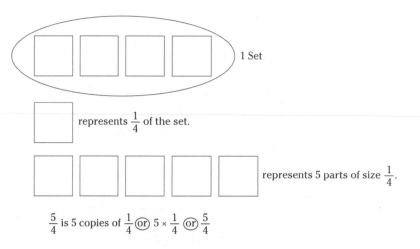

$\frac{5}{4}$ is 5 copies of $\frac{1}{4}$ (or) $5 \times \frac{1}{4}$ (or) $\frac{5}{4}$

The Measure Meaning of $\frac{a}{b}$

The concept of the whole underlies the concept of a fraction.
Merlyn J. Behr & Thomas R. Post (1992, p. 213)

From *part of a whole* to *compared with a whole*. Barnett-Clarke, Fisher, Marks, and Ross (2010) noted, "The interpretation of rational number [fraction] as a measure pushes us beyond our interpretation of a fraction as a *part of a whole* to the broader idea of a fraction as a *quantity compared with a whole*" (p. 23). When a child says, "I ran half a kilometer," the measure $\frac{1}{2}$ km tells us the distance the child ran *compared with the whole*, 1 km, which in this case is a unit of measure for distance. When a child says, "I'm five and a half," the inferred unit of measure (which the child is too young to know!) is one year. The measure $\frac{11}{2}$ years, or the mixed number $5\frac{1}{2}$ years, therefore, tells us the amount of time the child has lived since birth—or the child's age—*compared with the whole*, 1 year. A good way of making children aware from a young age of the importance of associating a number to the unit of measure (which is often not specified but merely implied) in any measurement is to probe with questions such as, "Do you mean five and a half *days* old?"

Measuring is a multiplicative process par excellence. The process of measuring requires multiplicative thinking in two ways:

- **In the unit conversion:** Students "use their knowledge of relationships between units and their understanding of multiplicative situations to make conversions, such as expressing . . . 3 feet as 36 inches" (NCTM, 2000, p. 172). Indeed, if 1 foot is 12 inches, then 3 feet is three times more, or 36 inches.

- **In the nature of the measuring process itself:** Calculating the length of a book in non-standard units, such as staples, means figuring out *how many times* the staple (or *unit of length*) fits in a straight line, end to end, from one end of the desk to the other. When sufficient copies of the unit of measure are available, lining them up offers a nice visual of this multiplicative process.

An important inverse relationship. In measuring, there is an important relationship between the *size* of the unit of measure and the *number* of units it takes to measure a quantity. For example, if the trapezoid in Figure 1.1, which is half the area of the hexagon, is selected to be one unit of area, then the hexagon has an area of two units. On the other hand, if the triangle, which is three times smaller than the trapezoid, is selected as the new unit of area, the same hexagon now has an area of six units, or *three times greater than* the first measurement.

FIGURE 1.1
Area: An Example of Two-Dimensional Measure

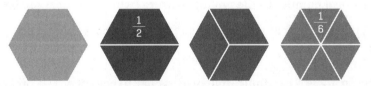

Note: Consider the size of the unit of measure for area: it is inversely proportional to the area measure of the hexagon.

An analogous situation in *linear* measure (length) is illustrated by different measures of the same stick, depending on the choice of unit (Figure 1.2). If the unit of measure is half of the stick's length, then the stick measures two units. But if the unit of measure changes to one-quarter of the stick's length—half the size of the first unit—then the new measure of the stick's length is four units, or twice the first measurement.

FIGURE 1.2
Length: An Example of One-Dimensional Measure

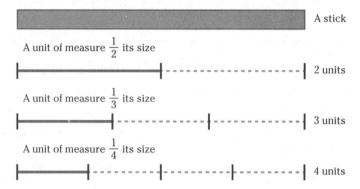

Note: Consider the size of the unit of measure for length; it is inversely proportional to the length measure of the stick.

At around age 7, students begin to observe this inverse relationship between the size of the unit of measure and the number of units it takes to express the measure of a given quantity. The role of instruction in helping students make their observation explicit is crucial. Use these measuring experiences to help students see why the ordering of unit fractions is the inverse of the ordering of whole numbers.

$$\frac{1}{1} > \frac{1}{2} > \frac{1}{3} > \frac{1}{4} \dots \text{ yet } 1 < 2 < 3 < 4 \dots$$

Fractions and measures: the importance of the unit. Another connection between a measure and a fraction, which, when made explicit, helps students better understand the meaning of a fraction, is the stated or implied unit. We saw that any measure, be it 4, $\frac{3}{4}$, or $5\frac{1}{2}$, is always stated in reference to a whole or a unit of measure, say, 4 quarts, $\frac{3}{4}$ of a mile, or $5\frac{1}{2}$ years. If the unit is unknown, then the number stated alone gives no sense of "How much?" This is also true for a fraction, which has no meaning if the whole or unit is unknown. Chapter 3 develops this important concept.

CCSS.Math.Practice.MP2: Reason Abstractly and Quantitatively

In all actions of measuring, we find structural similarities. Measuring is the process of assigning numbers to objects—it is understood that some attribute of the object (e.g., length, area, or volume) is being measured. The process consists of three steps:

1. Assign the number 1 to a selected unit of measure, non-standard or standard.

2. Express the measure of the object's attribute of interest as a certain number of "copies" of this unit (which is almost always a fraction, either less than or greater than 0).

3. Record the measurement as a number followed by the unit of measure.

For students to make sense of the use of fractions in their lives, they should experience multiple instances of measuring—both the process of measuring (the action) and the assignment of number to measurement (the product). They should understand how measurement instruments work so they can learn to use them to describe the physical world in meaningful ways. To construct the concepts of perimeter, area, and volume, they should actually wrap a diameter string around a circle, tile a region with different polygonal two-dimensional (2-D) shapes, or fill a container with unit cubes—and find that the result is almost never a whole number. In the process, students come to understand that *quantities* are actually attributes of objects (or phenomena) that are measurable. It is precisely our capacity to measure them that makes them quantities!

In 3rd and 4th grade, students assign whole numbers to these real-world objects, and then fractions and decimals: a length, a period of time, a price. In 5th and 6th grade, they begin to generalize perimeter, area, volume, and other measurement formulas, many of which contain fractional expressions, such as $\frac{1}{2}bh$ or $\frac{1}{2} \times base \times height$, for the area of a triangle. In 7th and 8th grade, measurement turns to more complex phenomena, such as rates of change (e.g., speed), which are also replete with fractional expressions.

More complex than simple numbers or expressions, the products of the measurement process in these grades are mathematical models (symbolic algebraic expressions, equations, systems of equations, etc.).

Measurement in grades 3–8 is thus a quintessential area of mathematical learning that requires students to juggle *quantitative reasoning* with *abstract reasoning*. We must offer students more quantitative experiences—and fewer computations with numbers disconnected from concrete situations—that help them ground their fractions, fractional expressions, and symbolic and algebraic expressions in the world they live in. If instruction fails to help students connect abstract symbolic representations with the problems or situations from which they emerged, students will not be able to build rich meanings of fractions. The students who do understand the principle of measuring attributes of objects and quantifying phenomena will have acquired insight into the important connection between real-world contexts and abstract mathematical models—the core of all scientific investigation!

The Quotient Meaning of $\frac{a}{b}$

Many students have difficulty conceptualizing division and its relationship to multiplication and fractions. In later chapters, we discuss division with fractions in more detail. Here, we focus on the interpretation of a fraction $\frac{a}{b}$ as referring to the division operation $a \div b$ and its resulting quotient. To this end, we review four situations in which students encounter division with whole numbers, where the dividend is greater than the divisor (as in $20 \div 4$).

The two big division ideas: *partitioning* and *grouping*. Consider the mathematical expression $20 \div 4$. What situations might it model? "We want to share 20 apples equally among 4 students. How many apples does each person get?" would be a classic example of *partitive* division, because we *partition* the 20 apples into 4 equal or fair shares, modeled by 20 ÷ 4. Partitioning or sharing is the action associated with this mental image of division; the result of the division action or the quotient $\frac{20}{4}$ is the equal share of 5. Both children and adults are most comfortable with this meaning of division; the number of containers is known (given), but the number or amount contained in each is unknown (sought), as shown in Figure 1.3.

FIGURE 1.3
Modeling 20 ÷ 4 as Partitive Division

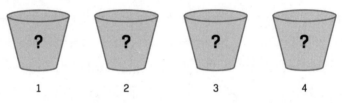

Now suppose we needed to pack all 20 apples in bags of 4 apples each. The new question would be "How many baskets do I need?" In this case, the number or amount contained is known (given), but the number of containers, modeled by 20 ÷ 4, is unknown (sought), as shown in Figure 1.4. The action associated with this idea of division is grouping, segmenting, or portioning: making equal groups of 4 apples until all 20 apples are used up.

FIGURE 1.4
Modeling 20 ÷ 4 as Quotative Division

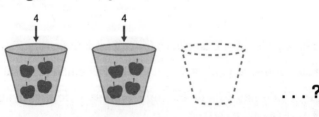

The result of the division action or the quotient of $\frac{20}{4}$ is the number of baskets required, which is 5. This less understood mental image of division is known as *quotative* or *subtractive measurement*.

Two other division ideas: deriving factors and reducing quantities. Even though students can easily parrot the sentence "Division is the inverse of multiplication," using this relationship to solve problems doesn't come naturally. In 3rd grade, students learn through exploration that the total number of square units in the area of a rectangle is the product of its two dimensions, later symbolized algebraically by the area formula $A = l \times w$. They are expected to know how to derive one dimension of a rectangle if they know the area and the other dimension.[1] Say, for example, that the area of a rectangle is 20 square feet and only one dimension, 4 feet, is known. The quotient of 20 ÷ 4 will express the length, in feet, of the rectangle's second dimension. Here, the division action is *deriving* one factor of a multiplicative formula, knowing the other factor and their product. The quotient, $\frac{20}{4}$ or 5, is the numerical value of the target factor.

A similar derivation process is required in Cartesian product situations—yet another conceptualization of multiplication. For example: "Jordan can make 20 different outfits by combining his shirts and his 4 pairs of pants. If an outfit consists of 1 shirt and 1 pair of pants, how many shirts does Jordan have?" Structurally, this problem is identical to the preceding one: O (# of outfits) = s (# of shirts) $\times p$ (# of pants). In this case, 20 = $s \times 4$. The number of shirts is derived by the division action 20 ÷ 4, and the quotient, $\frac{20}{4}$ or 5, is the number of Jordan's shirts.

---

[1] CCSS.Math.Content.3.MD.D.8: Grade 3, Measurement and Data: Solve real world and mathematical problems involving perimeters of polygons, including finding the perimeter given the side lengths, finding an unknown side length, and exhibiting rectangles with the same perimeter and different areas or with the same area and different perimeters (Common Core State Standards Initiative, 2010).

The difference, however, between the products of $l \times w$ and $s \times p$ lies in the nature of the units: $l \times w$ generates *square units*, mathematical units for measuring area (dependent on the generating *linear units*), whereas $s \times p$ creates completely new non-mathematical units called *outfits*.

Let's consider one more problem. Suppose you insert a 20 cm × 13 cm picture into a document on your computer; however, you need to reduce the picture's dimensions to a quarter of their original lengths so that its area is $\frac{1}{16}$ of its original area. Here, 20 ÷ 4 expresses the length of the reduced picture (Figure 1.5).

FIGURE 1.5
Modeling 20 ÷ 4 as Length Reduction

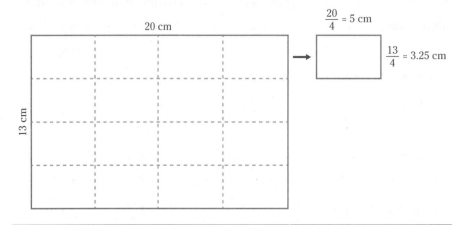

In this case, the division action is *reducing*; the dividend is the quantity being reduced, the divisor is the "shrinking factor" by which it is being reduced, and the quotient, $\frac{20}{4}$ or 5, represents the value of the quantity after the reduction. This interpretation of division involves one quantity rather than two, and there's no action of splitting the original quantity into parts: a single quantity (in this case, length) undergoes a transformation.

This "shrinking" effect of division is developed in the middle grades through the study of similar figures. Multiplication by a *scale factor* is used to denote the shrinking or stretching effect. In this example, from large to small, the scale factor for the shrinking or reduction of the picture's length is $\frac{1}{4}$, because $20 \times \frac{1}{4} = 5$. If we moved in the opposite direction, from small to large, the stretching or expansion scale factor is 4, because $5 \times 4 = 20$.

Connecting division and quotients to fractions. Operations are the means by which we express, describe, and solve problems in the social and physical world. Division metaphors give meaning to fractions themselves and are the foundation for division with fractions, which we will explore in later chapters.[2] The situations modeled by the same equation, $20 \div 4 = 5$, illustrate four distinct interpretations of the division action $20 \div 4$ and of its corresponding quotient $\frac{20}{4}$, which is a fraction greater than 1. In each case, the significance assigned to dividend, divisor, and quotient are different.

The challenge now is to revisit these metaphors for fractions less than 1 and explore if the meanings of *process* and *product* still hold. For example, consider $3 \div 4$ and $\frac{3}{4}$:

- Can we partition three things equally among four people? How do we express the equal shares?

- Can a rectangle whose area is 3 square feet have a side length of 4 feet? What would be the other side length?

- Can we imagine reducing a rectangle with a side length of 3 cm to $\frac{1}{4}$ of its length? How would we express this reduced side length?

- Do all interpretations work for $3 \div 4$ and $\frac{3}{4}$ as they do for $20 \div 4$ and $\frac{20}{4}$?

Investigate these questions with your students!

---

[2] For an in-depth analysis of multiplication metaphors for grades 3–5, see *Planting the Seeds of Algebra, 3–5: Explorations for the Upper Elementary Grades* (Neagoy, 2014, pp. 111–148).

A Bridge to Algebra:
"How many thirds do you need to make a whole?"

Through the repeated actions of partitioning a whole into b equal parts, students realize on their own that the larger the b value, the smaller the equal parts named $\frac{1}{b}$. They say things like "The more people who share a pizza, the less we each get to eat!" What they are learning from an algebraic perspective is that when a whole is divided by b, the answer is $\frac{1}{b}$. In a few years, they will express this symbolically as "$1 \div b = \frac{1}{b}$." When they are able to abstract this big idea to any number n, it will become $1 \div n = \frac{1}{n}$.

But there is a "companion" big idea that we could help instill simply by routinely posing the right questions as friendly reminders. For instance, when working with thirds, pose this question: "So, how many thirds do you need to make the whole?" When working with eighths, ask, "Remind me, how many eighths would I need to make a whole?" This will help automatize the reaction that it takes b b-ths to make a whole, or $\frac{1}{b} \times b = 1$. Generalizing as we did for any number n other than 0, we obtain $\frac{1}{n} \times n = 1$.

Taken together, these two algebraic equations summarize the process of dividing a whole by any number n, then multiplying the parts by n to get back the whole:

$$1 \div n = \frac{1}{n} \text{ (we partition, decompose, or divide)}$$

$$\frac{1}{n} \times n = 1 \text{ (we iterate, recompose, or multiply)}$$

Though this may seem obvious, I can assure you that many middle school students do not have the helpful reflex of thinking, "The number 1 can be written as the quotient of any number n over itself, or any algebraic expression E over itself":

$$1 = \frac{n}{n} = \frac{E}{E}, \text{ a conclusion drawn from } \frac{1}{n} \times n = 1$$

Routinely asking, "How many thirds do you need to make 1?" will go a long way!

The Ratio Meaning of $\frac{a}{b}$

Another possible interpretation of the symbol $\frac{a}{b}$ is a *ratio*. Although they have been relegated to the middle grades in the past, more and more math programs are including the concept of ratios prior to 6th grade, thanks to the Common Core State Standards. The word *ratio* is scary to some of us, as it conjures up negative emotions associated with complex ratio, rate, or proportion problems from our own middle school years. But it needn't be. Fifth grade students and even some 4th graders can develop an intuitive and informal notion of the ratio concept.

A ratio expresses a relationship, a *multiplicative* comparison, between two or more quantities. It compares their relative counts or measures. For example, suppose that a total of 12 people attended a picnic—3 chaperoning adults and 9 children. At least four ratios can be created from this information, two part-to-whole ratios, similar to fractions, and two part-to-part ratios, which are different from fractions.

- The ratio of children to the total number of people is an example of a part-whole ratio and can be denoted in a variety of ways, including 9 children to 12 people, 9 to 12, 9:12, and $\frac{9}{12}$. This ratio tells us that three out of every four people were children.

- The children-to-adults ratio, on the other hand, is a part-part ratio. This ratio, which can be expressed as 9 children to 3 adults, 9 to 3, 9:3, or $\frac{9}{3}$, tells us that there were three times as many children as adults at the picnic.

3 adults   9 children

Using A, C, and P for the number of adults, children, and people at the picnic, respectively, Figure 1.6 lists all four ratios.

FIGURE 1.6
Four Ratios Derived from the Picnic Problem

Part-to-whole ratios	Part-to-part ratios
$\dfrac{A}{P} = \dfrac{3}{12} = \dfrac{1}{4}$	$\dfrac{A}{C} = \dfrac{3}{9} = \dfrac{1}{3}$
$\dfrac{C}{P} = \dfrac{9}{12} = \dfrac{3}{4}$	$\dfrac{C}{A} = \dfrac{9}{3} = \dfrac{3}{1}$

A ratio need not be expressed in fraction notation, but it can be. When ratios are first introduced, many U.S. math programs use the colon notation to distinguish a ratio from the fraction notation—but then the fraction notation is quickly introduced. We will discuss the differences between ratios and fractions in more depth, but for now here are two distinctions:

- Fractions are always part-whole comparisons, but ratios can be either part-whole or part-part comparisons.

- Fractions that express part-whole relationships, quotients, measures, and multiplicative operators are always rational numbers, but fractions expressing ratios need not be. The four ratios in the picnic problem were all rational numbers. But a famous ratio, familiar to readers, that is not a rational number is π, the Greek equivalent for the letter p. Pi represents the ratio of the circumference to the diameter of all circles. The fact that circumference to diameter, $C : D$ or $\dfrac{C}{D}$, is 3.14159. . . simply means that the length of the circumference of any circle is about 3.14 times the length of its diameter. To express this in a more visual and child-friendly way: it takes three diameters plus a bit more to wrap around any circle.

The Multiplicative Operator Meaning of $\frac{a}{b}$

The final interpretation of a fraction in the intermediary grades is a *multiplicative operator*. In this sense, $\frac{a}{b}$ "changes or transforms another number or quantity by magnifying, shrinking, enlarging, reducing, expanding, or contracting it" (Barnett-Clarke et al., 2010, p. 27), depending on the nature of the quantity it's acting on. The action of change here is multiplication. Consider first a measurable quantity, such as a strip of tape of length l, and the fraction $\frac{2}{3}$. What does $\frac{2}{3}l$ mean from the operator perspective?

We can think of $\frac{2}{3}$ as having a *stretching-shrinking* effect on length l. First, we stretch l by a factor of 2 (the numerator as *stretcher*), and then we shrink the resulting length, $2l$, by a factor of 3 (the denominator as *shrinker*). The result is one-third of $2l$, or $\frac{2}{3}l$ (Figure 1.7).

FIGURE 1.7

The Stretching-Shrinking Effect of $\frac{2}{3}$ on l

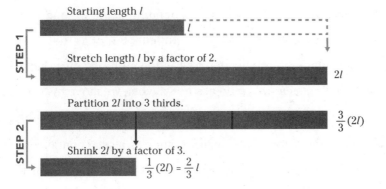

As students' understanding of fractions matures and they are able to see fractions as numbers and to quickly assess their magnitude with respect to the whole-number or fraction benchmarks they know well, instead of decomposing the operator effect of $\frac{2}{3}$ on l into two steps ($\times 2$ followed by $\div 3$), they simply shrink l in one step to the resulting $\frac{2}{3}l$. Similarly, they would stretch or shrink l in one step to get $\frac{7}{3}l$, $\frac{3}{2}l$, or $\frac{3}{4}l$, just as they would to get $2l$, $3l$, or $\frac{1}{2}l$ (Figure 1.8).

FIGURE 1.8
Whole and Fractional Multiplicative Operators Acting on Length *l*

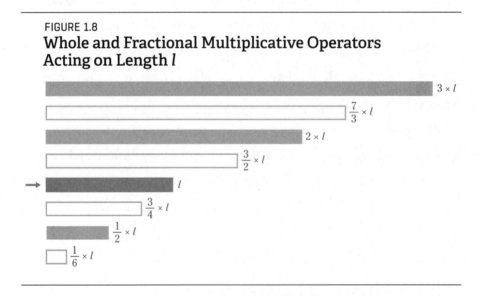

This stretching-shrinking metaphor of multiplication is more powerful than repeated addition and serves students better as they move from whole-number multiplication to fraction multiplication. Indeed, interpreting $3 \times n$ as $n + n + n$ breaks down when we move to $\frac{3}{4} \times n$, whereas stretching (e.g., $3 \times n$) or shrinking $\left(\text{e.g., } \frac{3}{4} \times n\right)$ works for any multiplier.

Next, consider a countable quantity, such as a set S containing six elements. Interpreting $\frac{2}{3}$ as an operator in the expression $\frac{2}{3}S$ means that $\frac{2}{3}$ has a *multiplier-divider* effect on the number of elements comprising S, which is six. First, we multiply 6 by 2 (the numerator or multiplier), and then we divide the resulting number, 12, by 3 (the denominator or divisor) to obtain 4, the number of elements in the set $\frac{2}{3}S$ (Figure 1.9).

FIGURE 1.9

Multiplicative Operator $\frac{2}{3}$ Acting on Set S

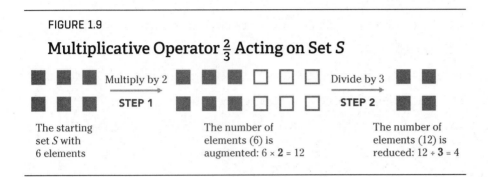

The starting set S with 6 elements

The number of elements (6) is augmented: $6 \times \mathbf{2} = 12$

The number of elements (12) is reduced: $12 \div \mathbf{3} = 4$

Again, as students move through the grades, their increasing familiarity with fraction values allows them to quickly see $\frac{2}{3}$ of 6 and therefore proceed from 6 to 4 in one step. That said, it is nevertheless important to understand the decomposition of multiplying a number or quantity by $\frac{a}{b}$ into two steps (multiply by a, then divide by b), as this process is not only applicable to all fractions but also especially useful with less familiar fractions.

Finally, since multiplication and division have equal status in order of operations, students will discover (with your prodding and questioning) that multiplying first and then dividing is equivalent to dividing first and then multiplying. Similarly, stretching first and then shrinking is equivalent to shrinking first and then stretching. As students become more comfortable with symbolism, they can translate these equivalent processes as follows:

- $n \rightarrow 2 \times n \rightarrow \frac{2 \times n}{3} \rightarrow \frac{2}{3}n$, which can also be thought of as
  $n \rightarrow 2 \times n \rightarrow \frac{1}{3} \times (2 \times n) \rightarrow \frac{2}{3}n$

- $n \rightarrow \frac{n}{3} \rightarrow 2 \times \left(\frac{n}{3}\right) \rightarrow \frac{2}{3}n$, which can also be thought of as
  $n \rightarrow \left(\frac{1}{3} \times n\right) \rightarrow 2 \times \left(\frac{1}{3} \times n\right) \rightarrow \frac{2}{3}n$

Teaching Tip: Math Talk

The mental processes employed by students engaged in fraction tasks are often quite different from the instructional procedures they are taught. Through quality mathematical discourse—lately referred to as *math talk*—we can access what students are really thinking and how they are producing their answers and then consider how those findings might modify our instruction. Regarding the interpretation of a fraction as a multiplicative operator $\left(\text{say}, \frac{2}{3}\right)$ operating on any number n, different views usually emerge within the same class, depending on students' prior experiences, knowledge, and instruction:

> **Alex:** I first multiplied the number by 2, and then I divided by 3.

> **Talia:** I put a 1 under the number $\left(\frac{n}{1}\right)$, and then I multiplied the numerator by 2 and multiplied the denominator by 3.

Alex's approach, the one explored in this chapter, uses whole-number multiplication and division. Note that if $2n$ is not divisible by 3, the answer remains in the fraction form $\frac{2n}{3}$. This approach is taught and learned well before the standard algorithm for fraction multiplication.

By contrast, Talia has clearly been taught the standard algorithm for multiplying a fraction by a number n and has applied it correctly—though it is unclear whether she fully understands it. The important pedagogical point here is to reconcile both approaches so all students see they are equivalent, even though they may hear Alex saying "*divided* by 3" and Talia saying "*multiplied* by 3."

A teacher's intervention at this point is crucial.

The Rational Number Meaning of $\frac{a}{b}$ Embodied by the Number Line

The rational-number concept is the outgrowth of extensive work on fractions over many years—the beautiful confluence of the part-whole, measure, division/quotient, multiplicative operator, and even ratio concepts. When conceptualizing a number in grades 3–8, be it whole, integer, or rational, students visualize its physical embodiment as a single point on a number line—a line with a selected point called the *origin*, *O*, composed of units of 1. ("Number" as an abstract concept occurs much later.) In locating or placing a fraction $\left(\text{say, } \frac{4}{5}\right)$ on the number line, we find aspects of all of the connected concepts we've discussed.

- **Part-whole.** The whole (the unit from 0 to 1) is sliced into five parts called *fifths*. We count four copies (iterations) of $\frac{1}{5}$, starting from the origin, and mark the point $\frac{4}{5}$.

- **Measure.** If we consider the unit of measure to be the line segment from 0 to 1, then the length of the line segment from 0 to $\frac{4}{5}$ represents the measure $\frac{4}{5}$ of the unit.

- **Division/quotient.** Partitioning the line segment from 0 to 4 into five equal "shares" yields five smaller line segments of length $\frac{4}{5}$. Try it!

- **Multiplicative operator.** There are two ways to consider this:

  1. Stretch the unit by a factor of 4 (i.e., land on 4) and then shrink the four-unit segment by a factor of 5 to land on $\frac{4}{5}$.

2. Shrink the unit by a factor of 5 $\left(\text{i.e., land on } \frac{1}{5}\right)$ and then stretch the $\frac{1}{5}$ segment by a factor of four to land on $\frac{4}{5}$.

- **Ratio.** This is more complex. We can form many ratios of lengths, such as $1{:}\frac{4}{5}$ and $4{:}\frac{4}{5}$. The ratio of 1 to $\frac{4}{5}$ is $\frac{5}{4}$ because 1 is $\frac{5}{4}$ $\left(\text{or } 1\frac{1}{4}\right)$ times longer than $\frac{4}{5}$. The ratio 4 to $\frac{4}{5}$ is 5 because 4 is 5 times longer than $\frac{4}{5}$. Take a moment to verify this!

Targeting Misconceptions with Challenging Problems

Even though there are ample fraction questions and problems available online and in books, many of them are rote problems that students carry out mechanically without deepening their understanding of fractions. We must formulate more thought-provoking problems that force students to change gears from number numbness to productive struggle. Seven such problems are suggested in the following list.

💡 **Problem 1: Multiple meanings.** Pick a fraction $\frac{a}{b}$ of your choice. For each of the following cases, describe a real-world situation, and then formulate a question to which your fraction is the answer:

- $\frac{a}{b}$ is a part of a whole.
- $\frac{a}{b}$ is a measure.
- $\frac{a}{b}$ is a quotient (the result of a division).
- $\frac{a}{b}$ is a multiplicative operator.
- $\frac{a}{b}$ is a ratio.

💡 **Problem 2: Part-whole meaning.** We know that a fraction can represent a part of a region or a collection.

- Draw, shade, or otherwise represent the fractional part of each figure.

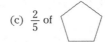
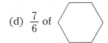

(a) $\frac{1}{3}$ of △

(c) $\frac{2}{5}$ of ⬠

(b) $\frac{3}{4}$ of ▭

(d) $\frac{7}{6}$ of ⬡

- Draw, shade, or otherwise represent the fractional part of each given set.

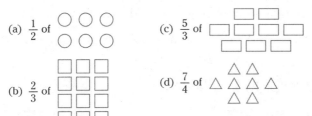
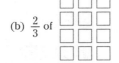

(a) $\frac{1}{2}$ of ○○○ ○○○

(c) $\frac{5}{3}$ of ▭▭▭▭▭▭▭▭

(b) $\frac{2}{3}$ of ▢▢▢ ▢▢▢ ▢▢▢ ▢▢▢

(d) $\frac{7}{4}$ of △△△△△△△

💡 **Problem 3: Number and linear measure meanings.** We know that a fraction can represent a number or a measure.

- Place a point on the number line that represents the number $\frac{4}{5}$.

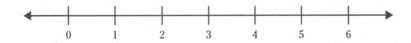

- This piece of packing tape is 5 units long (using the unit of measure in the previous number line). Draw a piece of tape below this one that is $\frac{4}{5}$ as long.

- In what ways are your number line and tape models similar? Explain.

- In what ways are your number line and tape models different? Explain.

Problem 4: Multiplicative operator meaning. Remember that a fraction can represent a multiplicative operator. Imagine that the figures below are flexible bands of fabric and that each piece can be stretched or shrunk to a desired length. Draw the result of the stretching or shrinking effect of each fraction on the given length of fabric.

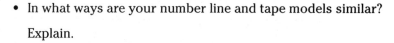

$\frac{2}{3}$ of $\frac{5}{2}$ of

$\frac{7}{4}$ of $\frac{2}{5}$ of

Problem 5: Connecting part-whole, quotient, and ratio meanings. Use everything you have learned so far about fractions to complete the following activities.

- Draw a rectangular chocolate bar, and shade $\frac{5}{6}$ of the bar, representing the part of the whole that you ate (i.e., the *part-whole meaning* of the fraction $\frac{5}{6}$).

- Draw five bars of chocolate that are the same size. Then model with a drawing or diagram how you might share the five bars equally among six people $\left(\text{i.e., the } \textit{quotient meaning} \text{ of the fraction } \frac{5}{6}\right)$.

- In what ways are the fractional meanings in the first two activities related? Are there other ways that they could be related? Explain.

- Drawing a rectangle for a chocolate bar once again, explain what a $\frac{5}{6}$ part-to-whole ratio might represent. Do the same for a $\frac{5}{6}$ part-to-part ratio.

💡 **Problem 6: Rational number meaning.** You have learned that a fraction can represent a rational number, which is shown by a point on the number line.

- Looking at this number line, cross out the fractions that clearly could not be represented by point *A*:

$$\frac{1}{2} \quad \frac{3}{5} \quad \frac{7}{6} \quad \frac{7}{10} \quad \frac{3}{2} \quad \frac{4}{5} \quad \frac{5}{4} \quad \frac{5}{7} \quad \frac{3}{4} \quad \frac{4}{3}$$

- Circle the fractions that could be represented by point *B*:

$$\frac{8}{5} \quad \frac{2}{3} \quad \frac{5}{4} \quad \frac{7}{10} \quad \frac{10}{7} \quad \frac{3}{2} \quad \frac{4}{3} \quad \frac{9}{7} \quad \frac{3}{4} \quad \frac{5}{3}$$

- Place point *C* on the number line to represent the number $\frac{7}{4}$. Explain how you used the values of the numerator and denominator of the fraction to find its place on the line.

💡 **Problem 7: Whole numbers and rational numbers on the number line.** Use everything you have learned so far about fractions to solve the following problems.

- The whole numbers 0, 2, and 3 segment number line N1 into four intervals. Place a fraction, as accurately as you can, in each of the four intervals.

- The fractions $\frac{1}{2}, \frac{5}{4}$, and $\frac{11}{3}$ segment number line N2 into four intervals. Place a whole number, as accurately as you can, in each of the four intervals.

💻 What's the App for That? *Fraction Math Match*

By playing the fun and addictive fraction memory game **Fraction Math Match** (www.apps4math.com), students come to appreciate various aspects of fraction representation, including visual, geometric, numeric, and artistic.

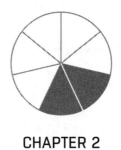

CHAPTER 2

Use Visual and Tactile Models

Invest time in building meaning for fractions by using multiple concrete models and meaningful contexts.

Kathleen Cramer and Stephanie Whitney (2010, p. 21)

Chapter 1 explored the meanings associated with the word *fraction*—the inner representations we develop to embody fractions, and the outer representations we use to express them. This chapter focuses on issues related to the use of visual and tactile models in fraction instruction. Which models are effective? Are all models equivalent? What limitations might they present? Should we use one or many models?

We'll also explore the actions that teachers model, the language we use, and the contexts we choose, all of which are fundamental to how instruction unfolds. The ultimate goal is to help students build an understanding of fractions as numbers in their own right—numbers like all others that can be manipulated with arithmetic. But before proceeding to computation algorithms, we must allow students the time to develop good fraction sense, which includes understanding fractions' magnitude, seeing how they can be used to describe situations, estimating the effects of operations on them, and visualizing their positions on the number line. That is the purpose of this chapter.

Note: The words *representation* and *model* are often used synonymously. However, representations can also denote students' personal mental images, which teachers cannot access. In this chapter, therefore, the word *representation* refers to the outer representations we use—drawings, pictures, objects, math manipulatives, diagrams, tables, and other learning tools—to help our students construct their understanding of new mathematical concepts.

Maya's Story

Maya, a seasoned 2nd grade teacher with a passion for learning and high expectations for all of her students, had recently accepted an offer to teach 4th grade in an international school. She conscientiously read the teacher guide for the math series used in her new school and learned that her students had previously represented fractions in various ways and in many real-world contexts. Here is a vignette from one of Maya's first lessons on fractions.

Maya writes the symbol $\frac{1}{4}$ on the board.

Maya: Does anyone know what this means? *[All hands shoot up.]* Carolina, can you tell us?

Carolina: One-fourth.

Maya: Cameron?

Cameron: One quarter.

Maya: OK, one more. Ali, what can you add?

Ali: One out of four!

Maya: I see you have many ideas about this. $\left[\textit{She points to } \frac{1}{4}.\right]$ Now you're going to imagine that *you're* the teacher, and you have to explain one-fourth to a younger student who's never seen this symbol before. You can use any representation you want.

Jaume: Can we use drawings?

Maya: Absolutely! You can express your ideas using words, drawings, math tools, actions—anything you think will help a young child understand. You're the teacher!

Perhaps influenced by Jaume's inquiry, almost all students took out their white slates and markers. But to Maya's disappointment, when show-and-tell time came, the majority of students had drawn a circle, divided it into four parts, and shaded one part. Although the words *one-fourth* and *one-quarter* had been voiced and heard by all students, the favorite verbal explanation that accompanied the drawings resembled this one: "I made a pizza, cut it in four parts, and ate one of them."

Her students' responses confirmed the research Maya had read on the impact of fraction instruction on student learning, leading her to two conclusions:

1. The main construct students used in their prior instruction of $\frac{a}{b}$ was probably the part-whole interpretation, verbalized by the phrase "*a* parts out of *b* equal parts of the whole."
2. The circle model was the model students retained best.

Beyond Misconceptions of Fractions

In this vignette, rather than misconceptions, we observe narrow conceptions of what fractions are and limited ways to model them.

Limited Repertoire of Fraction Models

The main advantage of the circular region is that it emphasizes the amount that is remaining to make up a whole.

John A. Van de Walle and Lou Ann H. Lovin (2006a, p. 254)

Circle models, representing pizzas or pies, are unquestionably the most commonly used area models in fraction instruction. Circle models are effective in early instruction, where they highlight the part-whole concept and clearly convey the relative size of part to whole. For example, in Figure 2.1, it's easy to see that $\frac{1}{5}$ of a whole pizza is smaller than $\frac{1}{3}$ of the same pizza.

But we must take students beyond a single visualization of fractions as pizzas. No single model alone can capture all meanings, but multiple models, used in combination, deepen students' understanding of fractions. Each new model offers an opportunity for students to learn something new or different about the complex concept of fractions.

FIGURE 2.1
Pizzas as Part-Whole Area Models

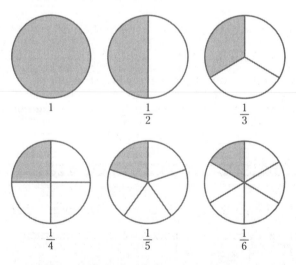

CCSS.Math.Practice.MP5: Use Appropriate Tools Strategically

Using mathematical learning tools strategically requires us to recognize the insight to be gained from each new tool and to discern its limitations. At least four limitations in *exclusively* using the circular-region model in grades 3 through 5 come to mind:

1. An overreliance on the circle model impedes students from progressing to the mathematics it serves to teach. A model is but a bridge to the mathematics—it itself is not the mathematics. Many older students still draw circles to justify, for instance, that $\frac{2}{3}$ is greater than $\frac{2}{4}$, rather than use mathematical reasoning.

2. It is difficult for students to see the unit or whole as anything other than one entire circle, as opposed to, say, thinking of the whole as two circles or a half circle.

3. With circle parts as the sole model for unit fractions, students are unable to see that whereas natural numbers (1, 2, 3, 4 . . .) are equidistant on the number line, their reciprocals $\left(\frac{1}{2}, \frac{1}{3}, \frac{1}{4} \ldots\right)$ are not.

4. It is difficult for children (and adults!) to precisely divide a circle into an odd number of equal parts, such as seven or nine.

Lack of Connectedness Among Models

Understanding is a measure of the quality and quantity of connections that a new idea has with existing ideas. The greater the number of connections for a network of ideas, the better the understanding.

John A. Van de Walle and Lou Ann H. Lovin (2006, p. 24)

Exposure to different visual, tactile, and other models does not suffice; the linking of these representations and the translation from one to another is of great importance. When teaching fractions, there are several ways to help students make connections for deeper understanding:

- Connect the informal knowledge that students bring to fraction instruction by relating new concepts, procedures, and symbols to real-world contexts and situations outside of school that are meaningful to students, and then build on them.

- Connect the different models used in instruction so students learn to seamlessly progress from one to another and back again, gradually coming to appreciate their similarities and differences.

- Connect the models used in instruction to the words articulated (new vocabulary, math talk), actions modeled (movements, gestures), and symbols manipulated $\left(\text{of the form } \frac{a}{b}\right)$. Students who experience a variety of ways to think, talk, and act about fractions, and who are expected to move back and forth between them, develop more flexibility in their fraction understanding.

Attending to all of these connections helps students construct a more integrated meaning for the big ideas that constitute the multifaceted concept of fractions (Figure 2.2).

FIGURE 2.2
The Multifaceted Concept of Fractions

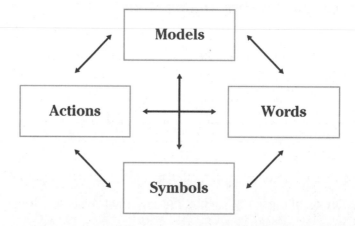

A Bridge to Algebra: Modeling Takes Center Stage

A central characteristic of human beings is our perpetual desire to understand our world. Nearly every explanation of our past or present (or prediction of our future) involves quantitative attributes: length, area, volume, mass, temperature, pressure, time, revenue, cost, profit, population, and so on. These quantitative attributes are modeled with numbers and variables, and relationships among quantities are modeled with equations. Much of the mathematics used today to describe, explain, or forecast was developed as a result of modeling real-world phenomena.

For these reasons, the NCTM placed the problem-solving process of mathematical modeling at the center of school mathematics. One of the four big ideas of the 3–5 Algebra standards is the ability to "Use mathematical models to represent and understand quantitative relationships" (2000, p. 158). To better understand NCTM's goal, let's revisit the four steps in mathematical modeling that uses mathematics to model and solve real-world problems:

1. Identify the problem of interest, P, in the real world.

2. Express the problem in mathematical language, using formulas, equations, and so forth. This is the *mathematical model* M.

3. Find the mathematical solution, S_M, of the model.

4. Apply the solution to the original problem, adjusting it as needed (S_R) to make sense in the real world (Figure 2.3).

FIGURE 2.3
The Process of Mathematical Modeling

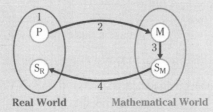

Unpacking the Mathematical Thinking

Despite their importance, models are a *means* to the mathematics, not the end (Clements, 1999). Though no model is perfect, we can overcome its limitations if we make a point of constantly connecting what we do in a meaningful way to the mathematics we wish to teach, embodied by the model we employ (be it a manipulative, picture, drawing, or problem situation). Let's look at some models we can use in grades 3–5 to help students represent and thus better understand the many meanings of fractions. The models are grouped into two categories: continuous models, including the special linear model known as the number line, and discrete models.

Continuous Models

Area models, commonly used to find the area of a circle, square, rectangle, or other polygonal shape, are often the first models students encounter. A given region, in theory, can be partitioned into any number of parts of equal area, since area is a continuous two-dimensional measurable quantity. In addition, drawings of regions offer more flexibility than manipulatives, such as pattern blocks, also used to represent area.

Use a variety of materials to embody regions: delineated sections of a sheet of paper, tag board, fabric, the classroom floor (especially if it's tiled), the blackboard or a whiteboard, and so on. You can also use commercial area models, but be careful to emphasize that you are focusing on the top face or top surface area of the objects, which are indeed 2-D measurable quantities.

Although area models are simple, basic, and appropriate for the early years of fraction instruction, they are nonetheless subject to mathematical misconceptions, as we will see in the second half of Maya's story later in this chapter.

Figure 2.4 illustrates some common (and one less common) area models showing the fraction $\frac{1}{4}$ of a shape's total area.

FIGURE 2.4
Area Models of $\frac{1}{4}$ of Each Shape's Total Area

Volume models are also fairly simple to understand, especially since the cross-section is similar to an area model. Simple containers in cubical, rectangular, or cylindrical shapes are accessible to elementary school students. Any amount of liquid, powder, or other substance, in theory, can be partitioned into any number of parts of equal volume, since volume is a continuous three-dimensional measurable quantity.

Use a variety of materials to embody volume, such as rectangular containers packed with unit cubes, calibrated beakers or other containers filled with liquid, solids that can be cut (e.g., apples), wooden Soma cubes that can be taken apart, or plastic multilink or connecting cubes that can be assembled to make a variety of shapes with measurable volume. Figure 2.5 illustrates volume models showing the fraction $\frac{1}{4}$ of a container's total volume.

FIGURE 2.5
Volume Models of $\frac{1}{4}$ of Each Container's Total Volume

  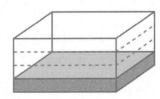

Length models are excellent ways to depict unit length and its unlimited fractional multiples or parts. You can draw line segments or narrow bars on paper, use pieces of rope or string, or cut out narrow strips of paper that can be folded into equal parts. Manipulatives, such as colored Cuisenaire® Rods and connected Unifix® cubes, despite their 3-D nature, are also designed to model length. Be creative with your choices. For example, if your classroom floor is tiled, point to the edge where the plane of a wall intersects the plane of the floor; have students measure that edge, and then find $\frac{1}{4}$ (or any other fraction) of its length. Figure 2.6 illustrates length models showing the fraction $\frac{1}{4}$ of a linear object's total length.

FIGURE 2.6
Length Models of $\frac{1}{4}$ of Each Object's Total Length

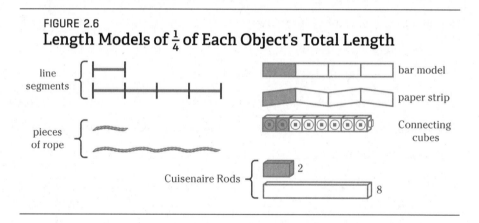

Again, as students' understanding of linear measure matures, when using concrete manipulatives, emphasize that you are not focusing on the volume of the rods or trains, or on the surface area of their faces, but rather on the length of their long edges, all of which are indeed one-dimensional (1-D) measurable quantities. When using imperfect models, making such clarifications about the object's geometric properties helps prepare students to learn about the dimensions of a solid (3-D) and its different components: 1-D, 2-D, and even zero-dimensional (0-D) (Figure 2.7).

FIGURE 2.7
Example of a 3-D Solid: A Cube

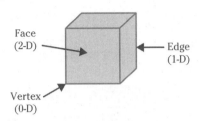

Face
(2-D)

Edge
(1-D)

Vertex
(0-D)

The **number line model** is an important, and specifically mathematical, linear model that deserves special mention, since it is alarmingly underused in elementary school classrooms. Mathematicians stress the importance of familiarizing students with the number line early on, as most of the mathematics in middle and high school is modeled on either one line (the x-axis), two lines (the x- and y-axes), or three lines (the x-, y-, and z-axes). However, it presents some difficulties for students, particularly in that the concepts of *number* (represented by a point on the line) and *linear measure* (represented by the length from the origin to the point in question) both converge in the number line concept.

Consider, for instance, the fraction $\frac{4}{5}$. We place the point on the number line that represents the number $\frac{4}{5}$ at precisely a distance (or length) of $\frac{4}{5}$ of a unit from the origin—so, any point P on a number line implicitly represents its distance from the point of origin. Often denoted by the letter O and at a distance of zero from itself, the origin therefore represents the number 0.

The progression from using cube trains in 1st and 2nd grade (3-D concrete models) to using bar models starting in 2nd or 3rd grade (2-D pictorial models) and ultimately to number-line segments as early as 3rd or 4th grade (1-D linear models) is an ideal example of a progression from concrete to pictorial to abstract representations of both number and length. Figure 2.8 illustrates this progression.

FIGURE 2.8
From Concrete (3-D) to Pictorial (2-D) to Abstract (1-D)

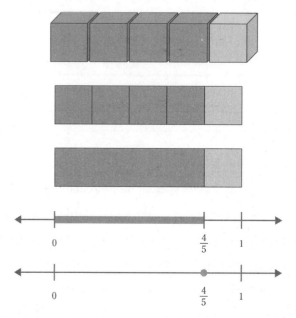

Note: Line segments (1-D) and points (0-D) on a line are challenging abstract concepts.

Since numbers are used to represent real-world quantities, the progression also helps students represent and understand *number as quantity*. Cube trains and bar models, used extensively in Singapore math classrooms, can therefore be thought of as "thickened" number line segments.

Discrete Models

Set or collection models can be puzzling to students, who often have little experience with tackling discrete quantities. For example, for students to see that the shaded discs on the left side of Figure 2.9 model $\frac{1}{4}$ of the total number of discs, they must mentally partition the 12 discs into subgroups. Some students may partition the array of 12 discs horizontally into three subgroups of 4 and reason in the following way: in each row of 4 discs, 1 disc is shaded. Since the fraction of shaded discs in each row is $\frac{1}{4}$, the fraction of shaded discs among all 12 discs is also $\frac{1}{4}$.

FIGURE 2.9

A Set Model of $\frac{1}{4}$ of the Total Number of Elements

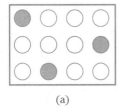 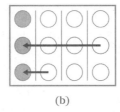

(a)   (b)

Note: Notice that (a) and (b) are the same set; (b) explains how one can rearrange the shaded discs to better see the fraction $\frac{1}{4}$ (as explained in the text).

For the students who don't see this, redrawing the 12 discs with three vertical lines to partition them into four subgroups of 3, and then shifting the 3 shaded discs to one column, helps them see that the fraction of 3 shaded discs out of 12 is the same as the fraction of 1 subgroup out of 4, namely, $\frac{1}{4}$.

Such models offer a useful springboard to fractions as ratios. Here, for instance, we could say that the shaded to white discs are in a 3-to-9 or 1-to-3 relationship (or a 1:3 ratio) and write $\frac{S}{W} = \frac{1}{3}$.

As always, when using a set or collection model with students, vary the nature of the discrete quantities you use as examples. You might include groups of students, backpacks, books or pens, classroom chairs, balloons, coins, baseball cards, toys, bracelets, buttons, cubes, or discs. To develop the notion of discrete quantities, select objects that cannot be arbitrarily subdivided (e.g., students, marbles) and ones that can be subdivided but would no longer be of interest if that occurred (e.g., stamps, pens).

Discussing and Connecting Models

We saw in Chapter 1 that "fraction as division" is an interpretation that few students in grades 3–5 readily grasp, partly because they witness little modeling of this meaning in the early grades. Yet, with some guidance, students in these grades are perfectly capable of connecting fractions to division.

Consider, for example, the fraction $\frac{3}{4}$. Ask your students for suggestions on how to share three small pizzas equally among four people. Even if they have no prior exposure to division, partitioning quantities for the purpose of fair sharing is rooted in early childhood experiences, and students will always have ideas about how to do this. One common student idea and two more sophisticated ones are illustrated in Figure 2.10.

When discussing solutions—both theirs and yours—ensure that students witness $\frac{3}{4}$ as both the *process* and the *product* of division: $\frac{3}{4}$ (3 divided by 4) represents not only the action of sharing three pizzas equally among four people but also the name of the resulting share (or quantity of pizza) each person receives.

FIGURE 2.10

Three Students' Ideas About How to Share Three Pizzas Equally Among Four People

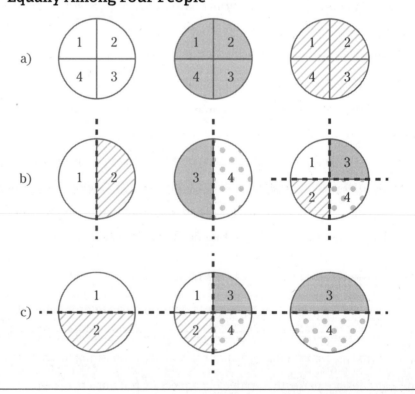

Teaching Tip: Partitioning and Iterating

Students must see teachers modeling both partitioning and iterating when we teach fractions. When showing $\frac{1}{4}$, we almost always begin with a whole, whether continuous or discrete, and then partition it into four equal parts. What students rarely see is teachers *iterating* to show $\frac{1}{4}$: repeating the action of appending to the original object or quantity a copy of itself three times until one composite unit of four parts is shown.

To illustrate, start with an object (e.g., a square, rectangle, or triangle) and then iterate it three times: draw, create, or fetch three more copies and then juxtapose or add them to the original one to make four. The original object now represents $\frac{1}{4}$ of the composite unit of 4 objects.

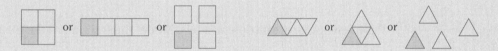

Students soon learn that *partitioning* reduces the size of the fractional parts but preserves the whole, whereas *iterating* preserves the size of the fractional parts but increases the whole.

Challenge your students to model the fractions $\frac{1}{3}$ or $\frac{2}{3}$ using two gray marbles and any number of white marbles. Since they can't partition, they will need to iterate: they may choose to add four white marbles to model $\frac{1}{3}$ gray, and one white marble to model $\frac{2}{3}$ gray.

Now that you have expanded their repertoire of knowledge and empowered them with new mathematical ideas, students will surprise you with their answers!

Targeting Misconceptions with Challenging Problems

Visual, tactile, and other models, while important, are not a guarantee to meaningful learning when teaching young students. The key to the effective use of models is the combination of the actions we take, the math talk we orchestrate around them, and the connections we help students make by posing good questions and assigning challenging problems. It is fundamental to use a variety of models that differ in how the unit, the fractional parts, and the fraction at hand are defined, perceived, and visualized. This forces students to keep changing gears, not rely on any one model, and ultimately move beyond the models themselves to construct rich mathematical ideas. The problems below are designed for these purposes.

 Problem 1: Using multiple models. Model the fraction of the pie represented by the shaded area, using the following models:

1. A length model of your choice

2. A collection model of your choice

3. A number line marked with 0, 1, and 2

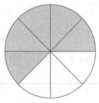

After completing your three representations of the fraction, specify in each case what part of your representation is your whole (or unit) and what part is your fraction.

Note: You can repeat this problem by replacing the circular model with the term *five-eighths* and then with the symbol $\frac{5}{8}$.

💡 **Problem 2: Modeling fair sharing.** Model how you would equally divide the sandwiches in the following situations:

1. Nine baguette sandwiches among three people
2. Six baguette sandwiches among three people
3. Three baguette sandwiches between two people
4. Two baguette sandwiches among three people
5. Three baguette sandwiches among four people

After modeling all five sandwich divisions, share in writing at least two mathematical observations.

💡 **Problem 3: Building and drawing models.** Let's work with the fraction $\frac{3}{4}$ (*3 one-fourths*).

1. **Cube trains–length model.** Build a train, using as many connecting cubes as you like, and call it Train A. Then build Train B such that Train A is $\frac{3}{4}$ of the length of Train B.
2. **Geoboard-area model.** Place a light-colored rubber band around the pegs that enclose the region with largest possible area on a 5-by-5-peg geoboard, and call it Region A. Then place a darker rubber band around a smaller Region B, whose area is $\frac{3}{4}$ of the area of Region A. Find three different shapes for Region B.
3. **Set model.** Select a number of counters of your choice, and call it Set A. Then make Set B such that the number of elements in Set A is $\frac{3}{4}$ of the number of elements in Set B.
4. **Number-line model.** Draw a number line and mark the origin O. Pick a point anywhere on the line, and call it Point A. Then place Point B on the line such that the distance from O to B is $\frac{3}{4}$ of the distance from O to A.

Which of these modeling activities were easier? Which were harder? Why?

💡 **Problem 4: Modeling fractions with paper strips.** Cut out two identical strips of paper of any length. Name the first one Strip *A* and set it aside. Take the second strip, fold it into eighths (hint: fold it in half three times), and then cut off $\frac{2}{8}$ of the length. Call the part left over Strip *B*.

- What fraction of Strip *A* is Strip *B*?
- What fraction of Strip *B* is Strip *A*?
- How did you figure out each fraction?

💡 **Problem 5: A nutty situation.** Imagine grabbing a handful of nuts from a bag. One-third of them are hazelnuts.

1. Use colored counters or make a drawing to model this situation. Call it Solution 1.
2. Use another set of counters or make another drawing that also models the situation but uses different numbers. Call it Solution 2.

For each solution,

- Explain how you selected the numbers (the number of hazelnuts and the total number of nuts).
- Give the number of hazelnuts.
- Give the total number of nuts.
- Identify what is different and what is the same in both solutions.
- Explain how many possible solutions there are, and justify your answer.

Problem 6: Partitioning and iterating. On each figure, show the fraction in two different ways: first by partitioning, and then by iterating.

- The fraction $\frac{1}{2}$

- The fraction $\frac{1}{3}$

- The fraction $\frac{1}{4}$

- The fraction $\frac{1}{5}$

 Problem 7: Hopping multiples of unit fractions on the number line.

Use a new number line for each part of this problem.

1. *Fourths*
   - Place $\frac{1}{4}$ on the number line. Making hops of $\frac{1}{4}$ on the number line, place $\frac{3}{4}$ and $\frac{7}{4}$.
   - Can you express the distance between the two fractions $\frac{3}{4}$ and $\frac{4}{7}$? How do you know?

2. *Thirds*

- Place $\frac{1}{3}$ on the number line. Making hops of $\frac{1}{3}$ on the number line, place $\frac{2}{3}$ and $\frac{5}{3}$.

- Can you express the distance between the two fractions $\frac{2}{3}$ and $\frac{5}{3}$? How can you be sure?

3. *Fifths*

- Place $\frac{1}{5}$ on the number line. Making hops of $\frac{1}{5}$ on the number line, place $\frac{2}{5}$ and $\frac{9}{5}$.

- While you haven't yet learned how to subtract fractions, can you see what $\frac{9}{5} - \frac{2}{5}$ would be? How did you figure it out?

Reflect on your work.

- Is $\frac{3}{4}$ harder to place on the number line than $\frac{7}{4}$, is it easier, or are they both the same? What about $\frac{2}{3}$ and $\frac{5}{3}$? What about $\frac{2}{5}$ and $\frac{9}{5}$? Explain your thinking.

- Write a paragraph explaining the process you learned for placing any fraction on the number line. Use the terms *top number* (or *numerator*) and *bottom number* (or *denominator*) in your explanation.

 Teaching Tip:
Hopping Multiples of Unit Fractions on the Number Line

Students will likely find Problem 7 challenging, not because it is particularly difficult but because the method is uncommon. Nevertheless, this problem teaches students many things:

1. It does away with different treatments of proper and improper fractions and consequently with those terms.

2. It equips students with a strategy for successfully placing any fraction on the number line.

3. It dispels the misconception that all fractions live between 0 and 1.

4. It reinforces the concept that whole numbers are also rational. Hopping from $\frac{3}{4}$ to $\frac{7}{4}$, for example, the student pauses at 1 and says, "$\frac{4}{4}$." The same is true for $\frac{3}{3}$ and $\frac{5}{5}$.

5. It confirms that equivalent fractions, though different in appearance, live at the same point on a line (like different family members who live together have the same street address). For instance $\frac{3}{3}, \frac{4}{4}$, and $\frac{5}{5}$ are all represented by the point at 1 on the number line.

6. It confirms the concept that despite the two numerals a and b that make up $\frac{a}{b}$, the fraction is a unique number represented by a single point on the number line.

Maya's Story, Part 2

After noting that many of her students had used or explained "one-fourth" of a circle in a rather rote way, Maya decided to spend the next day probing more deeply into her students' understanding of their favorite model—namely, the area of a single region. This time, she chose a square region to better assess the fraction shaded. She made three drawings on the board and asked if the shaded region of each square models $\frac{1}{4}$ (Figure 2.11).

FIGURE 2.11
Maya's Drawings of Three Areas of a Square Region

 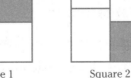

Square 1   Square 2   Square 3

Later, when Maya discussed this class with her colleagues, she noted how especially surprised she was that many students thought the shaded region in Square 1 *did not* model $\frac{1}{4}$ of the total area. Their reasoning: "Because there are only two parts." In addition, some students thought that the shaded region in Square 3 *did* model $\frac{1}{4}$ of the total area "because there are four parts." Their reactions to Square 2 were mixed.

Recognizing Misconceptions

Maya's follow-up helped her, and us, detect additional misconceptions about the most commonly used fraction model: the area model. Her inquisitive teacher mind helped uncover errors in student thinking that we seldom suspect.

The Parts Need Not Be Equal

Many students think that a shape divided into four parts represents fourths, even if the four parts don't have equal areas. This explains why some students thought that the shaded region in Square 3 represented one-fourth.

The Parts Must Be Clearly Delineated

Regions in which the equal parts are not clearly delineated by line segments pose particular challenges to students. Thus, Maya's students thought that the shaded region in Square 1 did not model $\frac{1}{4}$ of the total area because its complement—the larger part—although representing $\frac{3}{4}$ of the total square, was not clearly subdivided into three quarters.

The Parts Must Have the Same Shape

Many students are perplexed by problems in which the different pieces have equal areas but different shapes. They would have trouble seeing fourths in the following example, as the parts are not congruent shapes, even though each part is $\frac{1}{4}$ of the total area of the rectangular region.

The Shaded Regions Must Be Grouped into One Part

Many students also believe that the shaded or colored areas must be connected into a compact area. If, for instance, a rectangle is partitioned into four equal parts, two of which are shaded and two are not, and the two shaded pieces are separated by an unshaded piece, students will hesitate to call the shaded pieces (combined) $\frac{1}{2}$ of the total area.

I vividly remember a 4th grader reacting to Figure 2.9a (p. 61) by saying, "Oh, I thought the three shaded balls all had to be together!" It was a revelation to her that they could be scattered among the array of 12 balls.

Unpacking the Mathematical Thinking

Two key things become clear about teaching fractions with area models: (1) when discussing fraction $\frac{a}{b}$, we must clearly state that the b parts are *equal* in size; and (2) we must encourage students to focus on the *area* of each part (or combinations of parts) rather than be distracted by its *shape*.

The Importance of Equal Parts

In the early grades of fraction instruction, a common explanation for fraction $\frac{a}{b}$ often goes as follows: The number b tells the number of parts that a whole is divided into, so *b* plays the role of the *divisor* and names the fractional parts (e.g., fourths). The number *a* tells the number of these parts that are needed or used for the purpose at hand, so *a* has the role of *multiplier* $\left(\text{e.g., } \frac{3}{4} \text{ is } 3 \times \text{one-fourth}\right)$.

Although this is a beautiful explanation—and very mathematical—it fails to emphasize the equality among the fractional parts. We are all guilty of this. How often have we said "four parts" when what we meant was "four *equal* parts"? If the *b* parts are not equal, then we cannot be assured that each part actually measures $\frac{1}{b}$ or that $\frac{b}{b}$ will equal 1.

Area, Not Shape, Is the Focus

Children begin playing with shapes from a very young age. After color, which they see first, their attention is drawn to the visual perception of shape. They recognize shapes and name them: square, triangle, rectangle, circle, and so on.

The notion of area is learned later on and is more conceptual than visual. Area is based on measurement, which is a complex idea for elementary school students. They must pause and reflect when asked to figure out if the area (or the amount of 2-D space) in each piece is the same. This could explain, in part, why some of Maya's students thought that the shaded part in Square 3 in Figure 2.11 was in fact $\frac{1}{4}$ of the total area—after all, the four parts were all rectangular in shape!

Knowing this, we must remind students to focus on the area of *each part* in an area model. Analogies such as the "amount of carpet" or the "amount of paint" needed to cover each part can help students construct the concept of equal area.

Targeting Misconceptions with Challenging Problems

To support students in overcoming these basic misconceptions about area models, we need to be creative with the problems we pose and avoid always choosing the same examples. Seven problems are suggested below.

🔅 **Problem 1: What fraction is represented?** Kristin had afterschool activities three times a week. To help her remember the days that she had to do her homework at school, she shaded three columns of her calendar. What fraction of Kristin's calendar is shaded? Note: "Calendar" here refers to the totality of the cells making up the rectangle.

M	Tu	W	Th	F	S	S
30	1	2	3	4	5	6
7	8	9	10	11	12	13
14	15	16	17	18	19	20
21	22	23	24	25	26	27
30	31	1	2	3	4	5

🔅 **Problem 2: Find the fraction.** Describe the strategy you use to determine the correct figure(s) in each problem.

1. Circle the figures in which the shaded area represents $\frac{1}{2}$ of the total area.

2. Circle the figures in which the shaded area represents $\frac{1}{3}$ of the total area.

  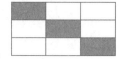

3. Circle the figures in which the shaded area represents $\frac{1}{4}$ of the total area.

Problem 3: Whose thinking is in line with yours? Jamie and Melissa made a hexagon sandwich with pattern blocks: one trapezoid and three triangles. They discussed the fraction of the hexagon modeled by one triangle:

Jamie: It's one-fourth because the hexagon is divided into four pieces.

Melissa: It's one-sixth because it would take six triangles to cover the hexagon.

Both Jamie and Melissa had arguments to justify their answers. Can you comment on their thinking? Which reasoning is closest to your own thinking about this question? Is Jamie correct? Is Melissa? Explain *your* thinking.

Problem 4: Pool problems. Use what you've learned about area to solve the problems below.

- The rectangular cover of public pool A is made of three different-colored fabrics, each one representing $\frac{1}{3}$ of the total area. Make a drawing of what the thirds might look like. Try to imagine and describe two other configurations.

- The rectangular cover of public pool B is made of eight equal-size pieces of fabric. Draw two possible configurations of the eight sections. In each drawing, shade $\frac{1}{4}$ of the total area green.

Variation: Pose the same questions, using a different shape and/or a different fraction.

Problem 5: Different? Or the same? Here two representations of $\frac{1}{4}$.

- How are these representations different? Explain.
- How are these representations similar? Explain.
- Describe a real-world context that would be well represented by each drawing.

Problem 6: Creative fourths. For this problem, you will need a 5-by-5 geoboard and rubber bands. Place a large rubber band around the pegs that will make the largest possible square. Imagine that this is your square garden.

1. Using two rubber bands, make two intersecting straight-line paths that cut through your garden. The two paths must "cut" your garden into four sections of the same shape and size (fourths!). Can you do this in three different ways?

2. *Challenge 1:* Remove the rubber-band paths. This time, you will again make two intersecting paths that cut through your garden and divide it into four sections of the same shape and size—but here is your challenge: the paths *cannot* be straight lines! Can you do this in three different ways? Explain.

3. *Challenge 2*: Can you divide your garden into four sections that are all fourths but not all the same shape? Explain.

Problem 7: Intersecting regions. Use what you've learned about area to solve the problems below.

- The shaded region represents the common area of two identical and overlapping rectangles; it measures $\frac{1}{4}$ of the area of each rectangle. What fraction of the area of the *entire figure* does the shaded region represent?

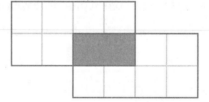

- The shaded region represents the common area of two identical and overlapping squares; it measures $\frac{4}{9}$ of the area of each square. What fraction of the area of the *entire figure* does the shaded region represent?

Maya's Story: Epilogue

Maya was determined to have her students develop for themselves new and varied models for fractions. She concluded the unit on fractions by assigning a Fractional Flower Poster project.

Make a poster of a big daisy. At the center, write the fraction $\frac{1}{4}$. Draw a petal for each different idea you have about the fraction. Use words, drawings, diagrams, or symbols to describe your thoughts. Make a few blank petals for new knowledge you will build this year about your favorite fraction.

Maya reserved a wall on which to post her favorite answers. By the end of the year, it looked like a sunburst with rays going in so many inspiring and creative directions (Figure 2.12).

I think Maya has given us a great idea to emulate! Happy fractioning!

FIGURE 2.12
Rendition of Maya's Wall

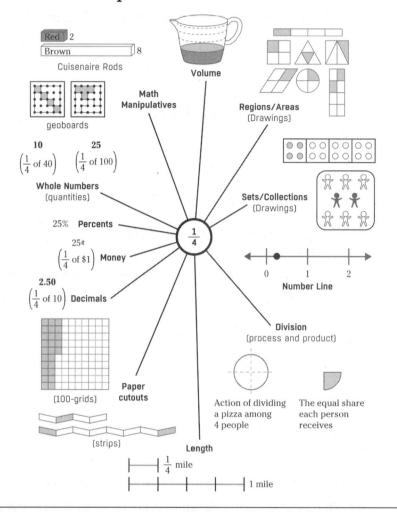

This multipurpose app helps students represent fractions using the first model students encounter in their fraction journey: the circular area model. The **Fraction Circles** app (www.apps4math.com) helps students visualize fraction magnitude and use the area representations to make sense of fraction operations.

CHAPTER 3

Focus on the Unit

Understanding that the magnitude of a fractional number is relative to the size of the unit is a key to understanding rational numbers.

Carne Barnett-Clarke, William Fisher, Rick Marks, and Sharon Ross (2010, p. 20)

The exercise of drawing a whole circle, square, or rectangle, dividing it into four parts, coloring in one part, and calling the colored part *one-fourth* is part of every American child's experiential knowledge by 3rd grade (Neagoy, 2012). This scenario typifies children's early school experiences with fractions, which focus primarily on partitioning wholes into n equal parts and then shading m of these parts, where m is chosen to be less than n. This early practice with partitioning wholes, grounded in children's early experiences with fair sharing—"How can I divide this cake equally among myself and my two sisters?"—is helpful for constructing fraction concepts.

However, if this is the only way that fractions are treated in the early grades—where the unit is always assumed to be 1 and of one type—then the approach can have unintentional detrimental effects on students' understanding of rational numbers later on. In this chapter, we look at some common student misconceptions related to the concept of the *whole* or *unit*, and we focus on the importance of the unit in developing foundational fraction concepts.

Note: The terms *unit* and *whole* are usually used interchangeably in most books on elementary school mathematics for students or teachers. That said, in linear models such as the number line, the chosen line segment between 0 and 1 is commonly called the *unit* or the *unit of measure,* rather than the *whole*, when used to measure lengths as integer or non-integer multiples of the unit length.

Ed's Story

After teaching 2nd grade for a few years, Ed was hired for a 4th grade position in another school. He was simultaneously excited and nervous— "Especially about teaching fractions," he confessed to me, even though he loved teaching math. I was conducting a grade-level working session on fractions at Ed's new school, and he arrived early, eager to pose a question. Pointing to one student's work (Figure 3.1), he lamented, "Tyler and a few others won't accept that this drawing represents three-halves. She insists it's three-fourths! How can I make her see three-halves?"

FIGURE 3.1

Tyler's Representation of $\frac{3}{4}$

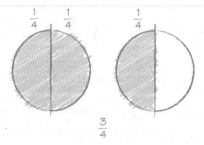

I could sense Ed's struggle and frustration. He genuinely wanted to help Tyler "see what she couldn't see." Modeling what I ask my teachers to do with their own students—namely, not to abort a constructive struggle—I opted not to provide an answer but rather ask a couple of probing questions, hoping that Ed would discover for himself what I could have just told him.

> **Monica:** Does this question come from your book?
>
> **Ed:** No, I made it up because I wanted to give them more examples of fractions greater than 1.
>
> **Monica:** Commendable objective. So, what did you ask?
>
> **Ed:** I just drew the two cookies on the board, shaded a part, and asked them what fraction it was.
>
> **Monica:** Do you remember precisely how you phrased your question?
>
> **Ed:** Yeah, I said, "What part of the cookies did I shade? Answer with a fraction."
>
> **Monica:** Did you add anything else?
>
> **Ed:** Like what?
>
> **Monica:** Did you specify anything about the unit?
>
> **Ed** [*after a pause*]: *Oh!!!*

Ed's seemingly simple question—and Tyler's answer—turned out to be more complex than Ed had thought. Ed had not paid attention to the role of the unit in defining a fraction when formulating his question; consequently, it was ambiguous. The next day, Ed further probed his students' reasoning. What silent assumptions had prompted the answers $1\frac{1}{2}$ or $\frac{3}{4}$?

Consistent with the research on students' beliefs about fractions, Ed found that the majority of his 4th grade students had automatically assumed one cookie to be the implied whole, and therefore answered $1\frac{1}{2}$. However, Tyler had assumed a different unit, and she eloquently used an analogy to explain her thinking to the class: "If I eat $1\frac{1}{2}$ cookies from a pack of two cookies, I eat $\frac{3}{4}$ *of the pack.*"

Ed's initial frustration quickly morphed into admiration. In the absence of any indication about the unit in his problem, he realized, either answer could be correct, provided that the students could explicitly describe their units. If one student said $1\frac{1}{2}$ cookies $\left(\text{or }\frac{3}{2}\right)$ and described the unit as one cookie, that was a correct response. If another surmised that both circles combined constituted the unit, then $\frac{3}{4}$ of the unit was indeed shaded.

 ### Teaching Tip: Creative Fraction Representations

Take the opportunity, from time to time, to depart from standard representations of area and to make more unusual, creative fractional shapes. Better yet, invite your artsy students—who may not be experiencing success with fractions—to share their creativity. The figures below show some examples you can use, and there are plenty of others.

Mathematicians who have received the Fields Medal (similar to the Nobel Prize for other sciences) often stress the importance of geometric visualization as an essential method for developing and expanding our mathematical minds. Moreover, by visualizing old ideas in new ways, we cultivate creativity and experience mathematical beauty.

I assure you that more than simple aesthetics will result from discussing, for instance, the shaded regions of the two squares versus the standard-looking representations for half a square. Questions about equality versus congruence and congruence versus symmetry will probably be raised.

Recognizing Misconceptions

Ed's story exhibits two common student misconceptions—one about the nature of the whole, and one about fractions with respect to the whole.

The Whole Is Made of One Piece

This widely held belief stems from students' introductory activities around fractions. They repeatedly engage in or witness the partitioning of single entitles: *one* cookie, *one* pizza, or *one* chocolate bar partitioned into n equal parts. Traditional assessments reinforce the erroneous notion that all units are of one piece by asking students to shade a fraction of one shape or to name the fraction for the shaded portion of one shape. Consequently, students struggle with questions or problems in which the unit or whole consists of more than one piece. Tyler was an inspiring exception to this rule.

A Fraction Is Smaller Than the Whole, the Unit, or the "1"

Another strongly held belief is that all fractions live between 0 and 1. Skip Fennell's pointed remark during a recent NCTM conference address ("Have you ever noticed that all number lines for fractions end at 1?") was met with a roar of laughter because we have all encountered this limited view among our students—and it can be hard to shake. For students who believe fractions are less than 1, a fraction such as $\frac{7}{5}$ has no meaning.

Again, this misconception can be traced back to children's initial explorations, which focus almost exclusively on the "part of a whole" definition of fractions. As we saw in Chapter 1, an obvious limitation of interpreting $\frac{a}{b}$ as "a parts out of b equal parts" is the tacit inference that the a parts must be smaller than the b parts, and therefore fractions with numerators greater than their denominators make no sense.

Difficulty Conceiving of or Writing Fractions Greater Than 1

Let's return to Ed's class. When he explored the reasoning behind his students' answers to the two-cookie problem, Ed discovered that among the students who wrote $\frac{3}{4}$, many were uncomfortable with fractions greater than 1; unlike Tyler, they gave the answer $\frac{3}{4}$ without having given much thought to the unit. So, although these students gave an answer that could be correct, if the pair of cookies were defined as the unit, they did so for the wrong reason: because they could not conceive of a fraction larger than 1. Ed also learned something more subtle: while he was using "$1\frac{1}{2}$" and "three-halves" interchangeably in the conversation, he realized that no student had actually opted for the notation $\frac{3}{2}$; they opted instead for the mixed-number notation $1\frac{1}{2}$, which contains a fraction less than 1. The students' comments revealed that they were uncomfortable even with *writing* $\frac{3}{2}$—the notation of a fraction with a numerator larger than the denominator.

Unease with fractions greater than 1 is understandable in grades 3–5, but it often carries over to middle and high school. During a 9th grade math lesson on linear functions that I once observed, I watched a student find $-\frac{11}{7}$ for the slope of his line, grab his calculator, and convert his rational number into a decimal to insert into his final linear equation. I later asked him why he didn't use $-\frac{11}{7}$ in his equation. His candid response: "I don't think of $-\frac{11}{7}$ as a number, so I prefer converting it to a decimal."

Limited Experience with Non-continuous Units

Often associated with the misconception that the unit must be one entity is the misconception that the entity is continuous. Modeling fractional parts of circular, square, or rectangular regions contributes to this belief. From the get-go, students should work with different kinds of units of quantity: continuous units, discrete units, fractional units, and composite units. We shouldn't shy away from posing questions in which the unit is a collection of things. In fact, the data suggest that discrete situations, which require well-developed counting procedures, are actually not that difficult for students (e.g., Post, Cramer, Behr, Lesh, & Harel, 1993).

Unpacking the Mathematical Thinking

Flexible reasoning about the unit is a key component of rational number sense, and it . . . develops over time and through many experiences.

Carne Barnett-Clarke, William Fisher, Rick Marks, and Sharon Ross (2010, p. 74)

Tyler exhibited such flexibility when she thought of the unit as a quantity other than 1 (cookie). Formal work on fractions begins in 3rd grade because by then children are able to think flexibly about the unit—or to *unitize*. With *unit* as its root, the verb *to unitize* means "to separate, transform, or classify something into discrete units." Students are encouraged to find or make a mathematical unit in one or more ways— such as counting, computing, measuring, or patterning—and then express their answer, whether it's a number, quantity, or pattern, in terms of these different units.

Unitizing also involves the ability to mentally decompose and then recompose quantities in different ways. For example, depending on what unit we focus on, the number 2,300 can be thought of as 2,300 ones; 230 tens; or 23 hundreds.

Considering a geometric example, the volume of a 3-by-3-by-3 cube can be viewed by chunking it in different ways, depending on what we choose for our unit: 3 layers of 9 cubic units, 9 columns of 3 cubic units, or 27 cubic units (see Figure 3.2).

FIGURE 3.2
Three Possible Choices of a Unit of Volume

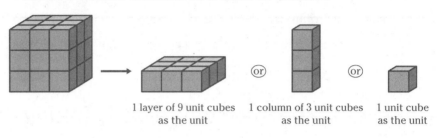

1 layer of 9 unit cubes   1 column of 3 unit cubes   1 unit cube
as the unit   as the unit   as the unit

In this section, we examine the central role of the unit in defining fractions, consider the different kinds of units that elementary school students should be exposed to, and revisit the interrelated process of partitioning and iterating that helps students develop the concept of unit.

 A Bridge to Algebra: From Units of 1 to Fractional (Rational) Units

From children's burgeoning ideas of number, which begin in infancy, through about age 8 or 9, the tacit assumption in the arithmetic of numbers is that all quantities are represented in terms of the unit 1: counting to three means three increments of the number 1, three dollars means three one-dollar units, and five granola bars means five one-bar units. This long-held assumption is a serious obstacle for upper elementary and middle school students when they enter the world of rational numbers, which can denote units other than 1.

Studies show that experiences with different types of units not only help students with whole-number arithmetic but also help them bridge more seamlessly to rational number concepts and operations, which are the prelude to algebra (Behr, Harel,

Post, & Lesh, 1994; Lamon, 1996). For example, after working with different types of units, students better understand that the number c (the amount they "carry") in the standard addition algorithm could represent c tens, c hundreds, c thousands, or some other unit.

Reflect on this example:

Take any fraction—say, $\frac{2}{3}$. We can think about this fraction in a number of ways. Using the four different units in Figure 3.3, see if you can visualize the equivalence between the following:

- One-third of a 2 unit

- Two-thirds of a 1 unit

- One $\frac{2}{3}$ unit

- Two $\frac{1}{3}$ units

FIGURE 3.3
Four Choices of a Unit of Length

A 2-unit : ▭ ▭

A 1-unit : ▭

A $\frac{2}{3}$-unit : ▭

A $\frac{1}{3}$-unit : ▭

This kind of mental gymnastics and flexibility is hard even for adults. But as you practice thinking of quantities in terms of different integer or non-integer units, you will begin to explore new kinds of questions with your students that will help them tremendously in their mathematical journey.

The Unit Is Defining

The concept of a whole underlies the concept of a fraction.

Merlyn J. Behr and Thomas R. Post (1992, p. 213)

Fractions are relationships: they are defined in relation to an implicit or explicit whole or unit. This is true regardless of which interpretation of fraction we consider. For example, the size of $\frac{1}{4}$ of a cake can be determined if the size of the whole cake is known; one and a half kilometers $\left(\text{or } \frac{3}{2} \text{ km}\right)$ is a well-defined length because the unit, 1 km, is a known, standard unit of measure for distance; the number $\frac{4}{5}$ can be placed on a number line only if the length of the chosen unit is given; and so forth. The unit is fundamental to understanding and proving equivalence between fractions (as we'll discuss further in Chapter 4), comparing and ordering fractions (Chapter 5), and operating on fractions (Chapter 6).

Working with a Variety of Units

Instruction on fractions is incomplete if it does not distinguish a fraction from the whole of which it is a part.

Merlyn J. Behr, Guershon Harel, Thomas R. Post, and Richard Lesh
(1992, p. 307)

Our goal should be to graduate students rather quickly from their beginning scenarios of the unit as just one circle, square, or rectangle. To spark student insight into fractions and deepen their thinking, we must challenge them with a variety of fraction contexts, using units of different types.

Continuous units. Continuous units include amounts of time, length, area, and volume. Varying the contexts of problems to include a variety of such units is enriching for students. I do suggest beginning with length before area, which is more accessible to upper elementary school students who are still constructing their concept of area. Furthermore, the notion of length converges with number on the number line.

Discrete units. Discrete units are sets or collections of elements, such as a group of pets, items in a suitcase, a set of geometric shapes, or a collection of stamps. Students learn that a set can have any (reasonable) number of elements and that the elements need not be identical, congruent, or equal.

 Teaching Tip: Continuous or Discrete?

It's important for students to become sensitive to the difference between continuous and discrete quantities early on. While this terminology is introduced much later in their mathematics education, elementary school students can understand the definition: a quantity whose magnitude can be determined by the act of counting is discrete, and a quantity whose magnitude can be determined by the act of measuring is continuous.

Here's another way to put it: a discrete quantity answers the question "How many?" while a continuous quantity answers one of many questions, including "How tall?" "How heavy?" "How long?" Routinely inquire about quantities: "Are they countable or measurable?"

Composite units. Composite units are single entities that contain within them a set of items, such as a can of 3 tennis balls, a hand of 5 fingers, or a box of 12 eggs. Like discrete units, such examples help students conceptualize a set of many things as one unit. One composite unit can serve a variety of purposes, depending on the fraction tasks we have in mind. For instance, when teaching thirds, 6 cans of 3 tennis balls offer students not only the option of finding $\frac{n}{6}$ of the cans (for different values of n) but also $\frac{n}{3}$ of the total number of balls, because the number of tennis balls is a multiple of 3. Dozens of eggs are likewise versatile, as they lend themselves well to the study of halves, thirds, fourths, sixths, and twelfths.

Fractional units. In problems using fractional units, the unit itself is a fractional quantity, such as a fourth of a kilometer, half an hour, or $1\frac{1}{2}$ pizzas. Just as counting by 2s, 5s, or 10s is helpful, so is counting by fractional units, such as $\frac{1}{2}$s, $\frac{3}{4}$s, or $\frac{3}{2}$s. And just as considering fractional parts of integer quantities is important, so is understanding what it means to take a fractional part of a quantity that is already fractional, such as $\frac{1}{2}$ of $\frac{3}{4}$.

Before students learn the formal algorithms for fraction computation, working with fractional units less than and greater than 1 is foundational for the later understanding of expressions such as $\frac{1}{5} \times \frac{2}{3}$ or $2\frac{3}{4} \div \frac{1}{2}$. For example, when considering $\frac{1}{5} \times \frac{2}{3}$, we can think of the starting unit as $\frac{2}{3}$ of an hour (or 40 minutes); multiplying it by $\frac{1}{5}$ means considering one-fifth of the unit (or 8 minutes). When considering $2\frac{3}{4} \div \frac{1}{2}$, one can think of the starting unit as $2\frac{3}{4}$ pizzas; dividing it by $\frac{1}{2}$ means counting the number of half-pizza portions that can be made from the unit. In the long run, these exercises foster the notion that a fraction $\frac{a}{b}$ is an entity in itself.

Revisiting the Partition and Iteration Process

Once students internalize that the denominator (b) of any fraction $\frac{a}{b}$ tells the number of equal parts $\left(\frac{1}{b}\right)$ into which the whole must be partitioned (hence, the divisor), and that the numerator (a) tells the number of copies or iterations of the fractional part $\frac{1}{b}$ that are desired or needed (hence, the multiplier), they can construct any fraction, be it less than or greater than 1, because the construction in both cases is similar. Figure 3.4 illustrates the related processes of partitioning and iterating to find fractions of three different units.

FIGURE 3.4
Finding Fractions by Partitioning and Iterating

Unit	Find	Step 1: Partition	Step 2: Iterate
	$\frac{3}{2}$	$\frac{1}{2}$ $\frac{1}{2}$	
	$\frac{2}{3}$	$\frac{1}{3}$ $\frac{1}{3}$ $\frac{1}{3}$	
	$\frac{9}{4}$		

◈ Teaching Tip: Moving from a Part to the Whole

Figure 3.4 shows the partition of the unit into equal parts followed by the iteration of one of the parts, an interrelated process that helps us find any fraction of any unit. Once students are comfortable moving from a unit to a fraction (using partition followed by iteration), encourage them to explore the reverse process: moving from the fraction to the unit, or from part to whole.

For example, tell students that the first column in Figure 3.4 represents the fraction shown in the second column, but the unit is unknown. To find the unit, what is their next step? Would they reverse the partition-then-iteration process? What would that look like?

When students seem comfortable moving from a part to a whole (and vice versa), ask them if they can generalize the process for *any fraction* of *any unit*.

Targeting Misconceptions with Challenging Problems

We challenge students' misconceptions about fractions by crafting judicious questions or problems to explicitly address them. The seven problems below will help you assess your students' misconceptions about the notion of a whole or unit and offer them opportunities to deepen and broaden their perceptions and conceptions of the unit, as well as the relationship between fractions and their respective units. These problems focus on finding the fraction—given the unit—in varied contexts. The second set of problems, later in this chapter, focuses more on finding the unit given a fraction.

💡 **Problem 1: Discrete and continuous sets.** Solve the problems.

1. For each diagram, circle a subset of objects that represents the given fraction:

    - $\frac{1}{3}$ of the set

    Set A

    - $\frac{4}{5}$ of the set

    Set B

    - $\frac{2}{7}$ of the set

    Set C

2. For each problem, draw the figure stated as the unit, then shade the given fractions:

- The unit is a square: Draw $\frac{1}{4}$ of the unit. Then draw $\frac{5}{4}$ of the same unit.

- The unit is a rectangle: Draw $\frac{2}{3}$ of the unit. Then draw $\frac{7}{3}$ of the same unit.

- The unit is an equilateral triangle: Draw $\frac{5}{6}$ of the unit. Then draw $\frac{11}{6}$ of the same unit.

Problem 2: Line segments, squares, and circles. Solve the problems.

1. The line segment PQ is the unit length. Draw a line segment corresponding to each of the following fractions:

- $\frac{1}{2}$ of the unit length, then $\frac{3}{2}$ and $\frac{5}{2}$ of the unit length
- $\frac{1}{4}$ of the unit length, then $\frac{3}{4}$ and $\frac{9}{4}$ of the unit length

- $\frac{1}{8}$ of the unit length, then $\frac{7}{8}$ and $\frac{10}{8}$ of the unit length

2. The three squares form the unit. Draw a picture corresponding to each of the following fractions:

   - $\frac{1}{3}$ of the unit, then $\frac{2}{3}$ and $\frac{5}{3}$ of the unit
   - $\frac{1}{6}$ of the unit, then $\frac{5}{6}$ and $\frac{7}{6}$ of the unit
   - $\frac{1}{9}$ of the unit, then $\frac{5}{9}$ and $\frac{13}{9}$ of the unit

3. Two and a half pizzas form the unit. Draw a picture corresponding to each of the following fractions:

   - $\frac{1}{5}$ of the unit, then $\frac{3}{5}$ and $\frac{6}{5}$ of the unit
   - $\frac{1}{10}$ of the unit, then $\frac{7}{10}$ and $\frac{12}{10}$ of the unit
   - $\frac{1}{15}$ of the unit, then $\frac{12}{15}$ and $\frac{18}{15}$ of the unit

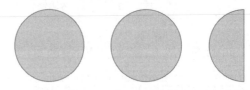

Problem 3: Cuisenaire Rod fractions: fractions as lengths. Cuisenaire Rods come in lengths of 1 cm through 10 cm, as shown below.

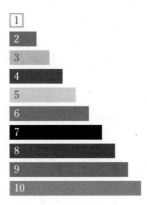

Use either actual Cuisenaire Rods or these drawings to answer the following questions:

- If rod #6 is the unit, what fraction does rod #2 represent? What about rod #3?

- If rod #9 is the unit, what fraction does rod #6 represent? What about rod #10?

- If rod #8 is the unit, does rod #2 represent $\frac{1}{4}$? Explain your answer. Use this information to explain why rod #10 does or does not represent $\frac{5}{4}$.

- If rod #10 is the unit, do 5 copies of rod #5 placed end to end represent $2\frac{1}{2}$? Explain your answer. Write $2\frac{1}{2}$ as a fraction.

- Rod #10 is still the unit. Five copies of another rod, placed end to end, represent $3\frac{1}{2}$. Which rod is it? Explain your choice.

- Place rods #2 and #10 end to end to form a new unit. Write two questions using this new unit and answer them. In the first question, the fraction must be less than 1, and in the second, the fraction must be greater than 1.

Problem 4: Neighbors on the number line: fractions and whole numbers. On each number line below, place the three given numbers. Place the numbers as precisely as you can, and explain your strategy in each case.

- Place $\frac{2}{3}$, $\frac{4}{3}$, and $\frac{7}{3}$ on this number line:

- Place 0, 1, and 3 on this number line:

Which exercise did you find more difficult? Explain why.

 Teaching Tip: Drawing Number Lines

Whenever you draw a number line on the board for the purpose of placing fractions, model for students the following actions:

- Make tick marks for at least the three whole numbers 0, 1, and 2. More whole numbers are always welcome!

- Place arrows at both ends of the line segment you draw.

The first visual cue conveys the subliminal message that fractions live everywhere and anywhere on the number line, not just between 0 and 1, even if students don't yet know how to place them all. The second suggests that numbers extend indefinitely in both directions.

You may also extend the number line to the left of 0, even if by very little. This suggests that unknown numbers yet to be discovered live there, which piques students' curiosity. If they inquire about these numbers, don't hesitate to oblige them. You might say something like, "Later, you will learn about numbers that are less than zero." Some students may have intuitive ideas about negative numbers, which you should welcome and build on: "Yes, we use them to express a loss of money, a loss of points in a game, or a fall in temperature. Say I lose 50 cents; that's the same as losing half of a dollar. That would be one interpretation of the fraction $-\frac{1}{2}$, which is the same distance from 0 as $\frac{1}{2}$, but in the opposite direction." Such an approach lays the groundwork for notions to come, demystifies negative numbers, and helps children cultivate friendliness with *all* numbers. It also sets off their imaginations!

Problem 5: Composite regions: tangram pieces representing area.

Use the seven pieces of a solid or paper tangram, labeled here as *A* through *F*, to help you find the following fractional relationships.

- If the area of the entire tangram is 1 square unit, express the areas of regions *B*, *G*, and *F* as fractions of the unit.

- If the area of region *A* is 1 square unit, express the area of region *G* as a fraction of the unit. Are there other regions that have the same area as *G*? If so, explain how you know.

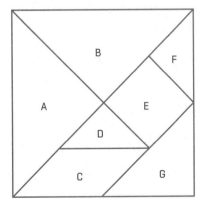

- Suppose the area of the combined regions A and B is 1 square unit. Using one or more pieces, make the following:

  ○ A square whose area is $\frac{1}{2}$ of the unit

  ○ A triangle whose area is $\frac{1}{4}$ of the unit

  ○ A rectangle whose area is $\frac{1}{4}$ of the unit

  ○ A right trapezoid whose area is $\frac{3}{8}$ of the unit

  ○ A pentagon whose area is $\frac{5}{4}$ of the unit

  ○ A shape of your choice, whose area is $\frac{3}{2}$ of the unit

Problem 6. Cultivating unitizing. The online company ZeaTea ships 36 packets of loose green tea in 1 large box.

- If you were an online customer who only bought a couple of packets, you would consider the individual packet of tea as the unit. How many units are in half a box? What about $\frac{1}{4}$ of a box?

- If you were the ZeaTea wholesaler, however, with thousands of boxes in your warehouse, you'd consider 1 large box as the unit. How would you express 1 packet of tea as a fraction of the unit? What about 4 packets of tea? How about 6 packets?

- Pick a third possible unit and describe it. Express 1 packet of tea as a fraction of that unit, and then express the large box as a fraction of that unit.

- Is it useful to be able to think about quantities in terms of different units? Explain your thinking.

Problem 7: Sharing pizzas. Two sisters, Rachel and Madison, are trying to figure out how to share two large pizzas equally among the five members of their family. They disagree on the fraction name for the equal share. Can you help them? Here are their arguments:

Rachel: I think it's two-fifths because we sliced each pizza into five, and we each get two one-fifths.

Madison: I don't think so. I think it's one-fifth because there are ten slices in all and we each get two, and two out of ten is one-fifth!

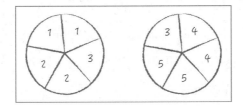

- Do you agree with Rachel's thinking? Is she correct? Explain your answers.

- Do you agree with Madison's thinking? Is she correct? Explain your answers.

- Could they both be correct? If so, explain how.

Two Vignettes

Following are two situations I witnessed during classroom visits, both on the topic of unit. I trust that you have had similar experiences.

Linda's Story

Linda, a 3rd grade teacher, was getting ready to teach a lesson on fractions. She began the lesson by holding up the isosceles trapezoid block from her bin of pattern blocks (see Figure 3.5) and asking, "What is this fraction?"

FIGURE 3.5
The Seven Pattern Block Pieces

Note: These pieces are known by most U.S. students and teachers.

Almost in unison, the students called out, "One-half!" Linda kept a poker face. She then held up a small green triangle and asked, "What about this block?" Again, many students said, "One-sixth!"

The students were pleased, thinking they had provided the answers that Linda expected. To their surprise, they learned that the correct answer was actually "It depends" (an answer we should all use more often in mathematics!). Linda then engaged her students in a lesson on the importance of the unit when comparing fractions.

Jason's Story

Jason, a 4th grade teacher, arranged his students in groups of four and gave each group an envelope, a piece of string, and a pair of scissors. Each group received a different length of string. Their task was to fold the rope in fourths, cut off and discard one-fourth, and then place the remaining piece of string in the envelope. After giving students a few minutes to complete the task, he asked the group, "Do you think that you all have the same *fraction* of string in your envelopes?" Everyone agreed that the new piece of string represented $\frac{3}{4}$ of the original piece.

Jason's big question came next: "Do you think that all of your pieces of string are the same length?" Before resolving the suspense, he quickly polled the group. About two-thirds of the class thought they were. I found this an original and engaging way to help students become mindful of the unit!

Recognizing Misconceptions

First, students need to grasp the key idea that fractions name the relationship between the collection of parts and the whole, not the size of the whole or its parts.

John P. Smith III (2002, p. 8)

In Linda's story, we saw that students had assigned fraction values to specific pattern blocks, as a result of prior experiences in which the hexagon was always taken to be the whole. In Jason's story, we saw that many students believed that the fraction $\frac{3}{4}$ corresponded to a fixed length of string, overlooking the relationship of the fraction to the original string length. Such misconceptions among young students are not unusual. Following are two additional difficulties students have with attending to the unit, which often lead to misconceptions.

Difficulty Going from Part to Whole

Reconstructing the whole, given a fractional part of the whole, is more difficult than the more common task of partitioning a given whole or unit to find a specific fractional part. Again, one reason for this difficulty is that students are almost exclusively asked to find, compute, or shade a part, given a whole. If they were asked to perform the reverse process more often, they would develop strategies and become more proficient with part-to-whole tasks.

Difficulty Discriminating Between What Is Relevant and What Is Not

The extensive research done by the Rational Number Project team (Behr, Lesh, Post, & Silver, 1983) reveals that students are easily affected by "distractors." Consider the task of placing $\frac{1}{3}$ on a number line with a clearly marked unit. If the units are already subdivided into thirds, then this task is almost trivial. Even if the units are not subdivided, it's relatively easy for students to partition the unit into three equal parts and then mark the first third. But what if the units are subdivided into something other than thirds? Placing $\frac{1}{3}$ on a number line whose units are divided into, say, halves or fourths is now a difficult task for students, as they are distracted by subdivisions that are not the ones they need.

Unpacking the Mathematical Thinking

Now that we have identified some key misconceptions, let's consider how we might address them mathematically.

A Fraction Is a Relation Between Two Quantities

A fundamental idea about fractions that students must understand sooner rather than later is that a fraction does not represent a size, a quantity, or an amount in itself; it only informs us about the relationship between the part and the whole. One-half of one whole does not represent the same quantity as one-half of another, different whole. Fractions have *relative* value, not absolute. Teachers can help students understand this subtle notion by drawing a parallel with whole numbers. For example, when we say the number 4, we don't have a sense of how big, how much, or how long 4 actually is until we know what unit we're referring to. Four miles is much longer than 4 inches!

Proceeding from Part to Whole

Problems like the pizza-sharing situation (Problem 7, earlier in this chapter) prompt students' thinking. Asking them to draw a border around the implied whole or unit area makes them realize that a same quantity can represent different fractions, provided the unit varies accordingly (Figure 3.6).

FIGURE 3.6
Same Quantity, Different Units and Fractions

Task: The students' task is to outline the implied unit in each diagram.

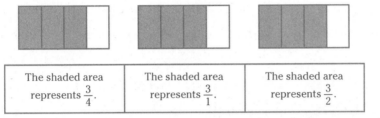

The shaded area represents $\frac{3}{4}$.	The shaded area represents $\frac{3}{1}$.	The shaded area represents $\frac{3}{2}$.

Figure 3.4 (p. 91) illustrated the partition-then-iteration process that we can use to find any fraction of any unit. Let's examine what is involved in proceeding from part to whole. Suppose this rectangle represents $\frac{2}{3}$ of a rectangular chocolate bar, and we wish to draw the unit bar.

- First, we partition the fractional amount into two parts to find one-third (since the amount we're looking at is *two*-thirds).
- Next, we take three iterations of one-third to obtain three thirds, or 1, which is the unit bar.

Notice that the numerator (2) indicates how to partition, and the denominator (3) indicates how to iterate. In sum, we divided by 2 and then multiplied by 3 or, in one step, multiplied by $\frac{3}{2}$. That makes sense since $\frac{2}{3} \times \frac{3}{2} = 1$! Given a variety of similar tasks, students will soon discover this pattern and learn to generalize it.

Infusing Problems with Distractors: Trapping or Stimulating Students?

Causing students to pause, hesitate, and get thrown off guard a bit is not a bad thing as long as the challenge is reasonable and not beyond their reach.

From the Rational Number Project, we learn that "a 'good' manipulative aid is one that *causes* a certain amount of confusion. The resultant cognitive disequilibrium leads to greater learning" (Behr et al., 1983, p. 122). Thus, don't hesitate to make problems difficult. Down the road, your students will be grateful that you "pushed the envelope" and probed the limits of their abilities.

Targeting Misconceptions with Challenging Problems

This second set of much-needed problems focuses on finding the unit, given a fractional part. These problems will give students pause and, with your judicious guidance, push them to the limits of their fraction sense.

💡 **Problem 1: The quantity changes, but the fraction remains the same.** Consider the fraction $\frac{1}{6}$.

- Shade $\frac{1}{6}$ of the area in each of the following regions:

- Shade $\frac{1}{6}$ of the elements in each of the following sets:

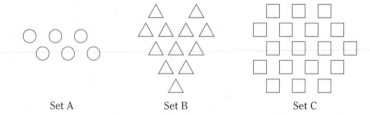

Set A   Set B   Set C

- Reflect on the *meaning* of the fraction $\frac{1}{6}$, and make two observations, based on what you just did.
- Repeat what you did with the fraction $\frac{2}{3}$.

Problem 2: The fraction changes, but the quantity remains the same.
Use colored tiles to construct rectangles. Note: For each instruction, "the tile" refers to a single square tile.

- Construct a rectangle in which the tile represents $\frac{1}{2}$ of the entire area.
- Construct additional rectangles in which the tile represents $\frac{1}{3}, \frac{1}{4}, \frac{1}{5}, \frac{1}{6}$, and $\frac{1}{7}$ of the entire area. Place the rectangles from smallest to biggest on your desk.
- Make two observations about the growing pattern of shapes.

Next, you will draw squares and rectangles in your notebook.

- Draw a square in your notebook and shade it in. Draw a rectangle around the square such that your shaded square represents $\frac{2}{3}$ of the area of the entire rectangle.
- Draw another rectangle in which your shaded square represents $\frac{4}{5}$ the total area.
- Were the last two activities harder than the first two? Explain why or why not.

 Problem 3: Overlooking distractions. Can you draw the fractions requested without being "distracted" by how the items are grouped?

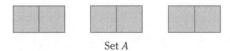

Set *A*

- Draw $\frac{1}{2}$ of Set *A*, then draw $\frac{3}{2}$ of Set *A*.
- If Set *A* represents $\frac{1}{2}$ of Set *B*, draw Set *B*.
- If Set *A* represents $\frac{3}{2}$ of Set *B*, draw Set *B*.

Set C

- Draw $\frac{2}{3}$ of Set C, then draw $\frac{5}{3}$ of Set C.
- If Set C represents $\frac{2}{3}$ of Set D, draw Set D.
- If Set C represents $\frac{5}{3}$ of Set D, draw Set D.

💡 **Problem 4: Drawings don't speak for themselves.** Consider the discrete example shown here:

- Say that the unit is the whole collection of four squares. What fraction does this example represent? Can it represent another fraction? If so, which one? Explain.
- Next, suppose the unit is the collection of the three shaded squares. What fraction is represented by the single white square?
- If the unit is still the three shaded squares, draw extra white squares so that the part represented by all of the white squares is $\frac{2}{3}$ of the unit.
- Repeat the last problem so that all of the white squares represent $\frac{5}{3}$ of the unit.

Let's now consider a continuous example, shown here:

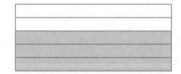

- Pick four possible regions that could be the unit, and describe each one.
- In each case, what fraction does the shaded region of the rectangle represent? Explain.

- In each case, what fraction does the white region of the rectangle represent? Explain.

 Problem 5: Resolve the dilemma. Joshua and Amy disagree on the fraction representation shown here:

Joshua says the shaded region represents the fraction $\frac{5}{6}$, but Amy insists it shows $\frac{5}{3}$.

- Do you agree with Joshua or with Amy? Why?
- Imagine Joshua's mathematical reasoning that led him to $\frac{5}{6}$. What is Joshua thinking?
- Imagine Amy's mathematical reasoning that led her to $\frac{5}{3}$. What is Amy thinking?
- Could they both be correct? Explain how.

 ### CCSS.Math.Practice.MP3: Construct Viable Arguments and Critique the Reasoning of Others

In our standards-based era, whether NCTM, CCSSM, or state standards, classroom math cultures are changing—moving from collections of isolated individuals to communities of learning. Here are two salient changes I've recently witnessed.

- Knowledge is not merely dispensed by the teacher and received by students. Students instead discuss, explore, and discover, as they actively construct new knowledge for themselves.

- Teachers are moving away from low-level, yes-or-no questions to deeper inquiries into student explanations and mathematical meanings.

But we still have a ways to go. Many teachers still find it challenging to make students *listen* to one another. Active listening is a prerequisite to critiquing the reasoning of others, as we first have to hear it! If this is also a challenge for you, these five pointers may help:

1. U-turn questions back to the class whenever possible, so that students learn to be attentive and become active in the learning of others. When a student is explaining, critiquing, or enlightening the class on an important issue, encourage good listening by saying, "Listen to the teacher!"

2. Post a list of indicators of good listening, such as "(1) Show that you are attentive; (2) Wait for an appropriate time to comment or ask a question; (3) If you disagree, do so in a respectful and constructive way; and (4) If you don't have a question, you can make a comment about what you heard."

3. Make it clear to students that you value their ability to reason, think, and critique, and that humans learn through social interaction. It is in and through productive discussions between two or more people that we clarify our own thinking.

4. Post a list of "sentence starters" to guide students: "I agree with ___ but I think differently about ___ because ___." "I heard your explanation, but I disagree because ___." "Your sharing helped me because ___." "I had another idea: ___." "That was interesting because ___."

5. On tests, quizzes, or in class, make it a habit to include tasks that require students to critique the work of real or hypothetical peers (such as Problem 5 on p. 107).

Problem 6. Use the model of your choice. Different fractions can represent the same quantity, depending on the choice of the unit.

1. Fractions $\frac{1}{2}$ and $\frac{2}{3}$

- Using these parallel number lines, which have equal units, place the two fractions, one per line, and show that they represent different lengths.

- Draw a second pair of parallel number lines with different units. Place the two fractions, one per line, and show that they can represent equal lengths.

2. Fractions $\frac{1}{2}$ and $\frac{3}{4}$

- Using these two sets of chips (A and B), which have an equal number of elements, shade to model the two fractions, one per set, and show that they represent different subsets.

- Draw a second pair of sets, Set C and Set D, with different numbers of elements; shade to model the two fractions, one per set, and show that they can represent equal subsets.

💡 **Problem 7: Mind the distractions!** Consider this number line.

- Color the line segment that represents the unit on this number line.

- Express 3 as a fraction of this unit (this fraction is greater than 1).

- Express the smallest subdivision drawn on this line as a unit fraction. How many of them make 3? Write 3 as a fraction that shows this relationship (this fraction is also greater than 1).

- Place the fraction $1\frac{1}{2}$ or $\frac{3}{2}$ on this number line.

Suppose that segment AB is this long:

- Draw a line segment that is 1 unit long if AB represents $\frac{1}{3}$ of a unit.

- Draw a line segment that is 1 unit long if AB represents $\frac{3}{4}$ of a unit.

- Draw a line segment that is 1 unit long if AB represents $\frac{3}{2}$ of a unit.

Now consider the two and a half discs represented here:

- Draw $\frac{1}{2}$, if these discs represent the unit (i.e., find a fraction, given the unit).

- Draw $\frac{5}{6}$, if these discs represent $\frac{1}{3}$ (i.e., find a fraction, given another fraction).

- Draw the unit if these discs represent $1\frac{1}{4}$ or $\frac{5}{4}$ (i.e., find the unit, given a fraction).

Teaching Tip: Move from "3 Parts Out of 4 Parts" to Three *One-Fourths*

The leap from simply reading the sentence, "Understand a fraction $\frac{1}{b}$ as the quantity formed by 1 part when a whole is partitioned into b equal parts" in the CCSSM (Common Core State Standards Initiative, 2010) to actually thinking this way ourselves, fostering this way of thinking in our students, and ultimately seeing our students perfectly comfortable and agile with this way of thinking requires several big leaps. The traditional fraction teaching model of "a parts out of b parts" is deeply engrained in the minds of both teachers and students. Even though this is the first model students see in the early grades, they must simultaneously experience the model of "a copies of $\frac{1}{b}$s," which is more mathematical, powerful, and helpful to them in the multiplicative world of middle school mathematics.

A Final Note

I will close this chapter with an amazing comment I heard from a student in Linda's class. She ended her lesson by saying, "Tomorrow we'll see how one-half can be bigger than a whole!" Almost immediately, Carlos, a young mathematician, responded: "Oh, yeah—like half of an elephant is bigger than a whole fly."

Carlos certainly had a strong intuitive sense about the impact of the unit on the "size" or "bigness" of a fraction! He reminds us that students are capable of sophisticated mathematical thinking—but we must invite them down that path.

 What's the App for That? *What's the Unit?*

Is $\frac{1}{2}$ larger than $\frac{1}{3}$? The answer is *yes*, provided the implied whole or unit is the same for both fractions. But what if the units are different? The **What's the Unit?** app (www.apps4math.com) helps students understand the necessity of knowing the unit when defining a fraction.

CHAPTER 4

Teach the Concept of Equivalence (Not Just the Rule)

Almost all of the essential fraction ideas surface in the concept of equivalent fractions.

Tom Bassarear (1997, p. 222)

Equivalence is a critical concept in mathematics, one that accompanies students throughout their mathematical journey. Examples from 3rd grade onward include equivalent notations for numbers, equivalent fractions, equivalent expressions, equivalent equations, equivalent functions, equivalent sets, and so forth, as shown in Figure 4.1.

Fraction equivalence is a poorly understood concept, yet it is foundational for comparing, ordering, and operating with fractions. In the late 1990s, an NAEP math assessment revealed that approximately one out of three 8th graders had difficulty shading areas or drawing pictures to model equivalent fractions and, conversely, selecting an equivalent fraction for a given pictorial model. To prevent such outcomes for our students, we must plant the seeds of understanding early on.

FIGURE 4.1

Equivalence in School Mathematics

Examples of Mathematical Objects		They are equivalent because...
Notations	3.00 and 3 (natural numbers)	They represent the same amount, quantity, or number.
	$\frac{1}{2}$, 0.5, and 50% (rational numbers)	
	$\frac{2}{3}$ and $\frac{6}{9}$	
Expressions	"$(2 \times 4) + (2 \times 3)$" and "$2 \times 7$" (numeric)	
	$2a + 2b$ and $2(a + b)$ (algebraic)	
Equations	$4x = 32$ and $\frac{x}{4} = 2$	They have the same solution.
Functions	$f(x) = \dfrac{4x^2 + 4}{(x^2 + 1)(x - 2)}$ and $g(x) = \dfrac{4}{(x - 2)}$	Their function values are equal for all inputs x (except 2).
Sets	$A = \{1, 2, 3\}$ and $B = \{x, y, z\}$	They have the same cardinality or the same number of elements.

But this does not mean simply teaching the equivalent fraction algorithm, a procedure that students quickly learn to parrot nonsensically, reciting or applying the following formula:

$$\frac{a}{b} \text{ is equivalent to } \frac{(n \times a)}{(n \times b)}.$$

Rather, when instruction moves flexibly among evocative representations—verbal, concrete, pictorial, contextual, and symbolic—students come to assign meaning to the procedure. Ultimately, they develop sophisticated reasoning about equivalent fractions that no longer depends on the use of physical models.

In this chapter, I'll discuss students' principal stumbling blocks with equivalence and show how we can build on their intuitive methods and understandings. As always, I'll caution against a premature telling of rules, which may seriously impede the natural development of fraction and operation sense. One of our greatest pedagogical challenges in teaching fractions is to help students both see with their eyes and understand with their minds that equivalence can be maintained, despite numeric or symbolic transformation. To this end, we must "spend whatever time is needed to ensure that students understand what it means for fractions to be equivalent at both the concrete and symbolic levels" (Cramer & Whitney, 2010, p. 21).

Lisa's Story

A year ago, I was working with the upper elementary school teachers of an American school in Europe, with a focus on improving fraction instruction. We often began our professional development sessions by observing a lesson as a group and then using the debriefing as a starting point for our discussions. On the day we attended Lisa's lesson on equivalent fractions, she gave her 3rd graders the following problem:

> Anna and Jeremy had 1 granola bar each. They were different
> flavors but the same size. Anna ate $\frac{1}{3}$ of hers and Jeremy ate $\frac{2}{6}$ of
> his. Who ate a bigger fraction of the bar—or did they eat the same
> amount? Explain your answer.

One student, Daniel, argued that Jeremy ate more. When asked to explain, he said, "Two is 2 times 1, and 6 is 2 times 3. So Jeremy ate double what Anna ate." To arrive at his solution, Daniel had made no drawing or diagram, nor did he use any concrete math manipulatives. I learned later from Lisa that Daniel was "quick with numbers and did most of his math in his head."

Lisa then called on Emma to share a different opinion. Emma had used pattern blocks to explain her answer: "One-third is like one diamond, and two-sixths is like two triangles. So they ate the same because two triangles are the same as one diamond—see?"

Using the pattern blocks, Emma demonstrated that two triangles fit perfectly on top of one rhombus. When asked which pattern block represented the granola bar, she said, "I pretended the hexagon was the granola bar."

For someone who was supposedly "struggling" with her fraction instruction, Lisa was holding her own. She didn't tell the students who was correct. Rather, she maintained a neutral expression as she listened to each explanation.

Opinions were divided among the students between Daniel's and Emma's rationales. Lisa asked for other ideas, but no more came forward. After all, it was their first lesson on equivalent fractions!

Before guiding the class toward a resolution, I asked a student named Ricky to go up to the whiteboard and share his work. I had noticed him quietly reflecting in a corner and saw he had the beginnings of a strategy that could empower his peers. Ricky obliged and drew two rectangles side by side on the board. On the first, he drew two vertical line segments to show three equal parts and shaded one; on the second, he drew five vertical line segments to show six equal parts and shaded two.

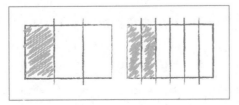

Lisa acknowledged Ricky's representations of $\frac{1}{3}$ and $\frac{2}{6}$ of a rectangular region as correct and then asked what he had concluded. Since his drawings were not precise, Ricky was hard-pressed to convince his peers of what he seemed to believe intuitively—namely, that the shaded areas in both drawings were in fact the same fraction of the rectangular granola bar.

Sensing his frustration, I probed further to assist him: "Ricky, is there another way you might cut the granola bar into six equal parts to show *two-sixths*?" Ricky was a quiet student but a deep thinker. However, before he could utter a word, Caroline blurted out, "We can divide the thirds in half!"

While Caroline's phrasing was not mathematically correct (she meant "divide by two" or "cut in half"), it resonated with Ricky. He promptly seized her suggestion and drew a horizontal line through the three thirds in his first rectangle.

Suddenly, the equivalence of $\frac{2}{6}$ of a bar and $\frac{1}{3}$ of a bar, modeled on the same rectangle, became more transparent. The total number of *equal fractional parts* had doubled, from 3 (thirds) to 6 (sixths), and so had the number of *shaded fractional parts*, from 1 (third) to 2 (sixths). The names of the parts had changed, but the shaded amount (representing the eaten amount) had not.

Recognizing Misconceptions

In 3rd grade, students develop preliminary reasoning about equivalence by working with simple fractions such as $\frac{1}{2}$ and $\frac{2}{3}$, with the help of visual and tactile models, in preparation for their work the following year. By

4th grade, according to CCSSM.4.NF.1, students must be able to "explain why a fraction $\frac{a}{b}$ is equivalent to a fraction of the form $\frac{(n \times a)}{(n \times b)}$ by using visual fraction models" (Common Core State Standards Initiative, 2010). But here is the problem we face: when the formula $\frac{a}{b} = \frac{(n \times a)}{(n \times b)}$ is provided *before* students have had ample opportunities to construct, see, and draw embodiments of fraction equivalence, students apply it mechanically without attending to either the presence or the meaning of the equals sign at center stage. The difficulties and misconceptions that follow are some that I have found to recur in classrooms and are abundantly present in the research.

Different Fraction Names for the Same Quantity or Number

One of the hardest aspects of learning fractions is understanding that "what looks like the same amount might actually be represented by different numbers" (Lamon, 1999, p. 22). The obvious reason students resist thinking that two different fractions can represent the same rational number is that a different pair of natural numbers constitutes each fraction. This takes us back to obstacles already discussed, including the difficulty many students have with (1) using different names or labels to denote the same number (or the same amount or quantity); (2) conceptualizing a fraction as a single number; and (3) focusing on the *relationship* between the two whole numbers that comprise the fraction, rather than on the numbers themselves.

Overreliance on Physical Models (3rd Grade and Up)

Many educators argue that even when students can generate equivalent fractions modeled with standard math manipulatives such as pattern blocks or ready-made fraction strips, they are not always able to explain the mathematics behind the fraction equivalence when questioned further. For example, Emma could explain that $\frac{1}{3}$ was equivalent to $\frac{2}{6}$ "because two triangles are the same as one diamond," and she could show that two small triangles $\left(\text{two } \frac{1}{6} \text{ of the hexagon, representing the granola bar}\right)$ fit perfectly atop one blue rhombus $\left(\frac{1}{3} \text{ of the hexagon}\right)$. But without further exploration, we can't draw definite conclusions about Emma's level of understanding.

Difficulty with Discrete Quantities (3rd Grade and Up)

When given one white cube alongside four gray cubes (Figure 4.2), a 3rd grader sees that $\frac{1}{5}$ of the cubes are white, using the part-whole inter-pretation of fractions: "one part of the five equal parts is white." But the challenge increases significantly when students are faced with a larger number of cubes representing the equivalent white-to-gray relationship—for instance, 3 white cubes alongside 15 gray cubes, which requires a good understanding of equivalence and a burgeoning sense of proportionality.

FIGURE 4.2
Discrete Examples of $\frac{1}{5}$

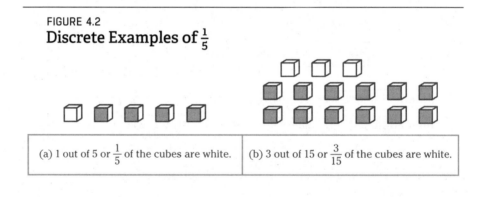

(a) 1 out of 5 or $\frac{1}{5}$ of the cubes are white. | (b) 3 out of 15 or $\frac{3}{15}$ of the cubes are white.

An analogous problem of the continuous type traditionally looks like Figure 4.3. Students can more readily see the 1-out-of-5 relationship in this case if they are able to unitize and lump together the three white unit squares (a) into one unit rectangle (b). If, however, the 3 white squares are dispersed among the 15 (c), students' difficulty in recognizing the equivalence between 3 out of 15 and 1 out of 5 then resembles or even exceeds that of our discrete example with the cubes.

FIGURE 4.3
Continous Examples of $\frac{1}{5}$

 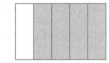 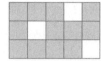

(a) 3 of the 15 unit squares are white.	(b) 1 of the 5 unit rectangles are white.	(c) 3 of the 15 unit squares are white, but dispersed.

Limited Concept of the Equals Sign (4th Grade and Up)

At the root of fraction equivalence is the meaning of equality. Let's turn for a moment to children's first experiences with the = symbol. From a very early age, they are presented with flash cards bearing symbols such as 2 + 3 = ☐ or questions such as "What is two plus three?", whose sole purpose is to produce the answer. Gradually, children come to view the equals sign as a command to act: the action is *to compute*, and the goal is *to produce the correct answer*. To most children, though, this action is transformative: they may see the equals sign with their eyes, but they think with their minds that the original expression has been somehow transformed by their action. Some researchers call this the process interpretation of equations (versus the object interpretation).

In their illuminating study, Falkner, Levi, and Carpenter (1999) alerted educators to this reality by proposing the equation 8 + 4 = ☐ + 5 to students in 30 typical elementary school classes, ranging from 1st to 6th grade. Fewer than 10 percent of all students gave the correct answer, 7. Popular answers were 12 and 17. Students found 17 by "transforming" further: 8 + 4 → **12** + 5 → **17**.

The equals sign as a process of transformation explains in part the common student thinking, typified earlier by Daniel, that the process of multiplying both numerator and denominator in the fraction $\frac{1}{3}$ by a factor of 2 cannot possibly produce a fraction *equal* to the original fraction. These students conclude that $\frac{2 \times 1}{2 \times 3}$ must be twice as large as $\frac{1}{3}$ $\left(\text{or that } \frac{4 \times 1}{4 \times 3} \text{ must be four times as large}\right)$. Lisa admitted that she too had a hard time believing at first that equivalent fractions are really the same number "because when you apply the formula, you're *multiplying*!"

Rote Application of $\frac{a}{b} = \frac{(n \times a)}{(n \times b)}$ (4th Grade and Up)

The rule, procedure, or formula for generating equivalent fractions—we will use the phrase *equivalent fraction algorithm* (EFA)—is frequently memorized too soon and then applied by rote rather than with under-standing. This is because we don't give students enough time to use their understanding of fractions to develop procedures that make sense to them. Nor do we give ourselves enough time to infuse the EFA with meaning by exploring how it plays out in different situations, where fractions have distinct interpretations. We must be mindful of the importance of unpacking for students—verbally, concretely, and visually—what "multiplying up and down by *n*" really *means* before presenting the symbolic equivalence equation $\frac{a}{b} = \frac{(n \times a)}{(n \times b)}$. In 3rd grade, this equation should not even be part of the equivalence discussion!

The Misuse of Language (All Grades)

The terminology used in fraction instruction can be confusing to children. One day we might say, "Two-thirds and $\frac{4}{6}$ are different fractions" and the next day say, "Two-thirds and $\frac{4}{6}$ are the same." Or, we might read the equation $\frac{2}{3} = \frac{4}{6}$ as "two-thirds *equals* four-sixths" yet say in classroom discourse that "$\frac{2}{3}$ *is equivalent to* $\frac{4}{6}$." Or, when discussing Emma's pattern block comparison (pp. 114–115), we might carelessly say, "The two triangu-lar pattern block pieces together are *congruent* to the one rhombus pattern block piece, so they represent the same fraction."

Though this is true, the subliminal message here is that when representing fractions (in 1-D, 2-D, or 3-D space), *congruence* is a necessary condition for *equivalence*, which we know is not true. Children interpret words more literally than adults, and we must be constantly mindful of the way we phrase mathematical statements in the classroom. Specifically, when discussing equivalence, the words *different*, *same*, *identical*, *equal*, *congruent*, and *equivalent* should be used with care.

 ## Teaching Tip: "Simplify" Rather than "Reduce"

When arguing that $\frac{2}{6}$ was more than $\frac{1}{3}$, Daniel insisted that "Jeremy ate double what Anna ate," because 2 is the double of 1, and 6 is the double of 3. You have no doubt heard students argue in this way. This misconception is related in part to another use of language that can be confusing. When teachers or students say, "I doubled the numerator and doubled the denominator," students are left with the impression that the fraction has doubled in value (see the next *A Bridge to Algebra* box on p. 129 for the correct mathematical language that resolves this common misperception).

There is yet another reason that students think a fraction increases in value when multiplying the numerator and denominator by a same number *n* to generate an equivalent fraction: because teachers commonly use the verb *reduce* when simplifying a fraction to its lowest terms—or, in other words, when dividing the numerator and denominator by a same number *n*. To reduce means to decrease in quantity, size, or value—but, in fact, nothing has been reduced. The fraction $\frac{1}{3}$ still has the same value as the fraction $\frac{2}{6}$. I recommend using the verb *simplify* in lieu of *reduce*. Simplifying a fraction means finding the simplest among all possible names—the one with the smallest whole numbers, whose sole common factor is 1. The numerator and denominator in this case are *relatively prime*.

A Partial View of the EFA (5th Grade and Up)

Have you ever given your older students (5th or 6th graders) a problem that came down to finding numbers that would make the following equation true?

$$\frac{\square}{6} = \frac{\square}{15}$$

In other words, can students find numerator values for both fractions that would make them equivalent?

Students typically say it's not possible because they can't find a factor n such that $6 \times n$ yields 15. We can respond to their assertion on two levels.

- Guide students to use their number sense to realize that *twice* 6 plus *one-half* of 6 will solve the problem $\left(\text{i.e., } 2\frac{1}{2} \times 6 = 15\right)$. Thus, any pair of numerators with the same relationship would work. For example, 2 and 5 would work, since $2 \times 2\frac{1}{2} = 5$, giving the solution $\frac{2}{6} = \frac{5}{15}$.
- Step back and pose some exploratory questions into the students' understanding of equivalence. Students will most likely answer by citing the *between ratio* of 1-to-2.5 between the two fractions and mention nothing about the *within* ratio—that is, the relationship between the numerator and denominator within each fraction of an equivalent pair.

This limited view of the EFA is due in great part to fraction instruction that focuses on the multiplicative relationship *between* equivalent fractions almost to the exclusion of the multiplicative relationship *within* each fraction (Figure 4.4).

Fraction instruction that insists on both relationships offers students a less restricted appreciation of the EFA and empowers their problem solving. Returning to our problem, selecting any natural number n and multiplying denominators "upward" by n in the equation $\frac{\square}{6} = \frac{\square}{15}$ yields the numerators, thus producing a solution. For example, for $n = 2$, the solution is $\frac{12}{6} = \frac{30}{15}$. To obtain the solution $\frac{2}{6} = \frac{5}{15}$, we divide denominators by 3, or multiply them by $\frac{1}{3}$.

FIGURE 4.4
Equivalent Fractions

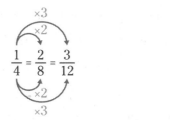

| (a) Emphasis on the *between* ratios | (b) Emphasis on the *within* ratio |

Additive Thinking

Another student misconception that teachers frequently encounter is the belief that adding any constant to both the numerator and the denominator produces an equivalent fraction.

$$\frac{6}{7} \xrightarrow[+1]{+1} \frac{7}{8} \quad \text{or} \quad \frac{12}{13} \xrightarrow[+10]{+10} \frac{22}{23}$$

In earlier chapters, we looked at the incorrect use of additive thinking in the multiplicative world of fractions. But because such errors are so widespread, we will revisit them from a new angle in Chapter 5.

Unpacking the Mathematical Thinking

Equivalence is a powerful tool for working with mathematical ideas, a major part of the process of developing mathematical concepts, and an indispensable stage in the mathematical journey toward abstraction. The process of establishing equivalences and recognizing similarities amid differences is foundational to students' learning of mathematics with understanding. Let's turn to some examples of equivalence that students encounter prior to 3rd grade and learn how we might build on these early experiences to help them make better sense of fraction equivalence.

Build on Students' Informal Experiences with Equivalence

Encounters with equivalence, in school and out, offer students many faces of the concept that two things are equivalent not only when they are identical but also when they are the same *in some important way*: in number, value, amount, quantity, solution, definition, significance, meaning, effect, and so on. Discerning similarities despite differences—isolating one important shared property among different exemplars—is a vital part of working with mathematical ideas.

In your instructional practice, draw analogies between simple instances of equivalence that students have understood and newer, more complex ones with which they are struggling. This will prepare students to understand that when two equivalent fractions are considered independently of any concrete or real-world model, they represent *the same rational number*—and ultimately to understand that a "number" is a concept and that fractions are among their infinite names.

Several ways that students routinely encounter and consider equivalence are described below and on the following pages.

Number concept. At an early age, children recognize that there is something similar between a collection of three children and a collection of three teddy bears: one teddy bear for each child. Although the elements of the sets are of a different nature, they share the property of "three." Thus, from multiple experiences with collections of cardinality, the concept of "three-ness" (or the concept of the number 3) gradually emerges. Students later learn in mathematics that two sets are equivalent if and only if they have the same number of elements. (Note that in the context of sets, equivalence is not the same as equality.)

Sums and products. In 1st grade, children learn that numerical expressions such as $7 + 8$, $5 + 5 + 5$, and $1 + 2 + 3 + 4 + 5$ share the property of yielding the answer 15 by addition. The numbers constituting the expressions may be different, as well as the number of addends in each, but their *sum* is the same. Similarly, four bags of three apples each are physically different from three bags of four apples each. However, the total number of apples, 12, is the same. We can write $(4 \times 3) = (3 \times 4)$ because the commutative property of multiplication states that the products of two numbers are identical regardless of the order in which they are multiplied. In the context of sums and products of numbers, equivalence *is* the same as equality.

Simple equations. Young students can figure out intuitively that the equations $2 + \square = 5$, $4 + \square = 7$, and $7 + \square = 10$ become true statements if 3 is substituted for the empty box in each case. The equations look different, but they share the same solution, 3. Students eventually learn that two equations are equivalent if their solutions are equal. Later, students learn to prove equivalence between two different equations by transforming one into the other, using properties of equality. In this example, adding 2 to both sides of the first equation $(2 + \square + 2 = 5 + 2)$ yields the second equation $(4 + \square = 7)$, and adding 5 to both sides of the first equation $(2 + \square + 5 = 5 + 5)$ yields the third equation $(7 + \square = 10)$.

Geometric shapes. Why is sorting such an important activity when we first introduce shapes to children? Precisely because it enables students to discover equivalences. Successfully grouping all triangles—large and small triangles; blue, red, and yellow ones; thick and thin ones; and so on—from a given set of shapes means that amidst all of the apparent differences among the shapes, a shared similarity has been perceived: all of the triangles have three "straight" sides and three "pointy" corners. In the context of geometric shapes, therefore, equivalence is not the same as congruence (having the same size and shape); rather, it refers to the sharing of defining geometric properties.

Measures. Students learn at a young age that a $1 bill, 4 quarters, and 100 pennies represent the same amount of money, and they see that a ruler is labeled 12 inches along one edge and about $30\frac{1}{2}$ centimeters along the other, long before understanding the inch-to-centimeter conversion formula. They hear adults talk about running a 5K or Olympics commentators report on hundred-meter races while they simultaneously know that distances in the United States are measured in feet, yards, and miles. And if they travel to foreign countries, they read temperature displays in degrees Celsius and can find the Fahrenheit equivalents on their parents' smartphones. In the context of measures, equivalence means different names that denote the same quantity.

Number notation. Children learn about equivalent ways of writing the same number: simple examples include $3 and $3.00; 0.5, $\frac{1}{2}$, and 50%; and $\frac{7}{2}$ and $3\frac{1}{2}$. They need not have formal fraction instruction to realize that taking seven half-pizzas and grouping them two by two to recompose whole pizzas results in three whole pizzas and one half-pizza $\left(\text{or } 3\frac{1}{2} \text{ pizzas}\right)$, thus yielding a new name for the seven halves $\left(\text{or } \frac{7}{2}\right)$. As with the context of measures, in the context of number notation, equivalence means different names that denote the same number.

Fraction equivalence. Students encounter instances of fraction equivalence in the early grades through playful explorations with math manipulatives such as pattern blocks, but they don't qualify those relationships as "equivalent fractions." For example, in 1st or 2nd grade, a child may say, "Two halves, three thirds, and six sixths are all the same as a whole."

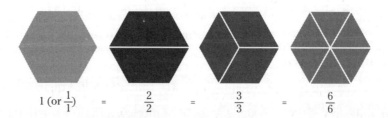

$1 \left(\text{or } \frac{1}{1}\right) \quad = \quad \frac{2}{2} \quad = \quad \frac{3}{3} \quad = \quad \frac{6}{6}$

Another child might say, "Two sixths make a third, three sixths make a half, or four sixths make two thirds"—provided of course that the hexagon is considered to be the whole or unit!

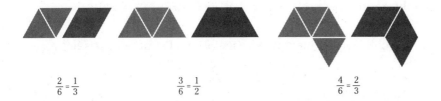

$$\frac{2}{6} = \frac{1}{3} \qquad\qquad \frac{3}{6} = \frac{1}{2} \qquad\qquad \frac{4}{6} = \frac{2}{3}$$

Cultivate the *Equivalence* Meaning of *Equality*

In order to foster the meaning of *equality as equivalence* throughout the elementary school grades, time would be well spent, in grades 3–5 and beyond, reflecting on equalities mathematically, rather than rushing to compute each side and compare numerical values. The following examples, which precede the learning of fractions, cultivate in students the notion of equality as a relationship between two equivalent expressions and exemplify powerful mathematical thinking.

Addition. How can I know that $(17 + 39) = (16 + 40)$?

- One child may think in this way: "If 17 'gives' 1 to 39 on the left side, the sum becomes $16 + 40$, identical to the right sum, so the two sides are equal."

- Another might think of the right sum as a *transformation* of the left sum across the equals sign and say, "17 has changed to 16 (1 *down*), while 39 has changed to 40 (1 *up*), so the left and right sides are equal because if you add 1 and then take 1 away, there's no change at all." The total change is in fact $(+1) + (-1) = 0$.

Children enjoy the "*n* up/*n* down" strategy (Neagoy, 2012). This algebraic way of thinking lays the foundation for later understanding of the *additive inverse* concept $(x + [-x] = 0)$ and the *additive identity* concept ($x + 0 = x$), which are both fundamental properties of addition. These two equalities hold for all x: whole numbers, fractions, and algebraic expressions.

Subtraction. How can I know that $500 - 297 = 503 - 300$?

- A child whose mental representation of subtraction is not merely "take away" might visualize subtraction as the distance on the number line between 297 and 500. In other words, the expression $500 - 297$ is the leap on the number line from 297 to 500. From that powerful perspective, a child might reason, "The jump from 297 to 500 is the same as the jump from 300 to 503, only it's 3 units to the right."

- Another child might visualize that leap as a "difference rod" and say, "If I shift the difference rod 3 units to the right on the number line, my difference becomes $503 - 300$" (Neagoy, 2012).

Multiplication. How can I know that $(35 \times 8) = (70 \times 4)$?

- A student who has learned about doubling and halving might say, "Thirty-five has been doubled while 8 has been halved, so the two products are equal because doubling and halving cancel out." In other words, $2 \times \frac{1}{2} = 1$, and multiplying by 1 brings about no change.

- Children are generally comfortable using the "doubling/halving," "tripling/thirding," "quadrupling/fouthing," and the "$\times n / \div n$" strategy for transforming products into simpler ones. This is algebraic thinking again, and it lays the foundation for later understanding of both the concept of *multiplicative inverse* $\left(x \times \frac{1}{x} = 1 \right)$ and the concept of *multiplicative identity* ($x \times 1 = x$), two important properties of multiplication that hold for all x ($\neq 0$): whole numbers, fractions, and algebraic expressions.

A Bridge to Algebra: Cultivating Algebraic Thinking About Operations in Grades 3–5

If you're thinking that it's unrealistic for elementary school students to reason in such sophisticated ways about numbers and operations in the lower grades, think again! Algebraic thinking is a high priority of the NCTM and CCSSM standards and an expectation for all students in the 21st century. There is ample evidence that young children are capable of sophisticated mathematical thinking and can learn to view equations not solely as implicit instructions to perform computations but also as equivalences between two quantities or expressions. These mathematical ways of thinking have been described as *early algebraic thinking*—about properties of numbers, relationships between numbers, meanings of operations, properties of operations, and more (Blanton, 2008; Carpenter, Franke, & Levi, 2003; Neagoy, 2012, 2014). Viewing equality as equivalence is fundamental to understanding fraction equivalence.

Starting in 3rd grade, foster the "doubling/halving" way of thinking at first: connect whole-number multiplication to geometric representation. Then generalize to any number, not just 2, which fosters algebraic thinking. For example:

- **Arithmetic:** $12 \times 5 = 6 \times 10 = 60$. We halved 12 and doubled 5 because 6×10 is simpler to compute mentally.

- **Geometry:** We cut the 12-by-5 rectangle in two, and rearrange the pieces.

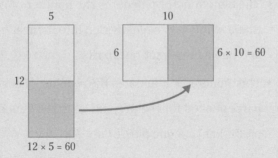

• **Algebra:** $a \cdot b = \left(a \cdot \frac{1}{2}\right) \cdot (b \cdot 2) = a \cdot \frac{1}{2} \cdot b \cdot 2 = a \cdot b \cdot \frac{1}{2} \cdot 2 = (a \cdot b)\left(\frac{1}{2} \cdot 2\right) = ab(1) = ab.$

Generalizing, $a \cdot b = \left(a \cdot \frac{1}{n}\right) \cdot (b \cdot n)$, since $\frac{1}{n} \cdot n = 1$ for all $n \neq 0$. *[Note that the symbol · is used here for multiplication, an alternative symbol for × in algebra. In fact, no multiplication symbol is needed at all between a number and a variable or between two variables.]*

In time, students transfer this way of thinking to fractional expressions as well.

Explain Equivalence by Connecting Fractions to Multiplication and Division

Many of us were taught fraction equivalence *solely* through the EFA formula application. It can thus be challenging to explain the notion to our own students without using that formula.

Helping children make sense of why fraction $\frac{a}{b}$ is equivalent to another one whose numerator and denominator have increased or decreased by the same factor, without giving the formula, requires highlighting the connection between the definition of a fraction $\frac{a}{b}$ and multiplication and division, a connection worth revisiting.

- The denominator b denotes the number of equal fractional parts that a whole has been divided into; hence, b plays the role of divisor and names the fractional parts.
- The numerator a denotes the number of copies of these fractional parts needed for the purpose at hand; hence, a plays the role of multiplier $\left(a \times \text{one } b\text{-th, or } a \times \frac{1}{b}\right)$.

Both multiplication and division reside within the "fraction" definition.

Consider the fraction $\frac{3}{4}$. How might we argue that $\frac{6}{8}$ is an equivalent fraction, using the concepts of divisor and multiplier? Here's one approach:

1. The change from $\frac{3}{4}$ to $\frac{6}{8}$ has caused the whole to be divided into twice as many equal parts (from 4 to 8). Consequently, the size of the parts is smaller—in this case, they are half as large as the original ones.

2. The number of copies needed has also doubled (from 3 to 6).

3. The effects of "twice as many copies" (2×3) and "fractional parts half as large" $\left(\frac{1}{2 \times 4}\right)$ cancel each other out. Therefore, the new fraction represents the same quantity or number as the original fraction; $\frac{6}{8}$ is simply a different form, or a new name, for the fraction $\frac{3}{4}$.

Wrapping our heads around the concepts of divisor and multiplier simultaneously is challenging, even for adults. Students eventually come to appreciate the important inverse relationship between the size of the fractional part that decreases or increases (D multiplied by n) and the number of copies of fractional parts needed that increase or decrease (N multiplied by n), if fractions are to remain equivalent. Seeing these verbal explanations embodied in different models and contexts is helpful.

Begin with Equal-Sharing Problem Situations

Many researchers recommend that we introduce equivalence through equal-sharing contexts (e.g., Empson & Levi, 2011; Fosnot & Dolk, 2002; Van de Walle et al., 2010). Equal-sharing problems engage students' attention because students can identify with similar situations they have personally experienced. Children are sensitive to fairness and have a good sense of when shares are equal or not. The notion of equivalence then emerges organically during the discussion and comparison of different solutions. You might begin with the simple case of halving, and then progress to sharing among four and among eight (powers of 2), all of which begin with the action of halving. You can then move to more complex partitioning cases that do not begin with halving, such as sharing among three, five, or seven people.

Let's place the same two fractions Lisa asked her students to compare in an equal-sharing context:

Suppose that six friends wanted to equally share two rectangular bars of chocolate. What fraction of the rectangular bar of chocolate did each person get?

As I have used this scenario countless times, I can tell you what I have witnessed in terms of how students go about solving the task, which generally happens in one of two ways.

- Rachel cuts each bar into six equal parts and gives each person two parts. When asked to name the equal share each person received, she replies, "Each person gets $\frac{1}{6}$ from one bar and $\frac{1}{6}$ from the other, so that makes $\frac{2}{6}$."
- Devon has another strategy. He cuts each bar into three equal parts and gives each person one part. "My fraction is $\frac{1}{3}$," he says.

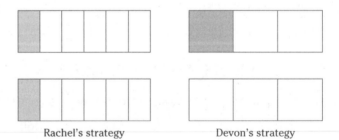

Rachel's strategy   Devon's strategy

Both strategies are convincing, so they are usually met with peer approval. From a simple yet relevant situation emerges the equivalence between the fractions $\frac{2}{6}$ and $\frac{1}{3}$, and students naturally find two different names to designate the same amount of chocolate. In addition to learning about equivalence, students are also exploring and constructing the idea that one-sixth of each bar, *times two*, equals two-sixths $\left(\text{later: } \frac{1}{6} \times 2 = \frac{2}{6}, \text{ or } 2 \times \frac{1}{6} = \frac{2}{6}\right)$.

But that's not all. Equivalent fraction discussions should always make explicit the unit or whole being referred to, as changing the whole generates additional examples of equivalent fractions. For example, in the chocolate problem, Lisa pushed the envelope: "Your answers assume the unit is *one* bar of chocolate. Suppose the chocolate bars come in a pack of two. How would we express Rachel's and Devon's solutions as fractions of the *pack*?"

After some reflection, LeAnh exclaims, "Rachel's way is two-twelfths and Devon's is one-sixth!" LeAnh has thus produced a second pair of equivalent fractions, $\frac{2}{12}$ and $\frac{1}{6}$, which are not equivalent to the first pair, as the unit has changed.

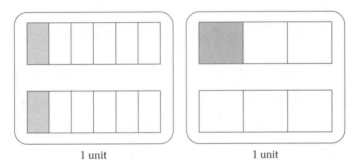

1 unit   1 unit

Some students may be puzzled over the two different names for Rachel's solution: $\frac{2}{6}$ and $\frac{2}{12}$. This presents a wonderful opportunity to revisit the importance of the unit: $\frac{2}{6}$ of one bar represents the same amount of chocolate as $\frac{2}{12}$ of two bars. Such concrete situations provide 4th and 5th graders with a model that gives meaning to multiplication of a fraction by a whole number: $\frac{2}{6} \times 1$ (bar) is equal to $\frac{2}{12} \times 2$ (bars).

Model Equivalence Using Different Interpretations of Fractions

We saw in Chapter 1 that the symbol $\frac{a}{b}$ has various interpretations. To help students construct a deeper meaning of equivalent fractions, starting in 3rd grade students need to see $\frac{a}{b}$ exemplified in more than just one of the different meanings of fractions: part-whole relationships, division/quotients, number/measure, multiplicative operators, and ratios. They also need to see equivalence embodied in different models: in 1-D models such as pieces of string, Cuisenaire Rods, connecting cubes, and fraction strips; in 2-D models such as pattern blocks, colored tiles, and polygonal regions drawn on or cut out of paper; in discrete models; and of course on the number line. Three-dimensional models can also be evocative. Below, we look at some of the many meaning-model instructional choices.

The part-whole meaning of $\frac{a}{b}$ modeled by a continuous 2-D area model. Let's go back to Ricky's model of the granola bar comparison problem (pp. 115–116) and see where he could have gone with his first drawing. Cutting a rectangular region into thirds, though not as easy as cutting it into halves, is nevertheless conceptually clear.

- Draw two line segments that cut the region into three smaller regions of equal area.
- Shade one region to represent $\frac{1}{3}$ of the whole.
- To produce any fraction equivalent to $\frac{1}{3}$, slice the first set of cuts perpendicularly—once, twice, three times, and so forth, depending on what equivalent fraction(s) one desires.

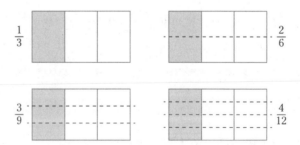

A few advantages of this model:

1. It's empowering to students, as it enables them to model any pair of equivalent fractions quite easily, unlike commercial manipulatives, such as pattern blocks, that can only model certain fractions.

2. The preservation of the original quantity is transparent.

3. The divisor and multiplier roles of denominator and numerator are nicely illustrated: as the size of the fractional parts decreases due to the repeated slicing (in this case, from thirds, to sixths, to ninths, to twelfths), the number of shaded fraction parts increases (in this case, from 1, to 2, to 3, to 4); thus, the original shaded amount is preserved.

To conclude our discussion of this problem, thinking of slicing one-third in half to make two-sixths is a far more powerful justification for equivalence than Emma's demonstration that two-sixths (two small pattern block triangles) fit perfectly when laid on top of one-third (one rhombus pattern block), because "it is based on mathematical relationships rather than a relationship between physical materials" (Empson & Levi, 2011, pp. 122–123).

CCSS.Math.Practice.MP7: Look for and Make Use of Structure

The opening sentence of Standards for Mathematical Practice 7 of the CCSSM reads, "Mathematically proficient students look closely to discern a pattern or structure" (Common Core State Standards Initiative, 2010). When we foster observation and discernment in our students, they develop the habit of mind to be mindful of what they do and say. In this early modeling of equivalent fractions, students notice several things:

- At the start, the numerator-denominator pair expressing the shaded area is, say, (1, 3).

- After drawing one horizontal line and slicing the rectangle once, the (N, D) pair (1, 3) turns into the pair (2, 6).

- After drawing two horizontal lines and slicing the rectangle twice, the (N, D) pair $(1, 3)$ turns into the pair $(3, 9)$.

- After drawing three horizontal lines and slicing the rectangle three times, the (N, D) pair $(1, 3)$ turns into the pair $(4, 12)$.

And so on!

The patterns generated by successive equivalent fractions are discernable:

- The successive counting numbers in the numerators express what happens to the number of shaded (fractional) parts: they double, triple, quadruple, and so on.

- The successive multiples in the denominators express what happens to the total number of (fractional) parts: they double, triple, quadruple, and so on.

From varied hands-on explorations of equivalent fractions, students begin to generalize patterns of behavior of the successive N and D values generated. Symbolizing any fraction as $\frac{N}{D}$, students may express *verbally* or *symbolically* that the family of infinite equivalent fractions share the same form, or structure:

$$\frac{\textit{Some number multiplied by } N}{\textit{The same number multiplied by } D} \text{ or } \frac{\textit{A multiple of } N}{\textit{The same multiple of } D}$$

And once their symbolization has matured, they will be able to write $\frac{n \times N}{n \times D}$.

Noticing patterns, articulating their common structure, generalizing, and ultimately symbolizing the generalization are quintessential elements of learning and doing mathematics. After all, is mathematics not "the science of patterns"?

The part-of-set meaning of $\frac{a}{b}$ modeled by a discrete collection.

Discrete models or collections of countable items are sometimes more difficult for students. Take the example illustrated here:

Grasping the equivalence between $\frac{3}{15}$ (3 gray cubes out of a set of 15) and $\frac{1}{5}$ requires the following:

1. Being able to unitize: to see equal "chunks of three" cubes (Lamon, 2005), think of these as new units, and conclude that one out of five units is a gray cube.

2. An appreciation of the multiplicative relationships—both the "times 3" relationship between the fractions $\frac{1}{5}$ and $\frac{3}{15}$ and the "times 5" relationship within each fraction.

3. A nascent sense of ratio: the ratio of 1 to 5 is the same as 3 to 15.

A 2-D array is a powerful visual way of organizing a collection of discrete items to make the equivalent fractions more apparent. The following array of 15 discrete cubes connects this part-whole example to the rectangular model seen previously:

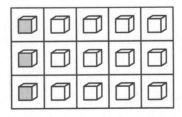

With the "chunks of three" cubes arranged vertically in the array, it's clear that one out of five columns are gray, and consequently that $\frac{1}{5}$ of the entire array of cubes is gray. This grouping helps students draw an analogy between a simpler continuous model (the 2-D area model) and the discrete model and to make the equivalent fractions $\left(\text{in this case, } \frac{1}{5}, \frac{2}{10},\right.$ and $\left.\frac{3}{15}\right)$ more apparent.

The quotient meaning of $\frac{a}{b}$ modeled by an equal-sharing situation. If we return to Rachel's explanation of how to share two chocolate bars equally among six people, we see that the fraction $\frac{2}{6}$ represents both the process and the result of the division operation:

- It denotes the *process* of partitioning two bars of chocolate equally among six people. Students first express this action of dividing with the mathematical expression $2 \div 6$. Later, $2 \div 6$ becomes $\frac{2}{6}$.
- It also denotes the *result*—the share of chocolate each person receives, or two of the one-sixth pieces. The result of the division action is called the *quotient*.

Measure or number meaning of $\frac{a}{b}$ modeled by a continuous 1-D length model. Using Cuisenaire Rods to model length is a good start, but, like other ready-made commercial manipulatives, it places limitations on the choices of fractional relationships that can be exhibited. A very efficient, versatile, and inexpensive fraction manipulative is the classic self-constructed fraction strips. The teacher or student selects a given length for the whole or unit. (The word *unit* is appropriate here, as it connotes linear measure and the number line.) By folding or cutting different-colored strips of the same size, students construct halves, fourths, and eighths by successive halving (Figure 4.5).

Students readily see that *one* $\frac{1}{2}$ strip and *four* $\frac{1}{8}$ strips represent the same amount of paper, despite their different sizes, colors, and numbers of pieces.

After exploring unit fractions of the form $\frac{1}{2^n}$, explore the relationship between thirds and sixths, thirds and ninths, and fifths and tenths. You might also build a fraction-strip poster of fractions between 0 and 1

FIGURE 4.5
Fraction Strips

$\frac{1}{1}$ or 1							
$\frac{1}{2}$				$\frac{1}{2}$			
$\frac{1}{4}$		$\frac{1}{4}$		$\frac{1}{4}$		$\frac{1}{4}$	
$\frac{1}{8}$	$\frac{1}{8}$	$\frac{1}{8}$	$\frac{1}{8}$	$\frac{1}{8}$	$\frac{1}{8}$	$\frac{1}{8}$	$\frac{1}{8}$

Note: Fraction strips illustrate equivalent fractions, such as $\frac{1}{2} = \frac{4}{8}$.

with denominators ranging from 1 to 10, which offers students a powerful visual tool for fraction equivalence and comparison.

Fraction strips are useful for a number of reasons:

- They allow students to develop a better understanding of fraction relationships, within and between rows.
- They serve as a precursor to fractions on the number line, as the unit strip easily morphs to the unit segment.
- There is no limitation to fractions between 0 and 1 (e.g., three $\frac{1}{2}$ strips is $\frac{3}{2}$, which is greater than 1) or on the choice of unit fraction representation: theoretically, a strip of paper can be folded or cut into any whole number of pieces.
- They serve as a model for "fraction as measure," as any strip is a nonstandard unit of linear measure.

Measure or number meaning of $\frac{a}{b}$ modeled on the double number line. Heeding the CCSSM's emphasis on the importance of modeling fractions on the number line, we should model equivalent fractions on the number line as well.

Suppose we wanted to model the equivalence between $\frac{2}{3}$ and $\frac{4}{6}$. After placing $\frac{2}{3}$ on the line, reinforcing what students learned with fraction strips, I might say, "I can think of the length from zero to two-thirds as *two* leaps of one-third each." I would then draw two arched arrows, labeling the first $\frac{1}{3}$, which is reminiscent of two $\frac{1}{3}$-long fraction strips (see L1 in Figure 4.6).

FIGURE 4.6

Modeling the Equivalents of $\frac{2}{3}$ and $\frac{4}{6}$

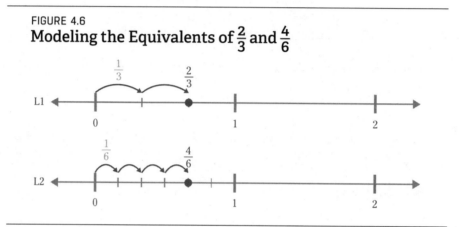

When I ask a class, "Could we make *shorter* leaps for the same distance?" students' first suggestion is usually to split the thirds in half. I like to draw a second number line (see L2 in Figure 4.6) beneath the first, indicating the corresponding key numbers 0, 1, and 2, and then adding three new tick marks of a different color at the center of each third to model sixths. "What might these shorter line segments be called?" I would probe, followed by "How do you *know* they're sixths?" An ideal answer would be "Because they're six leaps from 0 and 1," which reinforces that $\frac{6}{6}$ is another name for the unit.

To wrap up this equivalent fraction excursion on the number line, I might ask, "How many of these smaller leaps would get us to the same point, $\frac{2}{3}$?" The obvious answer, "four one-sixths," thus generates the equivalent fraction $\frac{4}{6}$, a new name for the same rational number. The four smaller arched arrows labeled $\frac{1}{6}$ are indicative of four $\frac{1}{6}$-long fraction strips.

Teaching Tip: Use the Number Line to Model Equivalent Fractions

The number line model, regrettably underused in the elementary school grades, is an extremely effective model for students.

- The actions of partitioning and then iterating to generate fractions are modeled.

- The roles of numerator as multiplier and denominator as divisor are made clear.

- The process of fractional parts decreasing in size while the copies of unit fractions increase in number, or vice versa, is visualized.

- There is a clear differentiation between the fractional measure of $\frac{2}{3}$, the length of the line segment from 0 to $\frac{2}{3}$, and the rational number $\frac{2}{3}$, which is a unique point on the line.

- The ability to partition to represent increasingly more precise measures is boundless.

- Creating equivalent fractions for any given fraction, be it less than or greater than 1, is easier through the use of the double number line (Figure 4.6).

Be Mindful That Models Lead to Concept Building

When helping students develop meaningful fraction concepts, we must be mindful of the interplay between model and concept. On one hand, the use of models should infuse our instruction. Models help students think about fraction relationships, solve fraction problems, and develop fraction concepts—their use should not just be an occasional event. On the other hand, as I've noted, models are not the mathematics—they are the *means* to the mathematics. Our instruction must support students, over time, to gradually move away from the need to always construct or use physical models and to move toward drawing or diagraming, internalizing the images of models, abstracting the mathematics, and, finally, developing the pure fraction concepts—the long journey of mathematizing.

Targeting Misconceptions with Challenging Problems

Creating contrived problems whose sole purpose is to have students apply a memorized rule serves no real purpose: the student doesn't construct new knowledge, and the teacher can't assess for conceptual understanding. Creating situations in which students can act like young mathematicians—making sense of the situation, conjecturing hypotheses, using models, figuring out solutions and discussing them, and learning in the process—is a better way to grapple with new ideas, including equivalence. Seven such problems are suggested below.

 Problem 1: Sharing pizza: an equal-sharing problem (for 3rd and 4th graders). On Sunday, Brian and his two friends stopped for pizza at an Italian deli. The three friends shared two large pizzas equally among them. The following Saturday, Brian stopped at the same deli, but this time he had five friends with him, and they shared four large pizzas equally.

- Assuming that all pizzas were the same size, draw circles and use shading to show the fraction of pizza Brian ate on each day. Name the fraction in each case. Compare and explain the two fractions.
- Draw a double number line, L1 and L2. On each, mark the whole numbers 0, 1, and 2.
  - On L1, draw a line segment that represents the amount Brian ate on Sunday.
  - On L2, draw a line segment that represents the amount Brian ate on Saturday.
  - Which representation of equivalent fractions was easier for you? Why?

Note: The difficulty in this type of problem depends on the relationship between the number of items shared and the number of people sharing them.

Problem 2: Fractions of the pentagon (for 3rd and 4th graders). Use your fraction sense to solve the problems below.

- Using this pentagon, represent the fraction $\frac{3}{5}$. On the same pentagon, show that $\frac{3}{5}$ is equivalent to $\frac{6}{10}$.
- On a new regular pentagon, represent the fraction $\frac{8}{10}$. On the same pentagon, show that $\frac{8}{10}$ is equivalent to $\frac{4}{5}$.
- In what ways are the processes you just used different? In what ways are they the same?
- Using one or more pentagons, show that $\frac{7}{5}$ is equivalent to $\frac{14}{10}$.

 Problem 3: Fractions on the multiplication table (for 3rd and 4th graders). On the multiplication table, observe the "times 4" and the "times 7" rows in relation to each other.

x	1	2	3	4	5	6	7	8	9	10
1	1	2	3	4	5	6	7	8	9	10
2	2	4	6	8	10	12	14	16	18	20
3	3	6	9	12	15	18	21	24	27	30
4	4	8	12	16	20	24	28	32	36	40
5	5	10	15	20	25	30	35	40	45	50
6	6	12	18	24	30	36	42	48	54	60
7	7	14	21	28	35	42	49	56	63	70
8	8	16	24	32	40	48	56	64	72	80
9	9	18	27	36	45	54	63	72	81	90
10	10	20	30	40	50	60	70	80	90	100

- How many fractions equivalent to $\frac{4}{7}$ can you find?
- Before now, have you ever made the connection between the multiplication table and equivalent fractions? Explain in words why

equivalent fractions for $\frac{4}{7}$ can be formed by using the "times 4" and the "times 7" rows of the multiplication table.

- Pick another fraction. Use the multiplication table to find equivalent fractions.

Problem 4: Different and the same (for 3rd–5th graders). Use your fraction sense to solve the following problems.

1. Miriam cut a small pie into eight equal slices and ate two. Isabella cut an identical pie into fourths and ate one piece.
   - Model with a drawing the different ways that Miriam and Isabella partitioned their pies, and shade the eaten portions. What can you conclude?
   - How might Ann slice an identical pie a third way yet still eat the same amount as Miriam and Isabella?

2. Andrew, Conner, Tina, and Kate attended a birthday party where there were several identical rectangular sheet cakes. They were sad to have to leave early, but they each got a doggy bag with some cake. The boys each got the same size rectangular piece of cake (light gray sections of the figure below), but Tina got one large triangular piece, and Kate got two smaller triangular pieces (dark gray sections).

Cake 1

Cake 2

   - Express the fractions of Cake 1 that Andrew and Tina each got. Share your thinking that led to your answers.
   - Express the fractions of Cake 2 that Conner and Kate each got. Share your thinking that led to your answers.

- Who got more cake—or did all four get the same amount?
- Did you use equivalent fractions to solve this problem? Fill out the table below and reflect on how the number, the shape, and the color of the pieces affect (or don't affect) fraction equivalence.

Party Guest	Number of Pieces	Shape of Piece(s)	Color of Piece(s)	Fraction of Cake
Andrew				
Tina				
Conner				
Kate				

💡 **Problem 5: Ways to partition: connecting unitizing with equivalence** (for 4th and 5th graders). Use your fraction sense to solve the following problems.

- Rectangle R is partitioned into 24 small squares. What fraction would you use to name one small square? What about all of R? Shade a region that is $\frac{20}{24}$ of R.

Rectangle R

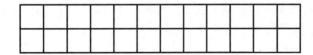

- Now think of partitioning R into *twelfths*. What fraction would you use to name one small rectangle? What about all of R? Shade a region that is $\frac{10}{12}$ of R.

Rectangle R

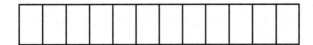

- Next, think of partitioning R into fourths. Draw a picture to show the fourths. Name all of R, using fourths. Shade a region of your choice and name it.

- Finally, think of partitioning R into eighths. Draw a picture to show the *eighths*. Name all of R, using eighths. Shade the region you chose above, and name it in eighths.

Problem 6: Different and identical (for 4th–6th graders). Suppose that you have to teach equivalent fractions to a friend who missed the lesson. Use this exercise to give her examples of equivalent fractions.

- Describe or draw a situation in which two different fractions have identical numerical values.

- Describe or draw a situation in which two identical fractions represent different quantities.

- Which of these two situations model equivalent fractions? What important concept does the other situation illustrate?

- In the first situation, we used "numerical value," and in the second situation we used "quantity." Is there a difference between the two? If so, describe this difference as best you can.

Problem 7: Modeling with sets and collections (for 4th–6th graders). The fraction $\frac{1}{3}$ is a familiar one.

- Draw three stamps, and color one red to represent that $\frac{1}{3}$ of the stamps in this collection are red.

- Draw a collection of nine stamps, where $\frac{1}{3}$ of them are red.

- In another collection, the fraction of red stamps is also $\frac{1}{3}$. If seven stamps are red, how many stamps in all are in this collection? Draw it.

- How do these three different sets of stamps illustrate fraction equivalence?

What's the App for That? *Can You See It?*

Visualizing fraction equivalence can be a challenge for students. To many of them, "multiplying up and down by 2" means *doubling* the fraction value. Using circular and bar models, the **Can You See It**? app (www.apps4math.com) helps students see, with their eyes and mind, that equivalent fractions are truly equal. It's a powerful springboard to the formal algorithm!

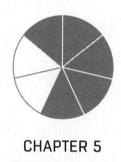

CHAPTER 5

Compare and Order Fractions Meaningfully

Many pairs of fractions can be compared without using a formal algo-rithm, such as finding a common denominator or changing each fraction to a decimal. Children need informal ordering schemes to estimate frac-tions quickly or to judge the reasonableness of answers.

Nadine Bezuk and Kathleen Cramer (1989, p. 162)

A fundamental property of our number system is that given any two num-bers, a and b, one of the following three cases is true:

$$a < b \qquad a = b \qquad a > b$$

This is true for all numbers—including fractions, which are positive rational numbers. But before knowing rational numbers deeply and being comfortable comparing fractions as abstract numbers, students in the elementary school grades work with quantities, observe measurable attributes, quantify those attributes using fractions, and then reason about the relative magnitude of the fractional quantities.

In order to compare two quantities or numbers judiciously, we must first have good number sense—and an important part of number sense is recognizing the relative magnitude of numbers. When it comes to fractions, research shows and classroom teachers confirm that this ability is direly lacking. An often-quoted test item on a past National Assessment of Educational Progress (NAEP) exam, known as the Nation's Report Card, asked 8th graders to approximate the sum of $\frac{12}{13} + \frac{7}{8}$ without computing it and to select the correct answer from among five choices. Over 50 percent of the students tested chose 19 or 21 as the best estimate of the sum. These students clearly had no sense that since each fraction is close to 1 their sum must be close to 2.

Just as we've seen when finding equivalent fractions or performing fraction computations, many students don't or can't compare or order fractions without resorting to a memorized algorithm. One reason for this unfortunate state is that algorithms for comparing fractions, like other fraction algorithms, are taught too soon. Students learn to rely on the mechanistic application of a rule rather than on mathematical reasoning to decide which of two fractions is greater or if they are equal.

Nicole's Story

Nicole, a seasoned 5th grade teacher, was teaching a lesson on fraction comparison. Her approach was memorable in that she did not ask her students, "Which fraction is greater, $\frac{3}{4}$ or $\frac{4}{6}$?" but instead asked them to work in pairs to come up with a strategy that would help them decide, without using the common-denominator algorithm. Nicole had set the stage with this real problem:

At Table A, four people equally share three rectangular vegetable casseroles for dinner. At Table B, six people equally share four same-size casseroles.

- The equal share of casserole at Table A is $\frac{3}{4}$, and at Table B it is $\frac{4}{6}$.
- Come up strategies to explain why $\frac{3}{4}$ of a casserole is greater than $\frac{4}{6}$.

Olivia and Cyril were the first to explain their strategy. They came up to the board and wrote a list of equivalent fractions for each of the two fractions (Figure 5.1).

FIGURE 5.1
Olivia and Cyril's Strategy

$$\frac{3}{4} \quad \frac{6}{8} \quad \frac{9}{12} \quad \frac{12}{16} \quad \frac{15}{20} \quad \cancel{\frac{18}{24}}$$

$$\frac{4}{6} \quad \frac{8}{12} \quad \frac{12}{18} \quad \cancel{\frac{16}{24}}$$

Cyril introduced the strategy: "We made a list of equivalent fractions and crossed out the common denominators because we couldn't use them. But you didn't say we couldn't compare same numerators, right?" Nicole nodded.

Olivia continued: "Then we saw that $\frac{12}{16}$ and $\frac{12}{18}$ had the same numerators. And since 18 pieces are smaller than 16 pieces, $\frac{12}{16}$ has to be the bigger portion." Like a good teacher, Cyril clarified and concluded, "That means $\frac{3}{4}$ is the biggest piece."

(Interestingly, the two lists didn't end with common *twelfths* but rather continued to common *twenty-fourths*. Perhaps Cyril and Olivia overlooked the twelfths and identified 24 as the "common denominator" because it is the actual product of the denominators 4 and 6.)

The class seemed satisfied. Nicole acknowledged the validity of the strategy and asked either Cyril or Olivia to state their strategy in words. Olivia obliged, saying, "You find same numerators by making lists, then you look at the denominators, and the small one is the big fraction." We, the observers, thought this sounded pretty good. Nicole revoiced what Olivia said, wrote the strategy on the board, and coined Olivia and Cyril's method the *Common Numerator Strategy*. As it was a new way of thinking for many students, Nicole took some time to discuss it and model it in a few different ways.

Fast-forward to Hugo and Sophie, who asked if they could explain their method. Sophie spoke for the pair: "We knew the two fractions are on the left side of 1 on the number line. What we did was, we compared the space left to get to 1. Three-fourths has another $\frac{1}{4}$ to get to 1, and $\frac{4}{6}$ has another $\frac{2}{6}$. But $\frac{2}{6}$ is really like $\frac{1}{3}$. So that makes $\frac{3}{4}$ bigger, 'cause there's less space to get to 1 on the number line" (Figure 5.2). Not bad for a 5th grade explanation of the "compare to a benchmark" strategy!

FIGURE 5.2
Hugo and Sophie's Strategy

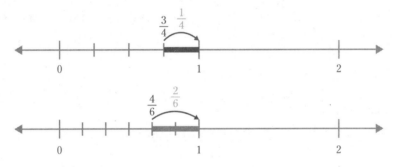

Note: Nicole drew number lines to help the class follow Sophie's explanation.

Nicole coined Hugo and Sophie's method the *Close to 1 Strategy*. She emphasized the power of visualizing and then comparing distances on the number line and encouraged all students to cultivate this way of reasoning about fractions. The fact that Nicole frequently used the number line in her own instruction was reflected by the ease with which Sophie could *see* the fractions $\frac{3}{4}$ and $\frac{4}{6}$ on the line with her mind's eye and discuss their proximity to 1.

Some students shared erroneous reasoning as well. Mark, for instance, objected to the stated answer $\left(\text{that } \frac{3}{4} \text{ is greater than } \frac{4}{6}\right)$ and shared his erroneous reasoning: "Isn't $\frac{4}{6}$ the bigger one because 4 is bigger than 3 and 6 is bigger than 4?" Nicole didn't want to discourage students from sharing, even if their reasoning was incorrect, so instead of correcting Mark, she gracefully responded with a prompt: "You know that $\frac{3}{2}$ is $1\frac{1}{2}$, so it's bigger than 1, right? And you also know that $\frac{4}{4}$ *equals* 1." Mark agreed. "Now look at how the numerators and denominators compare," Nicole suggested. This counterexample helped Mark realize that his reasoning was invalid.

Toward the end of the lesson, Tara voiced a lovely synthesis of both methods. She asked, "Can you use two strategies together?" Her teacher and peers didn't quite understand what she meant, so Tara proceeded to the board to explain. "If you take Cyril and Olivia's fractions, $\frac{9}{12}$ and $\frac{8}{12}$, and pretend you don't know the common denominator way, then you can do Sophie's way: $\frac{9}{12}$ is $\frac{3}{12}$ away from 1, and $\frac{8}{12}$ is $\frac{4}{12}$ away from 1. And $\frac{3}{12}$ is smaller than $\frac{4}{12}$, so that means $\frac{9}{12}\left[\text{or }\frac{3}{4}\right]$ is biggest 'cause it's closer to 1" (Figure 5.3).

FIGURE 5.3
Tara's Synthesis of the Two Strategies

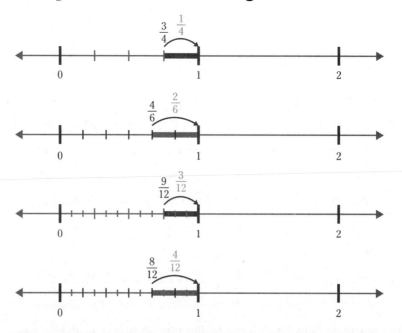

Note: Nicole added two more number lines to help the class follow Tara's explanation.

Tara's synthesis of the two methods that had been discussed in depth confirmed that she clearly understood the *Close to 1 Strategy*!

Nicole concluded the discussion with an assignment: "Think about comparing the two fractions to the benchmark $\frac{1}{2}$ instead of 1, and report back tomorrow."

 Teaching Tip: Develop Awareness of Ordering Different Kinds of Numbers

By the time students enter 3rd grade, they have a good sense of both the cardinal and the ordinal meanings of a whole number. They have developed a mental image of a number line with whole numbers 1, 2, 3, and 4 ordered as consecutive points, to the right of a chosen *O* point. Two properties are clear to them:

• Consecutive whole numbers correspond to equidistant points on the number line.

• Between any two consecutive whole numbers, there is no other whole number.

But the advent of fractional numbers shakes these solid foundations: there is no such thing as "two consecutive fractions." Students come to learn that between any two fractions, we can always find another fraction.

The kinds of questions you pose can play a big role in helping students shift gears from whole-number to rational-number thinking and can build a foundation for this subtle notion. Consider the following scenario:

Teacher: Three units are greater than 2 units, right? How does that help you compare $\frac{3}{4}$ and $\frac{2}{4}$?

Student: Three-fourths is greater than $\frac{2}{4}$ because *three* one-fourths is greater than *two* one-fourths.

Teacher: Nice justification. Now, can you find a whole number "in between" 2 and 3?

Student: No, the numbers go one, two, three, four . . . so there's nothing in between.

Teacher: Same question for $\frac{2}{4}$ and $\frac{3}{4}$: Can you find a fraction in between?

Student: [*gesturing to indicate uncertainty*]

Teacher: Here's a hint: Convert the fractions to eighths.

Student: Four-eighths and $\frac{6}{8}$?

Teacher: Yup, these fractions are equivalent to the original ones. Is there any fraction in between $\frac{4}{8}$ and $\frac{6}{8}$?

Student: [*taking it in*] Oh, yeah, you mean $\frac{5}{8}$?

Teacher: Exactly! Reflect on what we did, and then apply it to find a new fraction between $\frac{4}{8}$ and $\frac{5}{8}$.

Recognizing Misconceptions

When it comes to comparing fractions, student errors and misconceptions are both numerous and interrelated and therefore sometimes difficult to diagnose. Comparing fractions with meaning requires a solid understanding of foundational ideas, including the concept of the unit, the notion of equivalence, and the relational nature of fractions.

Overreliance on Ready-Made Models

Many commercial models, such as pattern blocks, are helpful beginning models for comparing fractions, but teachers must weigh the advantages against the disadvantages of these models. Take fraction strips, for instance: they have a built-in common unit and are already "sliced" into predetermined partition sets. A student using them to compare $\frac{3}{3}$ and $\frac{3}{6}$

can correctly conclude, without much difficulty or reflection about the need for a common unit, that $\frac{3}{6}$ is less than $\frac{3}{3}$.

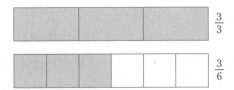

In the absence of fraction strips, students may construct their own models and then have to confront and perhaps struggle with the central idea of unit, as 4th grader Cecilia did here.

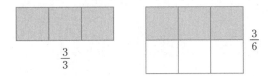

From this, Cecilia concluded (incorrectly) that the two fractions are equal.

Difficulty Comparing Fractions Without the Common Algorithm

As Nicole and many of us have noticed, students frequently use the method of converting to common denominators in fraction comparison problems. Many students simply memorize the rule and apply it without thinking. Worse, some students cannot even conceptualize the comparison of fractions without the use of an algorithm. Some researchers have concluded that this limited range of comparison and order strategies is directly related to both teacher and textbook instruction. As a case in point, a 3rd grade math book in a well-regarded series explicitly states that when comparing unlike fractions, "We have to change the fractions to equivalent fractions with a common denominator before we can compare." That is not true—and especially not in 3rd grade! Our students are more than capable of thinking without the support of a rule, but we must encourage and support them in doing so.

Lack of Attention to the Unit

We've seen that the concept of the whole or unit in defining the meaning of a fraction is hard for children to grasp. But when comparing two fractions, we must assume both units to be equal; otherwise, comparison is not possible. The previous example reveals the culprit of Cecilia's incorrect conclusion: she decided that $\frac{3}{6}$ is equal to $\frac{3}{3}$ because she paid no attention to the requirement of a common unit. Using unit fractions students know well, model for them some absurd conclusions we can arrive at if we don't pay attention to the unit. In the following example, if we disregard the unit, $\frac{1}{4}$ certainly looks greater than $\frac{1}{3}$!

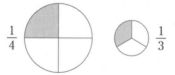

Moreover, remind students that a common unit is similarly implicit in statements regarding whole-number comparison. We know that 5 is greater than 4 precisely because 5 represents *five* iterations of the given unit 1, whereas 4 represents only *four* iterations of the same unit.

$5 = 1 + 1 + 1 + 1 + 1 = 5 \times 1$

$4 = 1 + 1 + 1 + 1 = 4 \times 1$

 Teaching Tip: Search Beyond the Correct Answer

We don't always take the time to probe students' reasoning behind their correct answers. But such time would be well spent, as correct answers sometimes stem from faulty reasoning. Furthermore, it sends the message to students that cultivating correct mathematical thinking is as important as getting the right answer, if not more so.

Correct numerical answers are not transferable to other similar problems, but sound reasoning can be applied over and over.

Suppose, for example, that Lyann states, "Five-sixths is greater than $\frac{2}{3}$." Asking questions like "How do you know?" or "How did you figure it out?" elicits her thinking. You might find that Lyann's statement is based on her (incorrect) reasoning with pattern block models.

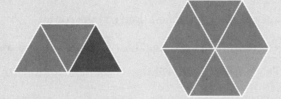

From this, Lyann concluded that $\frac{5}{6}$ is greater than $\frac{2}{3}$. Although her answer is correct, these two regions are not equal in area and thus their fractional parts cannot be compared in this way. By taking the time to observe Lyann's fraction constructions, you would conclude that she failed to select equal units. Then, rather than point out her flaw, you could react with another question that would prompt Lyann to discover her error on her own, such as "What would $\frac{2}{3}$ of *two* trapezoids look like? Compare that with your $\frac{5}{6}$."

Inappropriate Whole-Number Reasoning

Considering the complexity of fraction concepts, it is not surprising that students encounter difficulties when comparing fractions. After years of whole-number schema, they must learn to think in new ways that often conflict with their ideas about whole numbers. Some common examples are discussed below.

One-third is less than $\frac{1}{4}$ because 3 < 4. When ordering unit fractions, children learn that even though 3 is less than 4, $\frac{1}{3}$ is *greater* than $\frac{1}{4}$.

Students use erroneous arguments that are based on what they *see* rather than mathematical arguments that are based on what they *reason*.

Three-thirds does not equal $\frac{4}{4}$ because 3 ≠ 4. Equivalent expressions for 1 constitute another difficulty for students. Although they can see, using concrete models such as fraction circles, that $\frac{5}{5}, \frac{6}{6}, \frac{7}{7} \ldots \frac{10}{10}$ are all equal to 1, the increasing whole-number components of the fractions can nonetheless distract them. Don't be surprised if one day they assert that the fractions are all equal and the next day they say that $\frac{6}{6} < \frac{7}{7}$. Major changes in mindsets need time to take root.

Seven-ninths is greater than $\frac{5}{6}$ because 7 > 5 and 9 > 6. Recall that Nicole's student Mark exhibited a similar rationale; he argued that $\frac{4}{6}$ had to be greater than $\frac{3}{4}$ because 4 > 3 and 6 > 4. Such reasoning exemplifies a lack of relational thinking, which is at the core of the fraction definition. Repeatedly stress for your students that it is not the isolated numerator and denominator values that matter but rather the relation between the two. Examples of fractions composed of small whole numbers that are greater than fractions with larger ones, such as $\frac{1}{2}$ and $\frac{49}{100}$, can be illuminating. In this example, you can point out that 49 cents is less than half a dollar, which all students understand.

Predominance of Additive Thinking

Additive thinking is apparent in misconceptions related to just about all aspects of fraction work, including fraction comparison. Students learn, for instance, that multiplying the numerator and denominator of $\frac{3}{5}$ by 2 yields the equivalent fraction, $\frac{6}{10}$ (Figure 5.4). But they will invariably substitute adding for multiplying in the EFA and claim that $\frac{3}{5} = \frac{5}{7}$ because 3 + 2 = 5 and 5 + 2 = 7.

We saw that the 1-to-2 (or 2-to-1) relationship between $\frac{3}{5}$ and $\frac{6}{10}$, or between any two equivalent fractions, is often referred to as the *between ratio*. The *within ratio* is less obvious and for this reason is infrequently

FIGURE 5.4

Multiplicative Thinking and Additive Thinking

a) $\dfrac{3}{5} \xrightarrow[\times 2]{\times 2} \dfrac{6}{10}$; therefore $\dfrac{3}{5} = \dfrac{6}{10}$ b) $\dfrac{3}{5} \xrightarrow[+2]{+2} \dfrac{5}{7}$; therefore $\dfrac{3}{5} = \dfrac{5}{7}$

(a) Correct multiplicative thinking   (b) Incorrect additive thinking

discussed. Fractions $\frac{1}{3}$ and $\frac{2}{6}$ have a between ratio of 1 to 2, but a within ratio of 1 to 3: 1 *times 3* equals 3, and 2 *times 3* equals 6. Fraction $\frac{4}{10}$ has a 1-to-2.5 within ratio, since 4 *times 2.5* equals 10. We notice students substituting addition in this second occurrence of multiplication as well. They will claim that $\frac{6}{7}$ and $\frac{9}{10}$ are equal because they are both "one apart" or that $\frac{3}{5}$ and $\frac{4}{6}$ are equal because they are both "two apart." The expression "*n apart*" comes from mentally adding the same constant (1, 2, or any value n) to each numerator to obtain the respective denominator.

CCSS.Math.Practice.MP8: Look for and Express Regularity in Repeated Reasoning

Making it a habit of mind to look for and express regularity in patterns of numbers, patterns of shapes, patterns of thought, and so on is quintessential to thinking mathematically. Mathematics in the 21st century is often defined as "the study of regularity" or "the study of patterns." Consider these fractions:

$$\frac{1}{2}, \frac{2}{3}, \frac{3}{4}, \frac{4}{5} \cdots$$

Students may consider that these fractions are equal, as each numerator is "one apart" from its denominator. One way to help students become more familiar with one-apart fractions is to have them draw consecutive bar models for $\frac{1}{2}$ through $\frac{9}{10}$ and then model the part-whole relationships by shading all but one part of each whole.

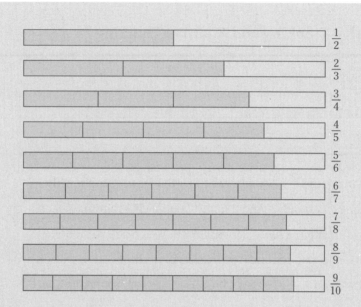

They will see that even though each fraction is less than 1 in value, they all grow closer to 1 as both the numerator and the denominator increase.

Ask, "What would $\frac{99}{100}$ look like? How far is $\frac{99}{100}$ from 1?" Something changes in this pattern (the individual values of the consecutive fractions), but other things remain the same (the "one-apart-ness" of the fractions and their gradual approach toward 1). A picture paints a thousand words!

Another approach to dissuading students from thinking that fractions with equal "apart-ness" are equal in value is to select a fraction $\left(\text{say, } \frac{2}{3}\right)$ and then generate a sequence of equivalent fractions by multiplying the numerator and denominator of $\frac{2}{3}$ by 2, 3, 4, and 5:

$$\frac{2}{3} \quad \frac{4}{6} \quad \frac{6}{9} \quad \frac{8}{12} \quad \frac{10}{15}$$

Ask students to examine the apart-ness of each fraction in this sequence. The additive differences between the numerator and the denominator follow the pattern of multiples used to generate them (1, 2, 3, 4, 5) because the initial difference between 2 and 3 was 1.

Conclusion? Fractions with distinct apart-ness can all be equal in value!

Unpacking the Mathematical Thinking

We want our students to be able to reason quantitatively about fractions—to have a good sense of the size, amount, or number a fraction represents. For this, we must use the informal knowledge of fractions that children bring with them and build on it through evocative experiences, multiple contexts, mathematical discussions, and sufficient time for children to develop strong fraction sense for themselves.

Strong fraction sense includes familiarity, fluency, and fluidity when working with fractions. But most importantly, it includes flexibility. First, we must ask ourselves if *we* model flexible thinking for our students when working with fractions—or any other math topic for that matter. Second, we must nurture flexibility when examining the relative magnitude of fractions by modeling a variety of ways of thinking and doing, rather than imposing rigid ways to solve fraction comparisons.

 Teaching Tip: Focus on the Strategy Rather Than the Answer

Like Nicole in the opening vignette of this chapter, rather than ask students convergent questions, such as "Compare $\frac{1}{2}$ and $\frac{2}{5}$" or "Compare $\frac{4}{6}$ and $\frac{5}{8}$," give students a list of fraction pairs and have them reflect on the most efficient strategy they could use to determine the relative magnitude of the fractions in each case. Have them group the fraction pairs according to strategies they name and describe, such as "Compare to 1," "Compare to $\frac{1}{2}$," "Common denominators," "Common numerators," "Unit fractions," "One-apartness," and so on.

Here are some pairs you can use:

$$\frac{4}{6} ? \frac{5}{8} \qquad \frac{4}{6} ? \frac{5}{6} \qquad \frac{3}{8} ? \frac{3}{10} \qquad \frac{3}{4} ? \frac{4}{5} \qquad \frac{1}{9} ? \frac{1}{10} \qquad \frac{2}{5} ? \frac{7}{12} \qquad \frac{7}{8} ? \frac{9}{8}$$

Please add to this list as you see fit!

Comparing fractions typically adds more rules to the meaningless jungle of rules students already need to memorize about fractions—but this need not be the case. Instead, we can hold off from introducing the common denominator rule and support students in discovering and developing for themselves informal but meaningful comparing schemes. Just like with computational algorithms, there is no one best algorithm for comparing fractions. It depends on the fractions in question. Consider this example:

$$\text{Which fraction is closest to } 1: \frac{1}{2}, \frac{2}{5}, \frac{7}{9}, \text{ or } \frac{13}{15}?$$

Converting all four fractions to respectively equivalent fractions with common denominators is certainly *not* the most efficient strategy for comparing them! Other strategies are not only more efficient but are also testimonies of sound mathematical reasoning.

We will now consider some of the different strategies that students actually do use when we give them opportunities to use their thinking. Note that these strategies are not mutually exclusive: two or more strategies can be used to compare the same pair of fractions.

Using Models

Working with concrete models—both continuous and discrete—helps students form mental images for basic fractions and the comparisons among them, such as $\frac{1}{6} < \frac{1}{3} < \frac{1}{2}$ (Figure 5.5).

FIGURE 5.5
Continuous and Discrete Models

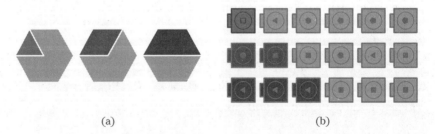

(a)   (b)

You can then progress to equal- or fair-sharing situations and ask questions about dividing sandwiches or pizzas, such as the problem Nicole posed to her class about different portions of casseroles. As students gradually detach from the fractional quantities, they are able to reason about fractions as pure numbers and learn to compare their magnitude just as they would whole numbers.

Reasoning with Unit Fractions

Unit fractions are special fractions with a numerator of 1 and a random whole-number denominator: $\frac{1}{2}, \frac{1}{3}, \frac{1}{4}, \frac{1}{5}$, and so forth. Reasoning with unit fractions involves comparing fractions that represent only one part of the respective partitioned units. Through multiple examples, students learn that the greater the number of equal parts (i.e., the denominator), the smaller the size of those parts.

This important inverse relationship between *number of parts* and *size of parts* is best learned if students construct the knowledge for themselves. Instead of simply stating it, offer students different explorations to familiarize them with unit fractions. For example, have students draw different unit fractions as equal shares of a common rectangular or circular whole, such as a loaf of sandwich bread or an apple pie.

Another good activity is to create a human number line, using unit fractions:

- Ask students to describe what a human number line would look like if each student were a consecutive whole number, say, from 1 to 25. Students will likely say that there will be an equal distance between neighboring people (points) and that the points (or number values) will move away from 0 and toward infinity as the numbers increase.

- Next, have students imagine a human number line with a huge unit length. If each student were a different unit fraction from $\frac{1}{1}$ to $\frac{1}{25}$, ask them how they see in their mind's eye the ordering of the 25 unit fractions.

- Prompt their thinking about the exercise by posing questions—for example, "What are the endpoints? What can you say about the distance between consecutive unit fractions? Where would $\frac{1}{1,000}$ be? Where would $\frac{1}{1,000,000}$ be?"

Students will be surprised to discover that unit fractions (1) get closer and closer to one another and (2) approach 0 as the denominator grows indefinitely (Figure 5.6).

FIGURE 5.6
Unit Fractions on the Number Line

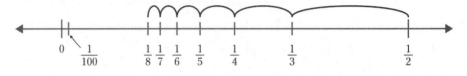

Using the Concept of Equivalence (Common Denominators or Numerators)

The problem of ordering two fractions [with different numerators and denominators] rests on considerable knowledge of fraction equivalence.

Merlyn J. Behr and Thomas R. Post (1992, p. 223)

Fractions with common numerators or denominators are either given in that form or can be generated using the EFA, as Cyril and Olivia did (see Figure 5.1 on p. 150).

Common numerators. When comparing fractions with common numerators, students must coordinate the inverse relationship between the size of the denominators and the size of the fractions: the greater the denominator, the smaller the fraction. This involves reasoning with unit fractions, as explained earlier.

Common denominators. When comparing fractions with common denominators, students can shift back to whole-number thinking and use their well-grounded ideas about counting. For example, the fraction $\frac{5}{8}$ is greater than $\frac{4}{8}$ because 5 *one-eighths* is greater than 4 *one-eighths*. The counting unit is *one-eighth*.

(Numerator 1) × n = numerator 2; and (denominator 1) × n = denominator 2. When considering the fractions $\frac{3}{4}$ and $\frac{9}{12}$, an insightful student would notice that 9 is a multiple of 3—in particular, 9 equals *three times* 3. A good habit is to check the denominators: in this example, 12 also equals *three times* something, in this case, 4. Consequently, each fraction can be generated from the other by using the EFA: multiplying the numerator and the denominator by 3 generates the second fraction from the first, and multiplying by $\frac{1}{3}$ or dividing by 3 generates the first fraction from the second. From this, we can see that the two fractions are clearly equal.

Comparing to Benchmarks

As students become more and more familiar with the number line, help them think of it as a road, with a starting point at 0, on which we can travel in two directions. For now, students travel to the right, into Positive Land. They encounter familiar landmarks along the way: $\frac{1}{2}$, 1, $\frac{3}{2}$, 2 . . . By 5th grade, comparing fractions to the benchmarks 0, $\frac{1}{2}$, and 1 should be second nature for students.

On opposite sides of the benchmark. Consider the fractions $\frac{3}{7}$ and $\frac{6}{10}$. Students should (or can be guided to) realize that $\frac{3}{7}$ is close to the benchmark $\frac{1}{2}$ but less than $\frac{1}{2}$, whereas $\frac{6}{10}$ is also close to $\frac{1}{2}$ but greater than $\frac{1}{2}$. Comparing 3 to $3\frac{1}{2}$, which is half of 7, and 6 to 5, which is half of 10, leads us to conclude that $\frac{3}{7}$ is less than $\frac{1}{2}$, and $\frac{6}{10}$ is greater than $\frac{1}{2}$. Rephrasing the latter inequality, $\frac{1}{2}$ is less than $\frac{6}{10}$. Consequently, from the double inequality, $\frac{3}{7} < \frac{1}{2} < \frac{6}{10}$, we gather that $\frac{3}{7} < \frac{6}{10}$. Students able to reason in this way have a quantitative understanding of fractions.

Note: Many students spontaneously see and mentally manipulate rational parts of denominators. For instance, they will say that "Three-sevenths is less than $3\frac{1}{2}$ sevenths." Even though $\dfrac{3\frac{1}{2}}{7}$ isn't written as a whole number over another whole number, it is nevertheless a rational number, since multiplying both the numerator and denominator by 2 yields $\dfrac{7}{14}$, which is assuredly a fraction! The ability to "chunk" a fraction or ratio while simultaneously preserving its multiplicative relationship (i.e., 1-to-2 equals $3\frac{1}{2}$ -to-7 equals 7-to-14) is a testimony of early proportional thinking. Encourage this kind of thinking when you witness it!

On the same side of the benchmark. The fractions $\dfrac{3}{4}$ and $\dfrac{4}{6}$ are on the same side of the benchmark $\dfrac{1}{2}$ $\left(\text{both are to the right of } \dfrac{1}{2}\right)$ and on the same side of the benchmark 1 (both are to the left of 1). Note that I am using Sophie's directional language of "left" and "right," which evokes a mental image of the number line as a road lined with numbers in ascending order as I travel to the right. But comparing $\dfrac{3}{4}$ and $\dfrac{4}{6}$ requires more subtle reasoning: we must assess *how far from the chosen benchmark* each fraction is. Sophie and Hugo chose the benchmark 0, but they could have also chosen $\dfrac{1}{2}$, as Nicole pointed out. Fifth grader Sophie beautifully explained that the space between $\dfrac{4}{6}$ and 1 is $\dfrac{1}{3}$, which is greater than $\dfrac{1}{4}$, the space between $\dfrac{3}{4}$ and 1. Therefore, since the "space to get to 1" (Sophie's language) is shorter from the fraction $\dfrac{3}{4}$, $\dfrac{3}{4}$ is greater than $\dfrac{4}{6}$.

Using Multiplicative Thinking

We have all witnessed students' predilection for additive thinking over multiplicative thinking in the realm of fractions and ratios.

Students are exposed to the between ratios of two fractions during their extensive work with fraction equivalence (as we saw in Figure 5.4 on p. 159). They use these ratios when converting given fractions to new ones with common denominators. But, as noted, seldom do we witness discussion around a fraction's within ratio—perhaps because we rarely address the concept ourselves. In 5th grade, we should.

Consider two simple equivalent fractions, $\frac{1}{3}$ and $\frac{2}{6}$. In addition to the "times 2" or "divided by 2" horizontal relationship, students' attention should also be drawn, whenever possible, to the "times 3" or "divided by 3" *vertical* relationship within each fraction: $1 \times 3 = 3$ and $2 \times 3 = 6$. Once students become aware of both multiplicative instances, they will learn to attend to both.

Let's revisit Nicole's fractions, $\frac{3}{4}$ and $\frac{4}{6}$, and look at them through these new lenses. Using strong number sense, a student may be prompted to see or say, "In the first fraction, 4 equals 3 [the numerator] plus 1 [one-third of the numerator], or one-and-one-third *times* the numerator. In the second fraction, 6 equals 4 [the numerator] plus 2 [one-half of the numerator], or one-and-one-half *times* the numerator." Thus, the denominator is greater compared to the numerator in the fraction $\frac{4}{6}$ than in the fraction $\frac{3}{4}$. Based on a good understanding of fraction magnitude, we conclude that $\frac{4}{6} < \frac{3}{4}$.

Granted, this way of thinking is sophisticated, but students are capable of sophisticated mathematical thinking. We must remember to articulate more explicitly both the between and within ratios when comparing two fractions.

Noticing Patterns

In mathematics, there are patterns, and in patterns, there is beauty. If for no other reason than an aesthetic experience, it can be valuable and powerful to tackle the most challenging sets of fractions from the pattern perspective. I've coined these classes of fractions by their "*n* apart-ness:"

- 1-apart: $\frac{1}{2}, \frac{2}{3}, \frac{3}{4}, \frac{3}{5}, \frac{5}{6}\ldots$
  (The numerator and denominator differ by $n = 1$.)
- 2-apart: $\frac{1}{3}, \frac{2}{4}, \frac{3}{5}, \frac{4}{6}, \frac{5}{7}\ldots$
  (The numerator and denominator differ by $n = 2$.)
- 3-apart: $\frac{1}{4}, \frac{2}{5}, \frac{3}{6}, \frac{4}{7}, \frac{5}{8}\ldots$
  (The numerator and denominator differ by $n = 3$.)
- *n*-apart: $\frac{1}{1+n}, \frac{2}{2+n}, \frac{3}{3+n}, \frac{4}{4+n}\ldots$
  (The numerator and denominator differ by any number n.)

Divide your class into groups, and assign each pattern to a different group as a project. As we did earlier with the one-apart sequence, ask students to examine what changes and what remains the same as the fractions progress through the sequence. They can use drawings, concrete models, calculators—any mathematical tool available that will help them come to know these fractions better.

Fraction sense, after all, means friendliness with fractions. If we think about each sequence as a class of fractions that share a common feature, we see that what can be learned about one fraction can be learned for all.

A Bridge to Algebra: The Power of Generalization

Students should be pattern sniffers.
Al Cuoco, E. Paul Goldenberg, and June Mark (1996, p. 378)

Algebraic reasoning has a defining feature of seeking generalization, from discerned repetition or regularity within patterns. Without this feature, there is no algebra. Generalizing is a human tendency, and children are not excluded from it. Shifting from making statements about *specific* numbers (or shapes) to asserting generalizations about *all* numbers (or shapes) is quintessential to algebraic thinking. We need to cultivate the habit of mind, in our students and ourselves, of searching for the general in the particular.

Generalizations are expressed by elementary school students in a number of ways—through natural language, physical gestures, concrete models, pictures or drawings, tables of numbers, graphs of points, or mathematical symbols. For example, consider these groups of Cuisenaire Rods:

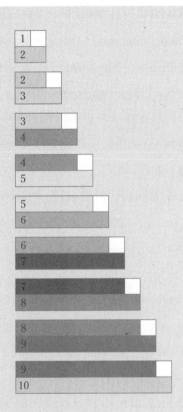

Suppose that the numerators (the top rods) represent the numbers of adults (1–9) at 9 different picnics taking place simultaneously, and the denominators (bottom rods) represent the numbers of children (2–10) at these same 9 picnics. The Cuisenaire Rods pairs depict the ratios of adults to children at the 9 picnics, ranging from 1-to-2 through 9-to-10. This graphic powerfully shows that as the numerator and denominator grow in value, their *constant difference of 1*—represented by the white unit cube—becomes less and less important relative to their size. The values of the consecutive pattern elements increase and approach 1.

Ultimately, students will come to see that all *n*-apart sequences increase in value (no matter the value of *n* other than zero) and get closer and closer to 1 but never reach it, thus forming their own generalization!

Looking Ahead: Visualizing the "Cross-Product" Method

Students learn in middle school, and sometimes earlier, the cross-product algorithm for comparing two fractions: for example, $\frac{2}{5} > \frac{1}{3}$ if and only if $2 \times 3 > 5 \times 1$. Since the products of 2×3 and 5×1 crisscross the two fractions, this algorithm is known as the *cross-product rule*. Students typically apply this algorithm with even less understanding than the common denominator algorithm.

In order to construct meaning for the two numerator-by-denominator products (in preparation for their middle school encounter with the cross-product algorithm), have students use the rectangle method, a visual representation for comparing any two fractions (Figure 5.7). In this case, a 3-by-5 rectangle will do the trick: shade two of the five columns to represent $\frac{2}{5}$, and shade one of the three rows to represent $\frac{1}{3}$.

From this, we can see that two columns of three squares each ($2 \times 3 = 6$) are dotted for the fraction $\frac{2}{5}$, and one row of five squares ($5 \times 1 = 5$) is shaded for the fraction $\frac{1}{3}$. This procedure, which is essentially an intuitive or informal cross-product algorithm, shows that $\frac{2}{5}$ is greater than $\frac{1}{3}$, since six squares is more than five squares.

FIGURE 5.7
The Rectangle Method: A Visual Way of Comparing Two Fractions

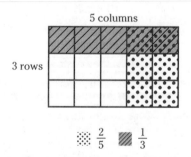

Targeting Misconceptions with Challenging Problems

Again, simple comparison problems can be found easily, online and in print. The problems that follow are more complex, and most require fairly sophisticated levels of mathematical thinking.

💡 **Problem 1: Comparing regions.** Each of these shapes represents a cake, and the white region of each represents the part(s) of the cake that has been eaten. Complete the following exercises for each *pair* of cakes, *A* and *B*.

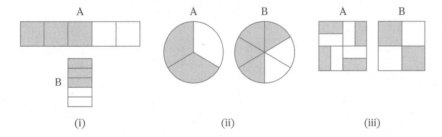

(i)   (ii)   (iii)

- Use a fraction to name the remaining fractional part of each cake.
- Compare the remaining fractional parts in each pair of cakes. Explain your reasoning.

💡 **Problem 2: An exercise problem.** Daniel surveyed 330 students to find which form of exercise they preferred among three choices. He found that $\frac{1}{5}$ of them liked swimming, $\frac{2}{3}$ liked basketball, and $\frac{1}{10}$ preferred running. The remaining students did not complete the survey.

- Which group is the largest, and how many students are in that group?
- Which group is the smallest, and how many students are in that group?

- Order the three fractions for survey participants in this problem from least to greatest.
- How many students did not complete the survey? How did you figure that out?
- How can you express this fourth subgroup as a fraction of the total group of 330 students surveyed? How does this fraction compare with the other three?

Problem 3: A growing pattern of fractions. These four fractions form a pattern on the number line between 0 and 1:

$$\frac{3}{4} \qquad \frac{3}{8} \qquad \frac{5}{8} \qquad \frac{1}{2}$$

- Figure out the pattern, and order the four fractions from least to greatest.
- Place the four fractions on the number line between 0 and 1.
- Name the next three fractions in this growing pattern, and place them on the line.

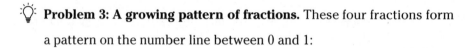

Problem 4: Recognizing the proximity to benchmarks. Separate each set of fractions into two groups, according to the directions:

- Separate the fractions into two groups: those less than 1 and those greater than 1.

$$\frac{4}{5}, \frac{6}{5}, \frac{4}{3}, \frac{4}{8}, \frac{1}{9}, \frac{7}{5}, \frac{2}{3}, \frac{3}{2}$$

- Separate the fractions into two groups: those less than $\frac{1}{2}$ and those greater than $\frac{1}{2}$.

$$\frac{1}{3}, \frac{3}{4}, \frac{4}{5}, \frac{2}{3}, \frac{4}{6}, \frac{2}{5}, \frac{5}{8}, \frac{3}{7}$$

- Separate the fractions into two groups: those closer to 0 and those closer to 1.

$$\frac{7}{8}, \frac{1}{9}, \frac{2}{11}, \frac{6}{7}, \frac{12}{13}, \frac{1}{10}, \frac{1}{8}$$

- Separate the fractions into two groups: those closer to $\frac{1}{2}$ and those closer to 1.

$$\frac{4}{5}, \frac{5}{9}, \frac{9}{8}, \frac{4}{10}, \frac{3}{5}, \frac{3}{6}, \frac{3}{8}$$

Summarize your learning by completing each sentence:

- I can tell if a fraction is close to 0 because _____.
- I can tell if a fraction is close to $\frac{1}{2}$ because _____.
- I can tell if a fraction is close to 1 *but less than* 1 because _____.
- I can tell if a fraction is close to 1 *but greater than* 1 because _____.

💡 **Problem 5: Three fractions in a row.** Given one fraction, find one on each side:

- *Use pattern blocks for halves and thirds:* The fraction is $\frac{2}{3}$; find one fraction greater than and one fraction less than $\frac{2}{3}$ whose denominators equal 2.
- *Use fractions circles for thirds and fourths:* The fraction is $\frac{3}{4}$; find one fraction greater than and one fraction less than $\frac{3}{4}$ whose denominators equal 3.
- *Use the number line for fourths and fifths:* The fraction is $\frac{3}{5}$; find one fraction greater than and one fraction less than $\frac{3}{5}$ whose denominators equal 4.

Now, given two fractions, find one in between:

- Find a fraction between $\frac{2}{2}$ and $\frac{3}{2}$, meaning, greater than $\frac{2}{2}$ and less than $\frac{3}{2}$.

- Find a fraction between $\frac{1}{3}$ and $\frac{2}{3}$, meaning, greater than $\frac{1}{3}$ and less than $\frac{2}{3}$.

- Find a fraction between $\frac{3}{4}$ and $\frac{4}{4}$, meaning, greater than $\frac{3}{4}$ and less than $\frac{4}{4}$.

In conclusion:

- Given any two fractions close in value, what can you conclude about the existence of a third fraction "between" them?

- Do whole numbers have this same "in between-ness" property? Share your thoughts.

- Explain a procedure that can help you find an "in between" fraction for any given pair of close fractions.

💡 **Problem 6: Ordering fractions, using the number line.** Use Set A and the number lines to solve the following problems.

$$A = \left\{\frac{2}{3}, \frac{10}{4}, \frac{6}{2}, \frac{7}{3}, \frac{1}{2}, \frac{8}{4}\right\}$$

- Place each fraction on one of the three number lines:

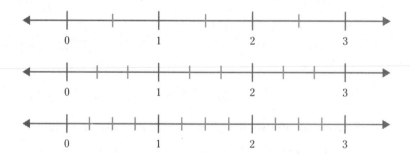

- Order the six fractions in ascending order:

___ < ___ < ___ < ___ < ___ < ___

Now, use the fractions denoted by the points P, Q, R, S, T, U, V, W, and X on the number lines below:

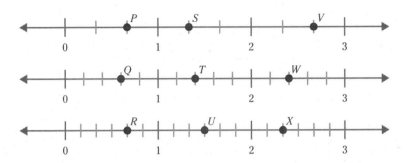

- Name the fractions represented by points P, Q, R, S, T, U, V, W, and X.

- Pick a pair of fractions with equal denominators, and compare them:

  ___ < ___.

- Pick a pair of fractions with equal numerators, and compare them:

  ___ < ___.

- Find a pair of equivalent fractions with different numerators and denominators: ___ = ___.

- Find a pair of fractions where the one with the greater numerator has the lesser value: ___ < ___.

- Find a pair of fractions where the one with the greater denominator has the greater value: one: ___ < ___.

- Did you learn something new from this exercise? If so, describe what you learned.

Problem 7: One-apart fractions. Ivan conjectures that fractions $\frac{5}{6}$ and $\frac{7}{8}$ are equal because they are both "one apart," meaning that their numerator and denominator values differ by 1 (in this case, the denominator is 1 greater than the numerator).

- Can you understand Ivan's thinking? Do you ever think in the same way? Explain.

- Analyze Ivan's conjecture: Are $\frac{5}{6}$ and $\frac{7}{8}$ really equal? Justify your answer.

- Take a one-apart fraction that you know well $\left(\text{say, } \frac{3}{4}\right)$. Multiply to generate four fractions equivalent to $\frac{3}{4}$:

$$\frac{3 \times 2}{4 \times 2} \qquad \frac{3 \times 3}{4 \times 3} \qquad \frac{3 \times 4}{4 \times 4} \qquad \frac{3 \times 5}{4 \times 5}$$

- What can you conclude about the equivalent fractions you produced?

- How might you use this pattern of fractions to help Ivan clarify his thinking?

 What's the App for That? *See It on the Line!*

Understanding fractions as numbers, represented by points on a line, can be challenging for some students. The **See It on the Line!** app (www.apps4math.com) enables students to manipulate and compare two or three fractions on the number line with ease and understanding.

CHAPTER 6

Let Algorithms Emerge Naturally

It is time to shift the emphasis and redefine the goal of fraction instruction in elementary school from learning computation rules to developing fraction operation sense.

DeAnn Huinker (2002, p. 78)

Mathematical algorithms are formidable inventions of the mind of man and woman. They are testimonies to mathematical insight, ingenuity, and efficiency. Yet mathematics educators, such as Kamii and Dominick (1998), warn us of their potential harm, as "they encourage children to give up their own thinking" (p. 135). But the algorithms themselves are not harmful—rather, the potential problems lie in *when*, *how*, and *in what context* we introduce them.

If there is one area of school mathematics in dire need of a shift "from rote to reason," it's fraction computation. Traditional instruction on fraction algorithms has essentially been rule based:

- "To add or subtract two fractions, first find common denominators."
- "To multiply two fractions, just multiply the numerators and multiply the denominators."

- "To divide two fractions, invert the second one, then multiply both fractions."

Lost in this nonsensical jungle of rules, students relinquish their own sense making and surrender to memorization. And if or when *why* questions are posed, they usually address operation procedures rather than meanings:

- "Why don't we need to find common denominators when multiplying fractions?"
- "Why doesn't fraction division work like fraction multiplication?"

Mirroring rule-based teaching, students sadly equate *learning fraction computation* with *knowing how to carry out algorithms* to produce the right answers.

A premature focus on the memorization of algorithms reinforces the erroneous but prevalent belief that mathematics is more about memorizing procedures than reasoning with or about powerful ideas. We must delay formal operations with fractions until students

- Have strong mental images for fractions.
- Appreciate the importance of the unit.
- Understand fraction equivalence deeply.
- Have a sense of the relative magnitude of fractions.

In preparation for learning standard algorithms, fraction operations should be explored in the context of problem situations that students can relate to. Students need ample time to do the following:

- Struggle productively with the many interpretations of operations.
- Build on their understandings of whole-number operations to construct new understandings.
- Devise their own algorithms that lead them meaningfully to solutions.

Rather than teach senseless rules, such as "Invert, then multiply" or "Flip the fellow that follows, then multiply," to better remember which fraction to invert, computation patterns can emerge naturally with a teacher's guidance. If we orchestrate challenges that engage students' sophisticated mathematical thinking and withhold telling them rules, our patience will be rewarded with students' pride in their new understanding: those "a-ha!" moments that come with productive struggle and build students' affinity for a discipline. Otherwise, when fraction teaching begins, students' love for mathematics often ends because they think mathematics is nothing more than committing random rules to memory.

Vignette 1: Division of a Whole Number by a Fraction

I posed the following question about the meanings of operations to a class of preK–5 teachers at a summer math institute: "Suppose a child who knows no algorithms turns to you for the *meaning* behind this string of symbols. What story might you invent that can be modeled by this expression?"

$$3 \div \frac{1}{2}$$

Initially, blank stares filled the room. It was a tough question, indeed. Finally, one group suggested a story of "splitting three pizzas in half and sharing them equally among two people, with each person getting $1\frac{1}{2}$ pizzas." Everyone seemed to agree, at first. But soon another group, who had worked out the algorithm, suggested that the answer was six pizzas, but they couldn't come up with a division story. The class was at a loss for an explanation that could reconcile the two answers: $1\frac{1}{2}$ pizzas, which seemed logical when "splitting three pizzas in half," and six pizzas, which seemed illogical but was produced by the standard algorithm.

Since the class was struggling, I called a time-out and reverted to an easier division question: "What story, modeled by this expression, would you invent to give meaning to division?"

$$22 \div 4$$

This time, smiles filled the room, as teachers felt confident about fulfilling the task. I handed a stack of plastic cups and 22 cubes to each group and asked them to clearly state what the cups and cubes represented when telling their story.

I then monitored the groups. Each group automatically took four cups from the stack, placed them at the center of the table, and discarded the extra ones. Teachers focused their discussions on the various scenarios that could be modeled by the cups and cubes. In most scenarios, the cups ended up representing four students. The predominant choice represented by the 22 cubes was some form of food item: cookies, candies, mini pizzas, and so on. One group chose 22 dollars.

After sharing their stories and discussing the different meanings of the remainder in context—two discrete objects such as two marbles that *could not* be split into halves, or two continuous quantities such as two cookies that *could*—the teachers thought they had uncovered the main point of the exploration: namely, the two possible answers depending on the nature of the 22 items (Figure 6.1):

- In the case of indivisible items, such as balls or rocks, the answer is 5—the remaining 2 items are simply discarded.
- In the case of divisible items, such as food, money, or time, the answer is $5\frac{1}{2}$ or 5.5.

The class was satisfied with these answers, but the best was yet to come.

"What do all your stories have in common?" I asked. "They're all about fair sharing?" tested one teacher. "Absolutely! And in this model, we must

FIGURE 6.1
Equal or Fair Sharing Stories for "22 ÷ 4"

(a) Sharing 22 marbles among 4 people: The equal share is 5 marbles and the remainder is 2.	(b) Sharing 22 cookies among 4 people: The equal share is $5\frac{1}{2}$ cookies and the remainder is 0.

emphasize to students that the shares must be *equal*," I replied. Then I prodded further: "OK, so, is fair sharing your only metaphor, model, or mental image for 22 ÷ 4?" As a hint, I related a different kind of division story: "I have 22 apples and wish to bag them, 4 apples per bag. How many bags do I need?"

It took the class a few moments to grasp the difference:

- In the *fair sharing* interpretation of division (partitive division), which all of my teachers selected, the number of "groups"— four people, in most of their stories—was known, but the share that each group (or "person," in their stories) received was unknown.

- In the *grouping* interpretation of division (quotative division, also called *measurement division* or *repeated subtraction*), it's the opposite: the number of elements in each "group"—four apples, in the example I gave—is known, but the number of groups ("bags," in my example) is unknown, as shown in Figure 6.2. I leave it to the reader to figure out the solution.

Equipped with this alternative *grouping* metaphor for division—which is simple for young children to grasp but less instinctive to adults, as it

FIGURE 6.2
Two Division Models for "22 ÷ 4": Sharing and Grouping

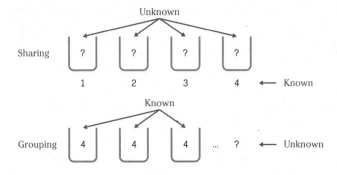

hasn't been traditionally taught from the get-go—together with the *sharing* metaphor, the teachers wrapped up their exploration by returning to my original question regarding "$3 \div \frac{1}{2}$." They imagined a variety of situations that can help students make sense of what it means to divide by a fraction. Figure 6.3 illustrates two such examples, to which I have added a third.

FIGURE 6.3
Visualizing Situations That Give Meaning to "$3 \div \frac{1}{2}$"

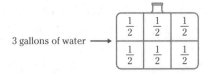

3 gallons of water

(a) How many half-gallon bottles can be made from 3 gallons of water?

Answer: 6 half-gallon bottles

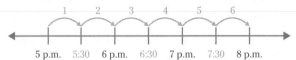

5 p.m.   5:30   6 p.m.   6:30   7 p.m.   7:30   8 p.m.

(b) How many half-hour TV episodes can I watch in a 3-hour span?

Answer: 6 half-hour episodes

(c) How many half-pizza portions can be made out of 3 whole pizzas?

Answer: 6 half-pizza portions

Vignette 2: Multiplication of a Whole Number by a Fraction

During a 5th grade math lesson, I had a discussion with Eric and Samantha about the multiplication problems they had completed for homework.

I said to Eric, "I see you got all your products correct. Bravo! Now take one problem—$6 \times \frac{2}{8}$, for instance—and tell me what it means."

Eric politely obliged: "Well, you put 6 over 1, then you multiply 6 and 2 to get 12, and 1 and 8 to get 8, and the answer, $\frac{12}{8}$, is $1\frac{1}{2}$."

$$\frac{6}{1} \times \frac{2}{8} = \frac{12}{8} = 1\frac{1}{2}$$

I said, "What you just explained perfectly is the *procedure* for multiplying six by the fraction two-eighths. Now suppose someone wanted to understand *why* you did what you did. Can you help them with a concrete situation or a drawing?" Eric paused for a moment and then said, "I never really thought about what it *means*."

While Eric was reflecting, his table partner, Samantha, gave it a try: she drew six rectangles to represent six candy bars and then tried to take two-eighths of it, without noticing that $\frac{2}{8} = \frac{1}{4}$. "It's hard to make eighths from six," she commented, "because it doesn't divide evenly like four would." Samantha too paused for a while.

Eric then emerged from his contemplation with an idea: "Can I draw two-eighths and then make six of them and see what that makes?" "That's a great idea," I said, adding, "Two-eighths of what?" Eric proceeded to draw six copies of two-eighths of a pie, counted the total number of eighths and was pleased with what he found: $\frac{12}{8}$, precisely what his algorithm had given him by rote. "Neat!" he exclaimed.

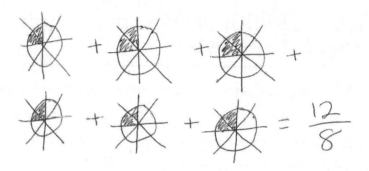

I also wanted to leave Samantha feeling empowered, as she too had a viable visualization, even though she got stuck halfway. "Samantha," I said, "what's a simpler fraction equivalent to two-eighths?" "One-fourth!" she replied. "Great," I said. "Now, can you please draw six chocolate bars in a row?" Samantha complied. "Can you show me half of the six bars by drawing a line segment to show the partition?" I asked. She separated the six bars into two groups of three with a vertical line segment. "If you now cut your halves in half again, what would the parts represent?" "Fourths," she replied instantly. And before I could formulate my next inquiry, Samantha suddenly smiled: "That makes one and a half [*pointing to the three halves she shaded in black*], like Eric's!"

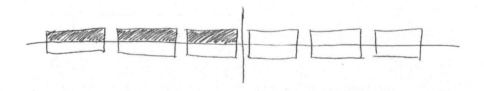

As she worked through the problem, Samantha noted, "$6 \times \frac{2}{8}$ and $\frac{2}{8} \times 6$ are equal." She chose the second expression, interpreted it to mean "$\frac{2}{8}$ of 6 bars" $\left(\text{or } "\frac{1}{4} \text{ of 6 bars"}\right)$, and obtained $\frac{3}{2}$ of a bar, or $1\frac{1}{2}$ bars. Eric, on the other hand, opted for $6 \times \frac{2}{8}$ and modeled the multiplication to mean 6 copies of size $\frac{2}{8}$, where 6 was the multiplier and $\frac{2}{8}$ the multiplicand. Both processes and products were logically interpreted and correctly carried out; they were simply modeled differently.

Recognizing Misconceptions

Traditional instruction of fraction algorithms begins with teaching the algorithms for adding and subtracting fractions (not always in context) and then progresses to multiplication and finally division. But under each operation, there are subcategories: under addition, for example, adding fractions with common denominators is distinguished from adding fractions with related denominators (e.g., 2 and 8), which is further distinguished from adding fractions with unrelated denominators (e.g., 2 and 5).

But that's not all—there are additional subcategories to further confuse the picture. Still under addition, there are rules for adding "proper" fractions (those less than 1), other rules for adding "improper" fractions (those greater than 1), and still more for adding mixed numbers—and such fragmentation occurs within each operation. The result is a litany of seemingly unrelated procedures that students must commit to memory, and their attempts to make sense of it all are soon relinquished.

It is not surprising, then, that difficulties, misunderstandings, and misconceptions have long accompanied the learning of fractions. Some key misconceptions are addressed below and on the following pages.

Difficulty Seeing Fractions as Numbers

Adding, subtracting, multiplying, and dividing rational numbers require that they be seen as numbers because in elementary school these operations are defined only for numbers.

National Research Council (2001, p. 238)

In problems involving fractions, if students don't see the symbols $\frac{a}{b}$ as denoting fractional quantities, they have trouble conceiving of operations on these quantities and consequently find it difficult to solve the problems. This is why mathematics educators stress the importance of first allowing students to develop rich mental images for the fractional symbols before asking them to combine fractions through computation.

Rote or Incorrect Application of Algorithms

Confusion among the rules. When algorithms are learned by rote and taught without contexts that provide meaning, it's easy for students to confuse them. For instance, carelessly transferring the multiplication procedure $\frac{a}{b} \times \frac{c}{d} = \frac{a \times c}{b \times d}$ to the addition of fractions commonly yields incorrect answers, such as $\frac{3}{4} + \frac{4}{5} = \frac{7}{9}$. If students simply considered the approximate size of the addend fractions, using fraction number sense, they would know that a sum of $\frac{7}{9}$ is incorrect. Since both $\frac{3}{4}$ and $\frac{4}{5}$ are greater than the benchmark $\frac{1}{2}$, their sum *must be* greater than 1. Given that $\frac{7}{9}$ is less than 1, it is therefore an incorrect answer.

Rigidity in rule application. Not only do students retain mechanically that when adding or subtracting fractions, they must find common denominators, they are also intent on finding the *least common denominator*. This heightened attention to the denominators distracts students from their sense of fraction magnitude.

Knowing Fractions Means Knowing the Algorithms

The conversation with Eric and Samantha, the two reflective 5th graders in Vignette 2, illustrates at least three points:

- For most students, *knowing fractions* has traditionally been equivalent to *knowing how to compute with fractions*.

- Knowing how to compute with fractions means knowing how to carry out the steps of algorithmic procedures to produce numerical results.

- Students are capable of sophisticated thinking about fractions if we take the time to let them think, listen to them, and help make explicit for them what is often only implicit.

> ### CCSS.Math.Practice.MP1: Make Sense of Problems and Persevere in Solving Them
>
> By definition, a *problem* is not solved instantly. We must help students accept that reflecting on a question or struggling with a problem is the *norm*, not the exception, in the mathematics classroom culture. We must deconstruct the myth that being good at math is synonymous with being *fast*. In the words of mathematics educator Cathy Seeley (2015), "Faster isn't smarter"—and mathematicians are the first to say they need time to think deeply about mathematics. Shifting from applauding speed to valuing perseverance is key to invalidating this common myth. We must keep in mind the model offered by Eric and Samantha, who attempted to make sense of the *why* behind their correct procedures and kept working until they found a convincing model to explain it—thus exhibiting the habit of mind described in CCSS.Math.Practice.MP1: "Make sense of problems and persevere in solving them" (Common Core State Standards Initiative, 2010).

Lack of Fraction Operation Sense

Due to the rush to teach fraction rules and tricks, students don't have time to cultivate the needed fraction operation sense. Students need time to think about what the operations *mean* and to develop mental images for each operation, aided by stories and contexts that illustrate them. Even the notion of fraction division, considered the hardest topic to teach and learn in elementary school, can be understood by 3rd graders if the teaching is built on the metaphors for whole-number division: sharing and grouping. The algorithm can emerge naturally later.

False Beliefs About the Effects of Operations on Numbers or Quantities

Students learn two golden rules early on: "Addition makes bigger, and subtraction makes smaller" and "Multiplication makes bigger, and division makes smaller." After years of whole-number computation, these rules-turned-beliefs are carried over into the middle grades, even as the number world expands to include rational numbers and integers. Students are perplexed when these rules no longer hold.

Lack of Attention to the Unit

One of the subtlest problems students have with fractions, which often goes unattended, is a lack of awareness of the units involved. When multiplying or dividing fractional quantities, for instance, students juggle more than one unit at a time and often don't realize it. This understated issue exacerbates any attempt at understanding process and result.

Unpacking the Mathematical Thinking

My goal here is not to address all algorithms under all operations, as readers already know them. Instead, with the goal of developing students' conceptual understanding (interwoven with procedural fluency), I will try to do the following:

- Offer four problem situations that are accessible to all children.
- Share students' invented strategies for solving these problems, divided into common types of problem-solving tactics.
- Review operation meanings, properties, and relationships.
- Highlight two important changes in ways of thinking that are brought on by rational numbers.

Begin with Problem Situations That Students Can Tackle

Thirty years ago, problem solving was a distinct topic in mathematics. Today, in the Standards era, it permeates all of mathematics and provides contexts in which new concepts and skills can be learned. Consider using the following problems—as I often have—with students who have no formal knowledge of fraction algorithms, and trust that they can tackle them.

Problem A. Suppose that one person eats $\frac{5}{6}$ of something, while another person eats $\frac{2}{3}$ of a similar thing. Decide what the "something" is, and explore these questions:

- Who ate a greater fraction of the thing?

- How much more did that person eat?

- What fraction of the thing did the two people eat together?

Problem B. (You can use ready-made plastic or wooden tangram pieces or cut out paper tangram pieces.) A developer has parceled out 1 square mile of land into 7 lots, each representing a fraction of the unit square. Explore the following questions and activities. Give your answers as fractions of the unit square (1 square mile).

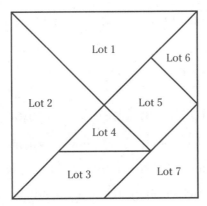

1. Write a fraction expression, using words or symbols, for Lot 1 and Lot 2 combined.

2. Mr. Lee bought Lot 2 and then sold half of it to his sister. What fraction of the square mile of land did he sell? Write a fraction expression, using words or symbols, for the area of Mr. Lee's remaining lot.

3. Compare the areas of Lots 3, 5, and 7, and express their areas as fractions.

4. Mrs. Halpern bought Lot 1. She wants to parcel out her lot into smaller lots—each equal in area to Lot 6. Show that she can make four such lots. Circle the sentence(s) that correctly model(s) Mrs. Halpern's action:

- (*Area of Lot 1*) divided by (*Area of Lot 6*) equals 4.
- $4 \times \frac{1}{4} = \frac{1}{16}$
- 4 copies of $\frac{1}{16}$ equals $\frac{1}{4}$.
- $\frac{1}{16}$ divided by $\frac{1}{4}$ equals 4.

Problem C. On a field trip, a teacher brought some large sandwiches for her nine students. Each student got $\frac{2}{3}$ of a sandwich. How many sandwiches did the teacher bring?

Problem D. On a field trip, a teacher brought six large sandwiches for her students. How many students can she feed if she makes equal portions of $\frac{2}{3}$ of a sandwich?

Allow Students to Devise Their Own Algorithms

When we move away from the traditional mechanistic approach to fraction learning, students are freed to begin their computation journey by inventing strategies (algorithms). These invented algorithms help students develop a conceptual knowledge base for fraction operation sense, on which the standard algorithms can be constructed.

To be clear: not every student "invents" a different way to solve problems. Students learn from one another, and some even learn the standard algorithms from relatives. So be it. Give students time to unpack all of them, make sense of them, compare them, and evaluate them. These will become the classroom repertoire of algorithms. As you begin weeding out the less useful ones, on the journey from invented to standard, address these questions:

- Do the invented strategies or algorithms make sense?
- Are they mathematically correct?
- Are they sufficiently efficient?
- Can they be transferred to and used with other, similar problems?
- Can they be generalized for all problems?

Allowing students to invent their own rules deemphasizes the teacher as demonstrator of the "correct" algorithm and emphasizes the students' role as young mathematicians. They learn that mathematics is about *doing* mathematics, not passively *receiving* it.

What follows are common student-invented strategies, along with examples of how students have applied them to make sense of and solve Problems A–D.

Making wholes. One of the first strategies students come up with when adding fractional quantities is to pack them together to "make wholes." By doing this, they demonstrate that the "need" for common denominators in order to add fractions is a myth.

To solve the third part of Problem A ("What fraction of the thing did the two people eat together?"), Ramsey, a 4th grader, drew two identical sets of six circles to represent two bags of six candies. To represent the eaten candies, he then colored five of one set $\left(\frac{5}{6}\right)$ and four of the other $\left(\frac{2}{3}\right)$. Combining the eaten candies, he completed $\frac{5}{6}$ with one candy to make $\frac{6}{6}$ (1 set), leaving three colored candies in the other set of six or $\frac{1}{2}$, for a total of $1\frac{1}{2}$.

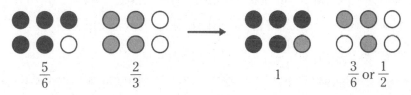

$$\frac{5}{6} \qquad \frac{2}{3} \qquad \longrightarrow \qquad 1 \qquad \frac{3}{6} \text{ or } \frac{1}{2}$$

In response to the same question, 3rd grader Jai also made wholes: he used two rhomboidal pattern blocks to visualize $\frac{2}{3}$ of a pizza, and five triangular pattern blocks for $\frac{5}{6}$ of a same-size pizza. He then exchanged one rhombus for two triangles: "I gave one triangle to the five-sixths, and that makes one whole and one half."

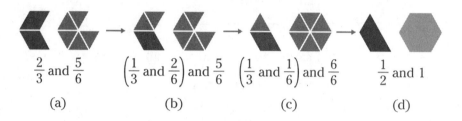

$\frac{2}{3}$ and $\frac{5}{6}$	$\left(\frac{1}{3}$ and $\frac{2}{6}\right)$ and $\frac{5}{6}$	$\left(\frac{1}{3}$ and $\frac{1}{6}\right)$ and $\frac{6}{6}$	$\frac{1}{2}$ and 1
(a)	(b)	(c)	(d)

Though they used different models to solve the problem, both Ramsey and Jai made one whole and were left with another half.

A final note about making wholes: making "whole hours" on a clock, a model less frequently used, would also be helpful in this problem. The sum of $\frac{2}{3}$ of an hour, or 40 minutes, and $\frac{5}{6}$ of an hour, or 50 minutes, gives 90 minutes, which is $1\frac{1}{2}$ hours. When adding fractions such as halves, thirds, fourths, sixths, and twelfths, encourage students to use the clock model, since by 3rd grade they know their minute equivalents.

Exchanging or renaming: using equivalent fractions. When left to investigate the meaning of problems, students naturally exchange a fractional quantity for other smaller ones, or combine smaller ones to make a larger one, and thus rename it. Here are a few instances of students using this strategy in order to tackle Problems A, B, and C (pp. 189–190).

As we saw in his solution to the third part of Problem A, Jai exchanged one rhombus for two triangles, going from a bigger fractional piece to a smaller one. Not with symbols but with actions, he decomposed $\frac{1}{3}$ into $\frac{2}{6}$; then, with words, he called the one-third piece "two-sixths."

To solve the third part of Problem B ("Compare the areas of Lots 3, 5, and 7, and express their areas as fractions"), 5th grader Sana did the opposite: having noticed that two small triangles $\left(\frac{2}{16}$ of the entire tangram$\right)$

matched up with each of the three medium-sized pieces, she placed the two small triangles (Lots 4 and 6) on top of the shapes corresponding to Lots 3, 5, and 7 and then concluded, "They're all the same."

parallelogram = Lot 3   square = Lot 5   triangle = Lot 7

When prompted for their equal area as a fraction of the tangram, Sana said, "I counted eight small triangles in half the tangram. That's $\frac{1}{16}$ of the big square. That means Lots 3, 5, and 6 are all $\frac{2}{16}$, or $\frac{1}{8}$."

For Problem C ("On a field trip, a teacher brought some large sandwiches for her 9 students. Each student got $\frac{2}{3}$ of a sandwich. How many sandwiches did the teacher bring?"), Ian, in 5th grade, listed $\frac{2}{3}$ nine times and grouped the fractions three by three. He said, "Three groups of two-thirds makes six-thirds; that's two sandwiches." He then added the three sets of two sandwiches and found six sandwiches.

$$\frac{2}{3} \quad \frac{2}{3} \quad \frac{2}{3} \qquad \frac{2}{3} \quad \frac{2}{3} \quad \frac{2}{3} \qquad \frac{2}{3} \quad \frac{2}{3} \quad \frac{2}{3}$$

Three $\frac{2}{3}$ or $\frac{6}{3}$, or 2   2   2

Fourth grader Tanya also used equivalent fractions to solve the first two questions of Problem A ("Who ate a greater fraction of the thing? How much more did that person eat?"). When asked which is greater, $\frac{5}{6}$ or $\frac{2}{3}$ of something, and by how much, Tanya used no concrete objects at all. Instead, she used her understanding of equivalent fractions and said, "Two-thirds is like four-sixths, so five-sixths is one [sixth] more!"

Through these problems, equivalent fractions come alive in concrete and coherent ways.

Teaching Tip: Why Insist on the "Simplest Form"?

Fraction problems often require that answers be given in the "simplest form." Consider the answers $\frac{4}{12}$ and $\frac{1}{3}$ to the fraction sum $\frac{1}{4} + \frac{1}{12}$. Both are viable answers because the fractions are equivalent and thus represent the same number. Insisting on the simplest form favors one fraction name over all of the valid fraction names, and it also contradicts the CCSSM emphasis on the importance of fraction equivalence.

A vital part of number sense is flexibility with numbers. Students develop flexibility when they are free to use whatever number form best fits the context at hand, makes sense to them, and is easiest to use. If we model flexibility with fractions, we will foster it in our students.

Matching to compare. Starting in 1st grade, children use matching to compare discrete quantities. If asked, for instance, which set of cubes is greater, the red or the blue, they'll line up the two sets side by side and match each red to a blue until there are no more of each or there are some left of one color.

To solve the first part of Problem A ("Who ate a greater fraction of the thing?"), 3rd grader Tess applied this principle to fractions: she used fraction strips to represent her two candy bars, $\frac{2}{3}$ and $\frac{5}{6}$, and lined them up to match the common shaded areas. This helped her easily see which was greater and by how much.

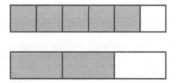

In her work on Problem B, we saw that Sana matched the two smallest triangles of the tangram with the square, then the parallelogram, and finally the medium triangle. Then she noticed that the two small triangles fit perfectly on top of each and concluded that the corresponding Lots 3, 5, and 7 were all equal in area. This approach commonly used by children in comparison problems translates later into addition or subtraction equations.

Iterating (repeated addition) combined with making wholes. A stepping stone from whole-number addition to whole-number multiplication is repeated addition. It's not surprising, then, that students use repeated addition for fraction multiplication.

Rachel, in 4th grade, approached Problem C ("On a field trip, a teacher brought some large sandwiches for her nine students. Each student got $\frac{2}{3}$ of a sandwich. How many sandwiches did the teacher bring?") by selecting a pair of rhomboidal pattern blocks as her representation of $\frac{2}{3}$ of a sandwich. She iterated such pairs nine times for the nine students, then grouped her 18 rhombi, 3 by 3, to make six hexagon sandwiches. Her conclusion: "The nine two-thirds came from six sandwiches."

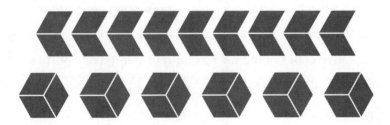

For the same problem, we saw that Ian, who is comfortable with manipulating fraction symbols, iterated $\frac{2}{3}$ nine times, made three subgroups of three $\frac{2}{3}$, computed each subgroup to find $\frac{6}{3}$ (3 two-thirds make 6 one-thirds), and used his knowledge of equivalent fractions $\left(\frac{6}{3} = 2\right)$ to conclude that there were 3×2, or 6 sandwiches. Rachel iterated the *figure* $\frac{2}{3}$, whereas Ian iterated the *symbol* $\frac{2}{3}$, but they both used repeated addition to find six sandwiches, thus solving what was, unbeknownst to them, a fraction multiplication problem.

Grouping. The less common division model students learn when working with whole numbers is grouping or segmenting (quotative division). We often see students apply this procedure to fractions without knowing that they are actually solving a fraction division problem.

To solve Problem D ("On a field trip, a teacher brought six large sandwiches for her students. How many students can she feed if she makes equal portions of $\frac{2}{3}$ of a sandwich?"), 4th grader Dante drew six long sandwiches, "cut" each into three thirds, and circled two-thirds at a time, thus making groups of two-thirds. He numbered each two-third portion to denote a new student and thus found that nine students had been fed.

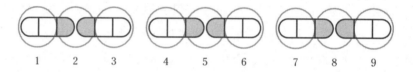

Brianna, in 5th grade, made six trains of three connecting cubes to model the sandwiches, with each cube representing one-third of a sandwich. Brianna symbolized her "groups of two-thirds" using color: every two consecutive cubes of the same color represented one portion—in this case, a student. She counted and numbered her pairs of colored cubes and found nine.

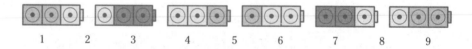

Both Dante and Brianna used grouping to solve a quotative division problem, a perfectly appropriate strategy, as we saw in Vignette 1.

Repeated subtraction. Another strategy students use to solve quotative division problems, again building on their understanding of division with whole numbers, is repeated subtraction.

Fifth grader Ethan used a more sophisticated mathematical representation to solve Problem D: the number line. He marked six intervals symbolizing the six sandwiches, labeled the linear units 1 through 6, and drew tick marks to divide them into thirds. He then modeled division as repeated subtraction on the number line, counting chunks of two-thirds backward from 6 until all six units were exhausted. He recorded nine hops and concluded that the answer is nine students.

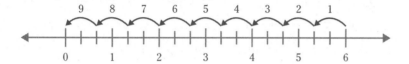

This strategy illustrates beautifully why quotative division is often called *measurement* division: it's as if we measure the line segment of length 6 with a unit of measure of length $\frac{2}{3}$. We can then conclude that the 6-unit segment measures 9 *two-thirds units*.

Using special sums. Like special whole-number sums etched in students' memory, such as $5 + 5 = 10$ (two hands) or $25 + 25 = 50$ (two quarters), certain fraction sums are automatic to some students as a result of their visual experiences with fraction manipulatives in their early work with fractions. When these sums arise in addition problems, students often explain, "I just know that." We could call them "fraction addition facts." The following figures illustrate four special sums well known by students who've done much work with pattern blocks.

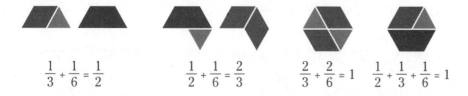

$$\frac{1}{3} + \frac{1}{6} = \frac{1}{2} \qquad \frac{1}{2} + \frac{1}{6} = \frac{2}{3} \qquad \frac{2}{3} + \frac{2}{6} = 1 \qquad \frac{1}{2} + \frac{1}{3} + \frac{1}{6} = 1$$

Partitioning and sharing. The four introductory problems, A–D, don't include a partitive division problem, but equal sharing is the foundation of students' basic understanding of division, built on two notions very real to children: the action of equally dividing a set or quantity between two or more people, and their sense of fairness. I will revisit this concept later in this chapter.

Revisit Meanings of Addition and Subtraction

The three interpretations of addition and subtraction still hold as we move from whole numbers to fractions (Figure 6.4). "Add to" and "take away" are the first and most basic meanings that students acquire for addition and subtraction. In these cases, the start number and end number play different roles: the end number is the result of some change made to the start number. In the other two meanings of addition and subtraction, the two numbers being operated on are present from the start. In "put together" or "combine," the sum or whole is being sought, whereas in "take apart" or "separate," the missing addend or part is being sought. In "compare" problems, the question of interest is "How much more?" or "How much less?

FIGURE 6.4
Meanings of Addition and Subtraction

Addition	Subtraction
1. Add to, change to more, change plus	1. Take away, change to less, change minus
2. Put together, combine, compose	2. Take apart, separate, decompose
3. Compare	

Comparison problems are more challenging, and the mental images of such problems that students retain will serve them later in algebra (Neagoy, 2012). Problem A is a good example. To find the difference between the two fractional amounts $\frac{2}{3}$ and $\frac{5}{6}$, and after establishing which is greater, the question "How much more?" may lead one student to think "addition" $\left(\frac{2}{3} + ? = \frac{5}{6}\right)$, whereas the question "How much less?" may lead another to think "subtraction" $\left(\frac{5}{6} - \frac{2}{3} = ?\right)$. Both approaches are equivalent and lead to the same answer, $\frac{1}{6}$. Students should ultimately see the difference between any two numbers, whole or fractional, as the distance between the points on the number line.

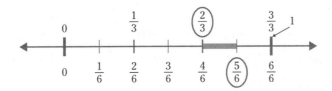

Here are some questions that can help students with fraction comparison:

- Which fraction is bigger? How do you know?

- How can you show me with a picture? On a number line? In a third way?

- Write two equations that will yield the difference between the two fractions, one with a + and the other with a –.

- About how much will the difference be? What whole number is it closest to?

Adding and subtracting similar fractions (with common denominators). Adding or subtracting like or similar fractional pieces, or fractions with equal denominators, relies on the definition of fraction and on the meaning of addition. For instance, $\frac{2}{7}$ means "2 *one-sevenths*," and $\frac{4}{7}$ means "4 *one-sevenths*," so $\frac{2}{7} + \frac{4}{7}$ equals 6 *one-sevenths* $\left(\frac{6}{7}\right)$.

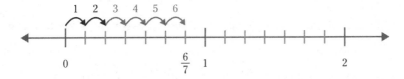

Expressions $2 + 4$, $\frac{2}{7} + \frac{4}{7}$, and $2x + 4x$ have the same structure—the only difference is the unit. The first is combining *ones*, the second *one-sevenths*, and the third *x*s. We can always convert two related fractions where one denominator is a multiple of the other, such as $\frac{2}{3}$ and $\frac{5}{6}$, by replacing one of them with an equivalent fraction. In this example, we'd replace $\frac{2}{3}$ with $\frac{4}{6}$.

A powerful model for adding or subtracting dissimilar fractions. Let's model fractions $\frac{1}{3}$ and $\frac{2}{5}$, with equal rectangles as the common unit.

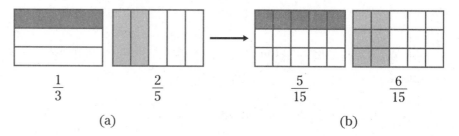

$\frac{1}{3}$ $\qquad\qquad$ $\frac{2}{5}$ $\qquad\qquad\qquad\qquad$ $\frac{5}{15}$ $\qquad\qquad$ $\frac{6}{15}$

(a) $\qquad\qquad\qquad\qquad\qquad\qquad\qquad\qquad$ (b)

The thirds are represented as three equal-size strips along one dimension of the rectangle, and the fifths as five equal-size strips along the other dimension. Both sets of strips have equal thickness. By superimposing both sets, we obtain a grid of 3-by-5, or 15 unit squares. The fractions $\frac{1}{3}$ and $\frac{2}{5}$ have different but equivalent names now: $\frac{5}{15}$ and $\frac{6}{15}$, respectively. Converted to similar fractions, they are easy to add or subtract: $(5 + 6)$ or $(6 - 5)$ *fifteenths*.

This is a powerful model for a number of reasons:

- It can be used to add or subtract *any* fractions or fractional quantities.

- It uses fraction equivalence, a common unit, and whole-number thinking.

- It parallels the steps in the U.S. standard algorithms for addition and subtraction.

- It is a powerful pictorial stage between the concrete and the symbolic stages.

Revisit Meanings of Multiplication and Division

Within the CCSSM framework, fluency with fraction multiplication and division and mastery of the respective U.S. standard algorithms are not expected until 6th grade. In grades 3–5, students take time to explore the meanings of combining a whole number and a fraction, or two fractions, by multiplication and division. The three basic interpretations of multiplication and the consequent four interpretations of division that students encounter $\left(\text{described in "The Quotient Meaning of } \frac{a}{b}\text{ "}\right.$ in Chapter $1\Big)$ still hold as we move from whole numbers to fractions (Figure 6.5).

FIGURE 6.5
Meanings of Multiplication and Division

Multiplication	Division
1. Adding equal groups	1A. Equal or fair sharing (partitive concept)
	1B. Equal grouping or segmenting (quotative, measurement, or repeated subtraction concept)
2. Increasing or reducing quantities	
3. Moving from factors to product or product to factors	

Adding equal groups **multiplication.** The CCSS for 4th grade math state that students will "apply and extend previous understandings of multiplication to multiply a fraction by a whole number" (Common Core State Standards Initiative, 2010). Students know that 6 × 4 can be interpreted as six equal groups of four, or 4 + 4 + 4 . . . (six times), or even six hops of four units on the number line, starting at 0. Similarly, $6 \times \frac{2}{8}$ means six copies or iterations of the quantity two-eighths. This was Eric's reasoning when he drew six copies of two-eighths of a pizza and counted them by repeated addition.

The CCSS for 5th grade math (Number and Operations—Fractions) state that students will "apply and extend previous understandings of multiplication to multiply a fraction or whole number by a fraction" (Common Core State Standards Initiative, 2010). Samantha's choice of the commuted factors is a good example: $\frac{2}{8} \times 6$, or $\frac{1}{4} \times 6$. We'd like students to think of $\frac{1}{4} \times 6$ as "$\frac{1}{4}$ of 6," as Samantha did, but too often they memorize "*of* means *times*," because we tell them that. The *equal groups of* meaning of multiplication helps make the connection: if 3×6 means three *groups of* six, and 1×6 means one *group of* six, then $\frac{1}{4} \times 6$ likewise means one-fourth of a group of six.

Division as the inverse of equal-groups multiplication. Since the two factors in equal-groups multiplication play different roles, and since division is the *inverse* of multiplication, two different division interpretations emerge: division by multiplier and division by multiplicand. As explained in Vignette 1, in the first or *equal sharing* interpretation, we know the number of shares (the multiplier), and we're looking for the amount of each share (the multiplicand). In the second or *equal grouping* interpretation, we know the amount in each group (the multiplicand), and we're looking for the number of groups (the multiplier). The following reviews both meanings, using the example $20 \div 4$:

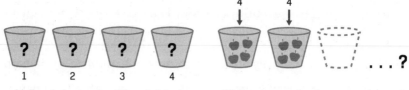

(a) Equal sharing (partitive division)   (b) Equal grouping (quotative division)

Consider the expression $3 \div \frac{1}{2}$. Since it is impossible to share three things equally among half a person, we would opt for the equal grouping metaphor of division. Three situations that give meaning to this division expression appeared in Figure 6.3 (p. 182). If the dividend were also a fraction $\left(\text{say, } \frac{3}{4} \div \frac{1}{2}\right)$, the reasoning is the same: How many one-halfs go into three-quarters? The answer is one whole and one-half more, or $1\frac{1}{2}$.

Now consider $\frac{1}{2} \div 3$. A whole-number divisor makes equal sharing possible. Consider this problem:

> A half-hour is left before bedtime, and you have three math exercises to finish. If you split your time equally, how much time will you spend on each exercise?

Figure 6.6 shows three ways of modeling the problem: (a) a linear model, (b) a clock model, and (c) an area model.

FIGURE 6.6
Three Models of $\frac{1}{2} \div 3$

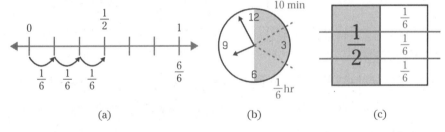

Note: (a) $\frac{1}{2}$ of a linear unit partitioned into 3 equal segments gives $\frac{1}{6}$ of the unit; (b) $\frac{1}{2}$ hour divided into 3 equal time periods is 10 minutes, or $\frac{1}{6}$ hour; (c) partitioning $\frac{1}{2}$ of a rectangle into 3 equal sections yields $\frac{1}{6}$ of the rectangle.

Increasing or reducing quantities (multiplication or division). Adding equal groups by repeated addition works well with whole-number multipliers. For fractional multipliers, as in $\frac{1}{4} \times 6$, the *operator* or *scalar* interpretation of the multiplier is more powerful. If 3×6 stretches a six-unit length to three times its original length, and 1×6 leaves it unchanged, then $\frac{1}{4} \times 6$ *shrinks* the six-unit length down to one-fourth its original length.

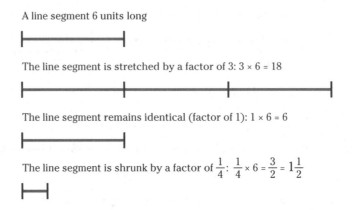

A line segment 6 units long

The line segment is stretched by a factor of 3: $3 \times 6 = 18$

The line segment remains identical (factor of 1): $1 \times 6 = 6$

The line segment is shrunk by a factor of $\frac{1}{4}$: $\frac{1}{4} \times 6 = \frac{3}{2} = 1\frac{1}{2}$

We must be mindful of what may seem contradictory to students. We *say*, "One-fourth of six is $\frac{1}{4}$ *multiplied by* 6," but what they *do* is partition the six units into four segments and then select one—and the action of partitioning is associated with *division*, not multiplication. An enlightening way to resolve this contradiction is to help them see that *multiplying by* $\frac{1}{4}$ is equivalent to *dividing by* 4. $\left(\text{Note: After trying a series of factors, students can then be guided to generalize that multiplying by any factor } \frac{a}{b} \text{ is equivalent to dividing by } \frac{b}{a}.\right)$

If the original length were a fraction, the reasoning would be the same:

My $\frac{4}{5}$ m woolen scarf was washed in hot water and shrank by $\frac{1}{4}$ its length. How long is it now?

It shrunk by $\frac{1}{4} \times \frac{4}{5}$, so its remaining length is $\frac{3}{4} \times \frac{4}{5}$. One-fourth of the scarf is $\frac{1}{5}$ of a meter, so $\frac{3}{4}$ of the scarf (what remains) is three $\frac{1}{5}$s, or $\frac{3}{5}$ m.

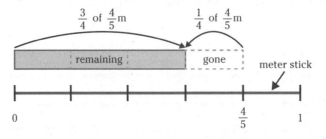

Here is a final, and more complex, consideration: What would $\frac{3}{5} \div \frac{3}{4}$ mean? Well, since $\frac{4}{5}$ m shrunk to $\frac{3}{4}$ its length and now measures $\frac{3}{5}$ m, and since division is the inverse of multiplication, $\frac{3}{5} \div \frac{3}{4}$ would magically restore the scarf to its original length of $\frac{4}{5}$ m. Try to make sense of this division, using a model like the one above.

$$\frac{4}{5} \text{ m} \xrightarrow{\times \frac{3}{4}} \frac{3}{5} \text{ m} \xrightarrow{\div \frac{3}{4}} \frac{4}{5} \text{ m}$$

From factors to products and back (multiplication or division). In 3rd grade, students explore the concept of area by tiling simple shapes, such as rectangles. By 4th grade, they know that the area is the product of the two side lengths. Similarly, the number of elements in an array is the product of the numbers of elements along each side. A multiplication problem gives the two dimensions and asks for the area, whereas a division problem does the reverse: gives the area and one dimension and asks for the other dimension.

In this third interpretation of multiplication, the two factors play symmetric roles, so searching for either dimension requires the same approach. If one or both dimensions are fractional, the reasoning is the same as with whole-number dimensions. The expression $2 \times 3\frac{1}{2}$, or $2 \times \frac{7}{2}$, would give the area of a rectangle with side lengths 2 and $3\frac{1}{2}$. Two times $\frac{7}{2}$ is $2 \times (7 \text{ one-halves})$, or 14 *one-halves*, or 7 square feet.

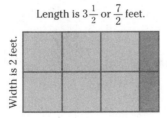

Length is $3\frac{1}{2}$ or $\frac{7}{2}$ feet.

Width is 2 feet.

The inverse division problem would state, "The area of a rectangle is 7 square feet. If one of its side lengths is $3\frac{1}{2}$, or $\frac{7}{2}$, what is the other side length?" The model $7 \div 3\frac{1}{2}$ or $7 \div \frac{7}{2}$ would yield the other side length. We would either see that $3\frac{1}{2}$ goes two times into 7, or use a model to see that two groups of seven halves fits inside of seven wholes.

Powerful models for multiplication and division. Borrowing from the rectangle model for whole-number multiplication, the product of any two fractions is the area of the rectangle produced by the fractional dimensions. In the following example, the product $\frac{2}{3} \times \frac{3}{4}$ is the shaded area $\frac{6}{12}$ or $\frac{1}{2}$.

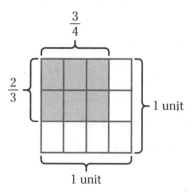

There is also a less-known rectangle model for division by a fraction. To solve the division $\frac{3}{4} \div \frac{2}{3}$ (as in, "How many $\frac{2}{3}$-gallons are there in $\frac{3}{4}$ of a gallon?"), we divide their equivalent fractions, $\frac{9}{12} \div \frac{8}{12}$, modeled by the first two squares seen here.

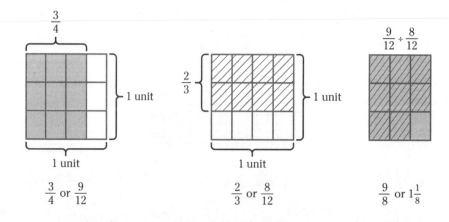

With similar fractions, we apply whole-number thinking: since $\frac{9}{12}$ and $\frac{8}{12}$ express similar unit fractions, 9 *one-twelfths* and 8 *one-twelfths*, and since $\frac{1}{12}$ goes into $\frac{1}{12}$ one time, solving $\frac{9}{12} \div \frac{8}{12}$ is equivalent to solving $9 \div 8$. We know that $9 \div 8 = \frac{9}{8}$ by the quotient meaning of fractions. Decomposing $\frac{9}{8}$, we can write $\frac{8}{8} + \frac{1}{8}$ $\left(\text{or, as a mixed number, } 1\frac{1}{8}\right)$. The third rectangle in the previous figure models this: the eight hatched units (*twelfths*) fit completely inside the nine shaded units (also *twelfths*), which gives $\frac{8}{8}$, or 1 whole. Note that there's room for one extra unit, and a common error is naming it $\frac{1}{9}$. It's actually $\frac{1}{8}$ because it's $\frac{1}{8}$ of the $\frac{8}{8}$ (hatched area) we're focusing on—namely, the divisor.

Teaching Tip: Discuss Students' Strategies Explicitly

As we watch students work with models to grapple with the meanings of operations, our challenge as educators is to be aware of and identify what is being learned from their "invented" algorithms *in addition to* simply executing the algorithms to solve the particular problem. Not discussing the strategies explicitly leaves to chance students' connecting their experiences to an ultimate formal algorithm.

The questions we pose are essential. Asking, "Why did you exchange a third for two-sixths?" may inspire students to connect their action with finding common fractional units (denominators) to facilitate the operation. Or, after repeatedly using the multiplication model, asking, "How do the numerator and denominator of the product compare to those of the factors? What's the relationship? Why is it so?" will help students generalize to $\frac{a}{b} \times \frac{c}{d} = \frac{a \times c}{b \times d}$ with understanding.

Emphasize That Relationships and Properties Still Hold

An understanding of the properties [of operations] for whole numbers becomes a critical component in developing a deeper understanding of algorithms for operations with rational numbers and in algebra.

Albert Otto, Janet Caldwell, Sarah Wallus Hancock, and Rose Mary Zbiek (2010, p. 60)

Relationships. It is important to stress the inverse relationship between the operations of addition and subtraction on the one hand and multiplication and division on the other, regardless of the numbers you're working with. Why? Because in mathematics, there are truly only two operations: addition and multiplication. Students will soon realize this fact. With the advent of fractions, and rational numbers in general, starting in 6th grade, they are already learning that any quotient $\frac{a}{b}$ is actually a product $\left(a \times \frac{1}{b}\right)$. Analogously, with the advent of negative integers in 6th grade, they will learn that any difference $a - b$ is actually a sum $(a + [-b])$. In other words, along their mathematics journey, the notions of subtraction and division gradually disappear. The more emphasis on the inverse relationship that binds each pair of operations—*what one does, the other undoes*—the more prepared students will be to let go of subtraction and division when the time comes.

Properties. Understanding the procedures of rational number computation is a prerequisite to success in algebra. We should therefore make explicit the properties of operations that explain the computational procedures with fractions, and later with decimals. Let's unpack some examples:

$$\boxed{\text{Why does } \frac{5}{9} + \frac{2}{9} = \frac{7}{9}?}$$

$$\text{Because } \frac{5}{9} + \frac{2}{9} = \left(5 \times \frac{1}{9}\right) + \left(2 \times \frac{1}{9}\right) = (5 + 2) \times \frac{1}{9} = 7 \times \frac{1}{9} = \frac{7}{9}$$

$$\qquad\qquad\quad \text{Step 1} \qquad\qquad \text{Step 2} \qquad \text{Step 3}$$

- Step 1: Fraction definition: $\frac{a}{b}$ = a copies of $\frac{1}{b}$, or $a \times \frac{1}{b}$; 5 and 2 *operate* on $\frac{1}{9}$ to increase it.

- Step 2: Distributive property of multiplication over addition: $\frac{1}{9}$ is the common factor *distributed*.

- Step 3: Addition of whole numbers (inside the parentheses).

$$\boxed{\text{Why does } \frac{3}{4} \times \frac{5}{7} = \frac{15}{28}?}$$

Because $\frac{3}{4} \times \frac{5}{7} = \left(3 \times \frac{1}{4}\right) \times \left(5 \times \frac{1}{7}\right) = (3 \times 5) \times \left(\frac{1}{4} \times \frac{1}{7}\right) = 15 \times \frac{1}{28} = \frac{15}{28}$

Step 1   Step 2   Step 3

- Step 1: Fraction definition: $\frac{a}{b} = a$ copies of $\frac{1}{b}$, or $a \times \frac{1}{b}$. The numerators *operate* on unit fractions.

- Step 2: Commutative and associative properties of multiplication: the first reorders the factors; the second groups whole numbers and fractions together, respectively.

- Step 3: Multiplication of whole numbers in the first parentheses. In the second, $\frac{1}{4}$ acts as an *operator* on $\frac{1}{7}$ and reduces the unit fraction to a unit four times smaller; hence, the $\frac{1}{28}$.

Teaching Tip: Help Students Become More Metacognitive About Their Work

Traditionally, students have looked for reactions indicating "right" or "wrong" from teachers regarding their math work. But more and more these days, teachers are U-turning students' questions about the correctness of their work back to *them*. Why? To help students become more metacognitive about learning. Opportunities arise daily for us to prod students to think more deeply about what they say, do, and find when doing mathematics.

An example regarding the properties of operations comes to mind. A 5th grader once explained the division $1 \div \frac{2}{5}$ to me in the following way: "I know that $\frac{1}{5}$ fits five times into 1, so $\frac{2}{5}$ fits half as much. And so half of 5 is $2\frac{1}{2}$." Reflect on that sophisticated thinking for a moment.

Rather than simply confirm his answer, I wanted him to be aware of the property he was using, so I asked him to explain why his reasoning worked. It wasn't easy. But after working together at the board, I helped him see that he had used "doubling and halving," based on the multiplicative identity. In other words, if "$\frac{1}{5}$ fits five times into 1," then $\frac{1}{5} \times 5 = 1$. If he doubles the first factor $\left(2 \times \frac{1}{5} = \frac{2}{5}\right)$, then he must halve the second factor $\left(5 \div 2 \ or \ 5 \times \frac{1}{2} = \frac{5}{2}\right)$ if he wants the new product $\left(\frac{2}{5} \times \frac{5}{2}\right)$ to still equal 1. The property $a \times b = (a \times 2) \times \left(b \times \frac{1}{2}\right)$ is based on the *identity element for multiplication*, 1, which in this case is $2 \times \frac{1}{2} = 1$.

As we help students become more metacognitive about their own learning, they gradually begin asking themselves the same kinds of questions. Consider hanging a list of questions on the wall to create an atmosphere that is more about mathematical thinking than about getting the right answer. For example:

In response to correct answers:	*In response to incorrect answers:*
How did you figure it out?	*Where do you think the error lies?*
How would the answer be different if . . . ?	*What do you know? What do you need?*
Can you share your thinking?	*What have you learned from this mistake?*
Can you show it in a different way?	*What might you do differently next time?*
Can you generalize your findings?	*How can you change the problem to yield your answer?*

Highlight Important Changes in Ways of Thinking

The expansion of our number universe from whole numbers to rational numbers introduces two significant changes that students must come to realize:

- In problems involving rational numbers, the units may be different.
- Multiplying doesn't necessarily make things bigger, and division doesn't necessarily make things smaller.

Each change is discussed in more detail below.

The unit is often different. Compare these addition problems:

- Sandra and Chloe each had 2 identical health bars. Sandra ate $\frac{1}{4}$ of hers, while Chloe ate $\frac{2}{3}$ of hers. What fraction of 1 health bar did the two girls eat together?

- Sam baked two different recipes on the same day. He filled a 1-cup measure with sugar. For the first recipe, he used $\frac{1}{4}$ of the sugar in the cup. For the second, he used $\frac{2}{3}$ of the remaining sugar in the cup. What fraction of a cup of sugar did Sam use altogether?

Both problems involve the fractional amounts $\frac{1}{4}$ and $\frac{2}{3}$, and both require the action of *combining*—hence, fraction addition. Nonetheless, the problems are very different. In the first, the two fractions refer to the *same unit*, one whole health bar. But in the second, the $\frac{1}{4}$ refers to one whole cup of sugar, whereas the $\frac{2}{3}$ refers to the remaining $\frac{3}{4}$ of a cup.

The units in division problems can be even more subtle. Consider this one:

- Richard is going to be home alone for 2 hours and 45 minutes, and he wants to figure out how many half-hour DVDs he can view. Can you help him?

Figuring out how many $\frac{1}{2}$-hour intervals fit in a $2\frac{3}{4}$ $\left(\text{or } \frac{11}{4}\right)$-hour interval is a quotative division problem modeled by $2\frac{3}{4} \div \frac{1}{2}$. With a number line modeling $2\frac{3}{4}$ hours (say, from 6:00 p.m. to 8:45 p.m.), counting the $\frac{1}{2}$-hour hops solves the problem.

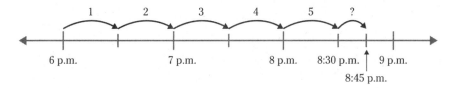

But when I pose this problem, there is always some hesitation from students around naming the fractional part beyond 5. Some of them opt for an answer of $5\frac{1}{2}$, and others say it's $5\frac{1}{4}$. To resolve the dilemma, I ask, "What's the unit?"

The dividend $\left(2\frac{3}{4}\right)$ is in *whole* hours, but the divisor, our counting unit, is in *half-hours*. So, while the remaining interval is $\frac{1}{4}$ of an hour, it is $\frac{1}{2}$ of a *half-hour*. The answer, then, is $5\frac{1}{2}$ DVDs. The time model helps students see that in the remaining 15 minutes, Richard can watch half of another half-hour DVD.

Multiplying need not make bigger, division need not make smaller. Throughout this chapter, we've seen examples that contradict the myths "multiplying makes bigger" and "dividing makes smaller," which students carry over from their whole-number computation. Using patterns is a powerful way to deconstruct these famous myths. Figure 6.7 uses bar models to represent the following problem:

Six-pound bags of flour are packed first in bags weighing 3 lbs., then 2 lbs., then 1 lb., then $\frac{1}{2}$ lb., then $\frac{1}{3}$ lb., then $\frac{1}{4}$ lb., and so on. Study the pattern of quotients and make three observations.

FIGURE 6.7
Breaking the Myth of "Dividing Makes Smaller"

Dividend	Divisor	Quotient	Verify
6	3	2	2 × 3 = 6
6	2	3	3 × 2 = 6
6	1	6	6 × 1 = 6
6	$\frac{1}{2}$	12	12 halves = 6
6	$\frac{1}{3}$	18	18 thirds = 6
6	$\frac{1}{4}$	24	24 fourths = 6
⋮	⋮	⋮	⋮

The first three cases are familiar, for they involve whole-number division. Notice that in the first two cases, "division makes smaller." As the individual packages decrease in weight to fractions of a pound, the quotients increase in number but the problem structure remains the same. To gradually deconstruct false beliefs, students should be prompted to visualize and verbalize surprising findings when they encounter them. Questions like "What is the quotient?" and "How does it compare with the dividend?" help students realize that *the quotient can be greater than the dividend*, which is a novelty! Another discovery students make by observing this pattern is the "invert and multiply" rule: $6 \div \frac{1}{2} = 12$, $6 \div \frac{1}{3} = 18$, $6 \div \frac{1}{4} = 24$, and so on. These findings emerge naturally!

Continuing this same pattern "upward" (in the opposite direction) by increasing the divisor leads to divisors such as 8, 9, and 10 and to corresponding quotients of $\frac{6}{8}$, $\frac{6}{9}$, and $\frac{6}{10}$. In this case, questions like "What is the divisor?" and "How does it compare with the dividend?" help students realize that *the divisor can be greater than the dividend.*

For multiplication, explore the pattern 3×6, 2×6, 1×6, $\frac{1}{2} \times 6$, $\frac{1}{3} \times 6$, $\frac{1}{4} \times 6$, and so on, and extend it at both ends, posing pertinent questions to attract students' attention to the novelty of what they are discovering.

 ## A Bridge to Algebra: Apply Algebraic Thinking to Demystify the "Invert and Multiply" Rule

Seeing *any* fraction $\frac{a}{b}$ as a product $\left(a \times \frac{1}{b}\right)$, which is emphasized by the CCSSM, has some consequences that often go unexploited. Two in particular are worth noting:

- The simple equivalence $\frac{a}{b} = a \times \frac{1}{b}$ can be used to demystify the invert-and-multiply division rule: substitute a fraction for the numerator a and another fraction for the denominator b. You now have a fraction of two fractions $\left(\text{say}, \dfrac{\frac{c}{d}}{\frac{e}{f}}\right)$ or a quotient of the two fractions. The equivalence $\frac{a}{b} = a \times \frac{1}{b}$ basically says "take the numerator and multiply it by the reciprocal (or *multiplicative inverse*) of the denominator." Since the reciprocal of the denominator is $\frac{f}{e}$, we obtain $\frac{\frac{c}{d}}{\frac{e}{f}} = \frac{c}{d} \times \frac{f}{e}$. Finally, since $\frac{\frac{c}{d}}{\frac{e}{f}} \Leftrightarrow \frac{c}{d} \div \frac{e}{f}$, we have just demonstrated why $\frac{c}{d} \div \frac{e}{f} = \frac{c}{d} \times \frac{f}{e}$.

- The equivalence $\frac{a}{b} = a \times \frac{1}{b}$ states that every quotient $\frac{a}{b}$ (assuming $b \neq 0$) can be written as a product $\left(a \times \frac{1}{b}\right)$, just as any difference $a - b$ can be written as a sum $(a + [-b])$.

Effect of addition and subtraction on numbers. In a similar fashion, students learn in middle school that adding negative numbers makes the total smaller, and subtracting negative numbers makes the total bigger.

Targeting Misconceptions with Challenging Problems

💡 **Problem 1: Which visual model can, and which cannot?** Use the visual models below to answer each question.

1. Which visual model(s) can be used to illustrate the sum $\frac{4}{5} + \frac{3}{5}$? Explain why any model you did not select is incorrect.

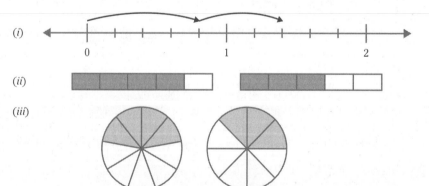

2. Which visual model(s) cannot be used to illustrate the
    difference $\frac{7}{3} - \frac{5}{6}$? Explain why some of these models are illustrative
    and some are not. Use the illustrative model(s) to find the
    difference.

(i)

(ii)

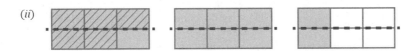

(iii)

💡 **Problem 2: Critique the work of other students.** In each scenario
below, read the problem and observe the student's model and answer.
If you agree with the problem representation and answer, explain why.
If you disagree, construct viable arguments that could help the student
better understand the problem and see his or her mistake(s).

1. Sarah wants to make a jam recipe that calls for 1 quart of grapes.
    She has $\frac{1}{2}$ of one quart of grapes and $\frac{2}{3}$ of another quart. Does she
    have enough grapes? Explain.

Student's model:

$$\frac{1}{2} \quad + \quad \frac{2}{3} \quad = \quad \frac{3}{5}$$

Student's answer:

Sarah needs more grapes to make one quart.

2. Sam's father drives him to school, taking the shortest route of $2\frac{1}{2}$, or $\frac{5}{2}$, miles. One day the car breaks down along this route, $\frac{3}{4}$ mile from home. How far must Sam walk to get to school?

Student's model:

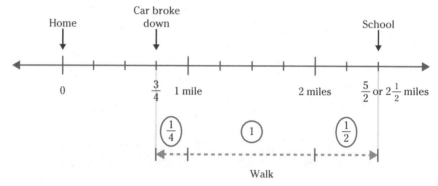

Student's answer:

$$\frac{1}{4} + 1 + \frac{1}{2} = 1\frac{3}{4} \text{ miles}$$

💡 **Problem 3: Which problem can, and which cannot?** Create pictures or diagrams to help you make sense of the following situations.

1. Which problem(s) can be modeled by the expression $3 \div \frac{1}{2}$?

   • I have 3 small cans of olives that I want to split evenly between 2 pizzas. I will sprinkle half of the olives on a cheese pizza and the other half on a vegetarian pizza. How many cans of olives will be on each pizza?

   • I have 3 pizzas that I plan to cut into halves. Assuming that I distribute one half-pizza portion per person, how many people can I serve?

   • A rectangle has an area of 3 square yards and a width of $\frac{1}{2}$ yard. What is its length?

   • A number N multiplied by 3 gives the product $\frac{1}{2}$. Express N, using 3 and $\frac{1}{2}$.

2. Which problem(s) cannot be modeled by the expression $\frac{1}{2} \times 32$?

- I have 32 dollars, and I want to split my money evenly between my two friends' birthday presents. What amount of money will I spend on each?

- The 32 students in a 5th grade class each bring 50 cents to contribute to a school project. How much money (in dollars) will the class contribute to the school project?

- How many half-pint containers can I fill using 32 pints of water?

- A rectangle has a length of 32 feet and a width of $\frac{1}{2}$ feet. Express the measurement of half of its perimeter.

💡 **Problem 4: Closest to or equal to 1.** For each operation, find the expression that is closest to or equal to 1. Don't compute. Instead, reason about the sizes of the fractions and the meanings of the operations, and use fraction equivalence. Explain your thinking. Use models if you wish.

Operation	Expression 1	Expression 2	Expression 3
Addition	$\frac{3}{4} + \frac{1}{10}$	$\frac{5}{6} + \frac{1}{7}$	$\frac{2}{3} + \frac{1}{8}$
Subtraction	$\frac{5}{4} - \frac{2}{8}$	$\frac{5}{6} - \frac{1}{9}$	$\frac{9}{4} - \frac{3}{5}$
Multiplication	$\frac{1}{6} \times \frac{9}{1}$	$\frac{1}{2} \times \frac{3}{1} \times \frac{4}{6}$	$\frac{5}{6} \times \frac{11}{12}$
Division	$6 \div \frac{1}{6}$ Hint: "How many sixths are in six wholes?"	$\frac{4}{5} \div 4$ Hint: "I share $\frac{4}{5}$ of a cake evenly among 4 people, What share does each one get?"	$\frac{1}{2} \div \frac{1}{3}$ Hint: "How many thirds are in one-half?"

💡 **Problem 5: Building number sense: Predicting the effects of operations.** Place a check in every cell that makes a true statement.

- Follow-up #1: For each cell you checked, give an example to illustrate the truth.
- Follow-up #2: For each blank cell, give an example to show that the statement is false.

	Always yields a whole number	Sometimes yields a whole number	Always yields a greater number	Sometimes yields a greater number	Always yields a lesser number	Sometimes yields a lesser number
Adding two whole numbers						
Subtracting two whole numbers, when the first number is greater than the second						
Multiplying two whole numbers						
Dividing two whole numbers, when the dividend is greater than the divisor						
Adding two fractions (any combination of fractions, < 1 or > 1)						
Subtracting two fractions (any combination of fractions < 1 or > 1)						
Multiplying a whole number by a fraction less than 1						
Multiplying a whole number by a fraction greater than 1						
Multiplying two fractions (any combination of fractions < 1 or > 1)						
Dividing a whole number by a fraction less than 1						
Dividing a whole number by a fraction greater than 1						
Dividing two fractions (any combination of fractions < 1 or > 1)						

💡 **Problem 6: Visualizing operations: From pictures to writing math expressions.** Use the visual models below to answer each question.

1. Suppose this figure represents $\frac{1}{3}$ of a unit. Name the amount represented by *one of the three unit squares* as:

    - A division expression

    - A multiplication expression

    - A subtraction expression

    - A single fraction

2. Suppose this figure is four iterations of the first one. Name the total amount represented as:

    - An addition expression

    - A multiplication expression

    - A fraction greater than 1

    - A mixed number

💡 **Problem 7: Visualizing operations: From math expressions to drawing pictures.** Create visual models for the problems below.

1. Draw a picture to model each operation, clearly identifying the resulting amount:

    - $3 \div 4$

    - $\frac{3}{4} \times 1$

    - $3 \times \frac{1}{2}$

- $2 \div \dfrac{1}{4}$
- $\dfrac{1}{2} + \dfrac{6}{4}$
- $\dfrac{7}{4} - \dfrac{3}{2}$

2. Use a different number line for each expression. Drawing arrows to show distances or hops, model the operation action. Cleary identify the resulting amount:

- $\dfrac{1}{2} + \dfrac{10}{4}$
- $\dfrac{6}{3} - \dfrac{3}{6}$
- $\dfrac{2}{3} \times 4$
- $9 \times \dfrac{1}{2}$
- $\dfrac{5}{2} \div 10$
- $5 \div \dfrac{1}{2}$

 What's the App for That? *Sweet Multiplication*

Visualizing fraction multiplication in a realistic context empowers students to appreciate the meaning of fraction multiplication and understand the logic behind the algorithmic procedure. The **Sweet Multiplication** app (www.apps4math.com) offers multiplication situations that are realistic, easy to understand, and fun to solve.

CHAPTER 7

Connect Fractions and Decimals

> *[A] survey of students' performance showed that the most common error for the addition problem 4 + .3 = ? was 7, which is given by 68% of sixth graders and 51% of fifth and seventh graders. Again, the errors show that many students have learned rules for manipulating symbols without understanding what those symbols mean or why the rules work.*
>
> National Research Council (2001, p. 234)

This book is about fractions, but it would be remiss of me not to mention decimals, which are an alternative notation for fractions and rational numbers in general. While not exhaustive, this chapter focuses on the whole number–decimal connection, the fraction-decimal connection, common student misconceptions, and recommendations for overcoming them.

Decimal fractions are ordinarily introduced in 4th and 5th grade and then developed intensely in 6th and 7th grade. A solid understanding of both fractions and place value is a prerequisite for students' understanding of decimals. The traditionally dismal performance of students with decimals, as with fractions, has prompted math educators to urge teachers to spend significant time cultivating decimal number sense and decimal operation sense.

The payoff can be huge. The real-world usefulness of decimals for measuring lengths, distances, areas, volumes, costs, and more seems obvious today, as decimals are everywhere: Olympians lose medals by hundredths of a second, a 0.25 percent difference in a mortgage interest rate can translate into thousands of dollars paid over the life of a loan, and drug dosages are measured in tenths or hundredths of milligrams— an error in administration by a percentage point can be fatal. Although some say that teaching math is not a question of life or death, situations such as these make us aware of how many small- and large-scale human misfortunes are (or could be) caused by simple and avoidable math errors.

A brief look back at history reveals the late entrance of decimals into the mainstream of mathematics. The Egyptians were savvy with unit fractions $\left(\frac{1}{2}, \frac{1}{3}, \frac{1}{4}, \frac{1}{5}, \ldots\right)$, but it wasn't until the 16th century that Flemish mathematician Simon Stevin introduced and explained the modern European decimal notation in his now famous booklet "De Thiende," first published in Dutch and then translated into French as "La Disme" (The Art of Tenths). This Old French word, from the Latin *decima pars*, or "tenth part," is at the origin of the U.S. dime: one-tenth of a dollar.

Decimal fractions are none other than unit fractions whose denominators are powers of 10: $\frac{1}{10}, \frac{1}{100}, \frac{1}{1,000}$, and so on. Over time, periods came to separate the decimal parts (tenths, hundredths, thousandths, etc.) from the wholes. Today, we still use these separations (e.g., 0.2, 3.75) and call the numbers *decimals*.

The purpose of this historic detour is to point out the long and challenging journey that mathematicians traveled before making commonplace what seems today an obvious extension of our decimal place value system. Keep in mind that while they may be familiar to *you*, decimals are difficult for children to absorb at first. Therefore, careful attention and ample time must be given to exploring their notation, meaning, terminology, and structure prior to embarking on decimal operations.

Denis's Story

The day I attended Denis's 4th grade math lesson, I saw a copy of the latest issue of *Teaching Children Mathematics* (the NCTM journal) lying on his desk. He told me that an article in this issue was his inspiration for today's lesson. I was eager to see what he had planned.

Denis: We've been practicing our places values with large numbers, and we saw that we can describe them in different ways, depending on what place we're focusing on. Who's going to tell Dr. Monica how many $100 bills are in $8,500?

Class [*in unison*]: Eighty-five!

Denis: How about $10 bills?

Class [*in unison*]: Eight hundred and fifty!

Denis: And now the tricky one: How many $1,000 bills, if we pretend they still exist today?

Tracey: Eight. But there's a half of one more thousand, so it's eight and a half.

Denis: Great! For the next couple of weeks, we're going to explore similar relationships, but this time between ones and quantities that are ten times, a hundred times, and even a thousand times *smaller* than ones. Today we'll focus on new ways of writing two small fractions we've seen, a tenth and a hundredth. $\left[\text{writes } \frac{1}{10} \text{ and } \frac{1}{100} \text{ on the board}\right]$

Grouped at tables of four, students had blank 10-by-10 square grids (100-squares—I'll discuss these further later in this chapter) and were sharing

Cuisenaire Rods from the containers on their tables. The square grid was the new unit, or the "one." Their first task was to place the rod that was one-tenth the area of the square grid and to explain how they knew it was one-tenth.

Ricardo: It's the orange one.

Denis: How did you decide on the orange one?

Ricardo: Because ten of them fit on the square. It's just like the long and the flat. [*Refers to the base-10 blocks the class frequently uses* (see below).]

Denis: You got it! Mathematicians use this symbol for one-tenth and call it the *decimal* form of the number. [*Writes "0.1" below* $\frac{1}{10}$ *and later tells me that he decided to postpone the alternate notation ".1" until the following lesson.*]

Denis: Now you know three names for one-tenth: the fraction, the decimal, and the number-word. Just like *water*, *ice*, and *steam* are three different names for H_2O. Let's practice using this symbol and write what Ricardo said: that 10 one-tenths make 1.

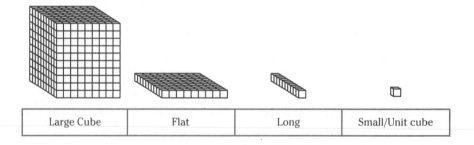

| Large Cube | Flat | Long | Small/Unit cube |

Some students added 0.1 ten times, then wrote "=1"; others wrote $10 \times 0.1 = 1$. No one asked any questions, so Denis moved on.

Denis: Now, find the next longest rod [*referring to the blue one*] and place it beside the orange rod. At your tables, discuss its fraction name as part of the whole.

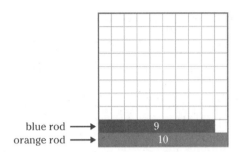

A discussion ensued. The first answer was "$\frac{1}{10}$ – 1." Calling the small cube "1" was probably due to the students' early work with Cuisenaire Rods, in which the shortest rod (the small white cube) and the longest rod (the orange one, 10 times longer) were always named "1" and "10," respectively. This is a difficult habit to break when changing units!

Sandra suggested, "One-tenth minus one-*hundredth*," which Denis wrote on the board as "$\frac{1}{10} - \frac{1}{100}$." Denis highlighted the *th* ending of the word *hundredth*. He then introduced "0.01" as the decimal notation for one-hundredth $\left(\frac{1}{100}\right)$. Students commented on the "strangeness" of the decimal notations for $\frac{1}{10}$ and $\frac{1}{100}$ yet noted the consistency in their structure.

Denis: How can we subtract these two fractions, the first in tenths and the second in hundredths?

[*After some give-and-take with a peer, Devon speaks up.*]

Devon: The orange piece is like ten-hundredths.

$\left[\textit{Denis writes "}\frac{10}{100} - \frac{1}{100}\textit{." A student then blurts out the answer, }\frac{9}{100}.\right]$

Denis: We don't blurt out answers, right?

Denis wanted his students to write this fraction in their newly learned decimal notation, but this was tricky. They had just learned how to write one-hundredth but were not sure about nine-hundredths. Having anticipated this difficulty, Denis asked them to line up nine little cubes $\left(\text{worth } \frac{1}{100} \text{ each}\right)$ alongside the blue rod and count together—one one-hundredth, two one-hundredths, three one-hundredths . . . up to nine one-hundredths. At the same time, Erika, whom Denis had selected wisely, wrote on the board what she thought were their decimal notations: 0.01, 0.02, 0.03 . . . 0.09. Students accepted the notation without objection—for the moment.

Denis probed further, "How would you write the next hundredth in the list?" Several students suggested 0.010, a natural extension to the list, prior to any place-value discussion of these new numbers. Erika, still at the board and playing teacher, said, "But one more hundredth makes the orange rod, and that's one-tenth, so it's gotta be 0.1." Good thinking!

Denis had his lessons for the next few weeks cut out for him. His students had provided much food for thought:

- Why is 0.010 *not* ten one-hundredths?
- How do 0.010 and 0.01 compare?
- How about 0.1, 0.10, and .1?
- What's the relationship between the digit values?
- How does decimal place value compare with whole-number place value?

In addition, out of the Cuisenaire Rods activity on 100-squares emerged decimal combinations that made sense and that Denis planned to explore further: "$10 \times 0.01 = 0.1$" for 10 small cubes equaling in length the longest rod; "$9 \times 0.01 = 0.09$" for the length of the next-longest rod, the blue one; and "$0.1 - 0.01 = 0.09$" for the length of the blue rod expressed as a subtraction.

Denis: Here's your last problem for today. You probably won't finish, so think about it tonight, and we'll tackle it tomorrow. Make a Cuisenaire staircase. Then think about how you'd write *each rod* as a decimal. Take a stab at the total staircase. Always ask yourself, "What fraction of the whole square is the entire staircase?"

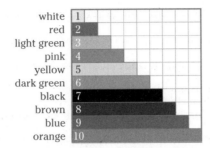

As Denis and I were chatting and the students were packing up for lunch, Igor came up to show us his grid, on which he was balancing his 10 rods.

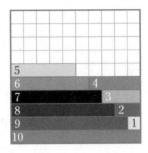

To our amazement, Igor said, "I found five tenths and a half," adding apologetically, "but I didn't write the decimals." A moment of beauty to crown a thoughtful lesson!

Recognizing Misconceptions

A number of studies reveal the many difficulties that students experience when learning decimals. Because they learn decimals relatively late, their misconceptions, if undetected, can accompany them through middle school and even high school. While it is impossible to address every misconception, I will discuss the main ones I have encountered or those noted in the research.

Scarce Contact with Decimals in Daily Life

After years of working with whole numbers, students learn to appreciate the difference between, say, 50 seconds and 5 seconds—they can *experience* that 50 seconds is 10 times longer than 5 seconds. By contrast, comparing 0.5 and 0.05 seconds is subtler. Both are very short time intervals, which makes it difficult for students to appreciate the ten-fold difference in duration. Nevertheless, given the structure of our place-value system, the difference between 50 and 5 seconds is identical to the difference between 0.5 and 0.05 seconds: in each case, the first is 10 times longer than the second. In 55.55 seconds, the sum of all four examples (50 + 5 + 0.5 + 0.05), the relationship between the digits *beyond* the decimal point is therefore the same as the relationship between the digits *before* the decimal point. Students need time to acquaint themselves with very small fractional quantities, such as $\frac{5}{10}$, $\frac{5}{100}$, and $\frac{5}{1,000}$, and to learn their new symbols: 0.5, 0.05, and 0.005.

Partly because our money system doesn't have coins representing one *one-thousandth* of a dollar, partly because thousandth parts of common items that students measure are quite small, and mostly because the concept of dealing with small fractional parts is challenging, students have particular difficulties with thousandths and ten-thousandths. Powerful models, such as those introduced in earlier chapters, can help. The models can lead students to discover the same mathematical relationships between tenths and hundredths, hundredths and thousandths, thousandths and ten-thousandths, and beyond.

Lack of Connectedness Between Fractions and Decimals

The U.S. curricular sequence of teaching fractions first, followed by decimals, is a logical one, since decimal fractions constitute the starting point for teaching decimals. Too often, though, the link between fractions and decimals is quickly lost after a few introductory lessons. We must continually connect for students the two ways of writing a same number: the fractional form that is familiar to them, and the decimal form that is new to them. This can be accomplished by starting with familiar fractions, such as $\frac{1}{2}$ and $\frac{1}{10}$, whose decimal notation is relatively easy, just as Denis did. The next step is an examination of our place-value system extending in both directions—to very big numbers *and* to very small ones.

Difficulty with Symbol Meaning

In previous chapters, we discussed the difficulties students have when first introduced to fraction notation, such as thinking that the fraction line is a separation between two distinct whole numbers. The decimal point, if not explained thoroughly, can be similarly difficult to grasp. Writing $\frac{1}{4}$ as 0.4, or $\frac{1}{5}$ as 0.5, is a common error. I've even seen $\frac{1}{5}$ = 1.5. These interpretations reveal a lack of decimal symbol meaning.

We saw another typical error in Denis's story. Students suggested that adding 0.01 10 times be written as 0.010, revealing whole-number reasoning: that adding a zero to the right of the decimal 0.01 makes the number 10 times greater. Or, since adding 1 to 9 gives 10, they assume that adding 0.01 to 0.09 gives 0.010.

Saying or reading decimals. Making sense of decimals is further complicated by the way we say or read them. To read the number 3.45, we use the name of the rightmost or smallest non-zero decimal place value for the decimal part of the number (in this case, *hundredths*) and join it to the integer part of the number with the conjunction *and*: "three and forty-five hundredths." Similarly, the decimal 3.456 is ordinarily read "three and four-hundred and fifty-six thousandths." This is of course the opposite of the method we use to name whole numbers, where we use the name of the leftmost or largest non-zero decimal place value.

If students initially read the numbers 3.45 and 3.456 as "three and four tenths and five hundredths" and "three and four tenths and five hundredths and six thousandths," respectively, don't discourage them! This oral form is a testimony of place-value understanding. (Note, though, that students whose native tongue is not English may have trouble hearing the endings in *ths*.) And in cases like the number pi, there is no other choice than to read it as "three point one four one five . . . ," which is an acceptable way of naming all decimals.

Writing decimals. Writing decimals can also be tricky. In the United States, .5, 0.5, and 0.50 are all acceptable decimal notations for $\frac{1}{2}$. In most countries, however, the first form is neither recognized nor used. For consistency across all decimals, I recommend using the 0 to the left of the decimal point, as in 0.2 rather than .2, as it signifies that there are zero units or wholes in the number. It also facilitates comparison with zero: 0.2 has two-tenths more than 0, so 0.2 > 0. Moreover, especially when handwritten, 0.2 is more legible than .2. That said, students should recognize that .2 is an alternative version of 0.2, since they may come across this form of notation on tests and elsewhere.

Overreliance on the Money Model

Money is an effective starting point for introducing decimals. Just as there are $10 and $100 bills, which represent quantities that are 10 and 100 times greater than $1, there are also familiar coins that similarly represent quantities 10 and 100 times less than $1. But many other models can and should be included in any unit on decimals, including base-10 blocks, 2-D 100-squares, meter sticks, the hundred chart, the place-value chart, and of course the number line.

Again, money is especially useful because it's familiar. Students know, for example, that there is a U.S. coin that represents one-half of a dollar, or 50 pennies out of 100; a quarter represents one-fourth of a dollar, or 25 pennies out of 100; and a dime represents one-tenth of a dollar, or 10 pennies out of 100. Therefore, once the conventional decimal notation is accepted for tenths and hundredths of a dollar (something that students frequently see in real and virtual contexts), using money to introduce basic fraction-decimal equivalent expressions becomes natural.

- $\frac{1}{2} = \frac{50}{100} = 0.5$
- $\frac{1}{4} = \frac{25}{100} = 0.25$
- $\frac{1}{10} = \frac{10}{100} = 0.1$

However, using money to explain decimals to the exclusion of other models may also cause misconceptions. First, decimals such as 2.5 or 3.178 are rarely seen in money contexts and thus have no meaning to children. Second, and more serious, students often conclude that the decimal point is a separator between two different kinds of whole numbers—the first whose unit is a dollar, and the second whose unit is a cent—rather than as an indicator of the single unit whose place is immediately to the left of it. These students must be guided to see that the cents unit is a fraction of the dollars unit.

Poor Understanding of Decimal Magnitude

It is when we assign decimal comparison tasks (and, later, decimal computation tasks) that we see most clearly the difficulty students have with the meaning of the decimal notation and the number magnitude it represents.

Difficulty estimating. Judith Sowder, a mathematics educator with many years of experience studying fraction and decimal instruction, gives some clear examples of the confusion students experience. Asked to estimate the sum of 148.72 + 51.351 (which is about 150 + 50, or 200), many middle school students gave absurd estimates, such as 150.470, "because one hundred forty-eight point seven two rounds to one hundred point seven and fifty-one point three five one rounds to fifty point four zero zero. Add those" (Sowder, 2002, p. 113). In another example, when several middle school students were asked to estimate the product of 789 × 0.52 (which is about 800 × 0.5, or 400), one said 789, and another said 0. Only 19 percent of the students rounded 0.52 to 0.5 or $\frac{1}{2}$.

Difficulty comparing. Decimals are actually easier to compare than fractions. It is more obvious and immediate to see that 5.2 < 5.5 than to see that $\frac{2}{5} < \frac{1}{2}$. The latter requires reflection to dispel the visual cues of 2 > 1 and 5 > 2. Nevertheless, there are pitfalls. Here are some typical examples of erroneous student reasoning when comparing decimals:

- Longer is bigger: the longer the decimal part, the greater the number (faulty whole-number reasoning). For example, 0.35 > 0.4, because 35 > 4.

- Longer is smaller: the longer the decimal part, the smaller the number. For example, 0.352 < 0.35, because thousandths are smaller than hundredths.

- Confusion of symbols: incorrectly translating decimals into fractions. For example, 0.7 > 0.1, because $\frac{1}{7} > \frac{1}{10}$.

- The place of zero: some students are unsure where to place zero in a list of decimals. They may think that since it's a whole number, it's bigger than a decimal, or that "zero point something is less than zero."

- Adding the digit zero makes bigger: students may say that 0.580 is greater than 0.58. This again is whole-number reasoning applied to the decimal part of the number.

Difficulty rounding. Once students accept the 5-to-9-rounds-up and 1-to-4-rounds-down rules, rounding decimals that contain only one non-zero decimal place to the nearest whole number is relatively easy. But rounding numbers that contain two or more non-zero decimal places, such as 7.48, to the nearest whole number can be challenging. Common flawed reasoning often goes like this: "The 8 rounds up, so we go to 7.5, and since

5 rounds up too, we go to 8." Thus 7.48, which is actually less than 7.5, is incorrectly rounded to the greater whole number, 8, rather than the lesser (and correct) whole number, 7.

Density or "in between-ness." In the early elementary school grades, students are asked to find numbers between any two given whole numbers. But when the two numbers are consecutive, students conclude that no other whole number lives between them. In late elementary school and middle school, students accept (sometimes with difficulty) that at least nine numbers exist between, say, 6 and 7—namely, 6.1, 6.2, 6.3 . . . 6.9—but they have a hard time believing that there are in reality *infinitely many* numbers between 6 and 7. This property is called the density of rational numbers, something that teachers can help students discover. Using the decimal form of rational numbers to find a number "in between" is slightly easier than using the fractional form, so the study of decimals presents a good opportunity to introduce the concept of density.

Rote or Incorrect Application of Decimal Algorithms

Decimal instruction, like fraction instruction, is plagued with rules and tricks. "Line up the decimal points first before adding or subtracting," "Add the number of decimal places in the factors to get the number of decimal places in their product," and "Convert the divisor to a whole number first before dividing" are notorious examples. The latter rule, for instance, evolves into the false beliefs that "you cannot divide by a decimal" or that "the divisor *must* be a whole number in order to divide" (Tirosh & Graeber, 1989, p. 92).

As with whole numbers and fractions, many students approach decimal operations from a digit perspective and thus develop a limited "digit procedure sense" rather than a profound "(decimal) number operation sense." Logical reasoning that invokes our numeration system and the fraction-decimal connection can easily avoid these limitations in understanding.

Unpacking the Mathematical Thinking

It is noteworthy that in the CCSSM, the decimal standards for 4th grade are under Numbers and Operations—Fractions, but for 5th grade they are under Number and Operations in Base Ten. Understanding how to add and subtract decimals, a focus in 5th grade, requires a good grasp of the meaning and value of each digit and, hence, of our place-value system. As Denis did, it is advisable to review the place values of whole numbers with your students prior to introducing decimals.

Extending Place Value to Tenths and Hundredths

The base-10 number system is a place-value system: any digit represents a different quantity depending on its *place* in the written number. To express numbers that contain amounts less than 1, we extend the base-10 system to the right of the decimal point. The structure of the place-value system applies to the digits to the right of the decimal point just as it does to the digits to the left of it: any digit represents a value 10 times greater than that represented by the digit to its right, and a value $\frac{1}{10}$ of that represented by the digit to its left (Figure 7.1).

FIGURE 7.1
Base-10 Place Value Numeration System

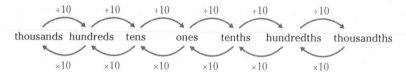

Fostering a good understanding of place value requires coordinating how we *write*, *say*, *read*, and *interpret* the digits of a number.

Symmetry. When thinking of the decimal point as a *separator* between two kinds of numbers, students fail to see the relationship between the whole and the decimal parts, or the symmetry that exists about the ones place (Figure 7.2).

- There is symmetry in the word roots (the bottom arrows).
- There is symmetry in the inverse growth ratios: × 10 and ÷ 10; × 100 and ÷ 100; × 1,000 and ÷ 1,000 . . . (the top arrows).

FIGURE 7.2
Symmetry About the Ones Place

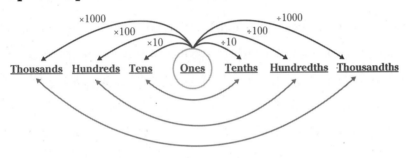

Note: By 6th grade, students should understand ÷ 10, ÷ 100, and ÷ 1,000 as $\times \frac{1}{10}$, $\times \frac{1}{100}$, and $\times \frac{1}{1,000}$.

The other problem with seeing the decimal point as a separator is the expectation of having *one-ths* on its right, just as it has *ones* (or units) on its left.

Increasing precision. Before decimal awareness, students understand that the whole number 342 has 3 hundreds, 4 tens, and 2 ones. With an expanded vision of the decimal place-value system in preparation for 6th grade, students should be more precise and see that 342 has 3.42 hundreds, 34.2 tens, or 342 units or ones. Similarly, the decimal 0.342 has 0.342 units or ones, 3.42 tenths, 34.2 hundredths, or 342 thousands (Figure 7.3).

The Models We Use Are Important

As with fractions, students need experiences with a variety of models. The questions they answer and the problems they explore should give them ample opportunities to establish connections between and among the decimal

FIGURE 7.3

An Expanded Vision of the Decimal Place-Value System

Hundreds	Tens	ONES	.	Tenths	Hundredths	Thousandths
		0	.	3	4	2
3	4	2	.			

Note: A more precise reading of place value includes "342 has 3.42 hundreds" and "0.342 has 34.2 hundredths."

representations, be they drawn from daily life, concrete, pictorial, verbal, or symbolic. Each new representation of decimals sheds more light on some aspect of decimal meaning. While many commercial manipulatives are limited in their ability to represent 100 or 1,000, there are a number of useful models.

1-D models: the meter stick and number line. Our 4th grade teacher, Denis, planned a few lessons on the meter stick as a way to progress beyond hundredths because he believed his students could tackle thousandths. A surprising fact about Cuisenaire Rods and the base-10 blocks is their metric measure: the edge length of the small cube is 1 cm, and the length of the long (base-10) or the orange rod (Cuisenaire) is 10 cm, or 1 decimeter. Lining up 10 longs or rods segues nicely to the meter stick.

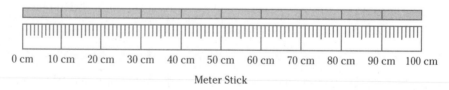

| 0 cm | 10 cm | 20 cm | 30 cm | 40 cm | 50 cm | 60 cm | 70 cm | 80 cm | 90 cm | 100 cm |

Meter Stick

In a subsequent lesson, Denis handed out ribbons made of fabric; using their Cuisenaire Rods, students made their own meter-long measuring tapes. Students thus experienced that a meter is made with 10 decimeters, and a decimeter is made with 10 centimeters. Following this by having students examine an actual meter stick allows them to see that this tenfold relationship continues—namely, that each centimeter is further divided into 10 millimeters, each about the thickness of a dime.

I recommend creating a measurement chart and having students measure different lengths in the classroom and then express them in three or four different ways (Figure 7.4).

FIGURE 7.4
Student Classroom Measurements

Length Measured	Meters (m)	Decimeters (dm)	Centimeters (cm)	Millimeters (mm)
Length of my desk	0.65	6.5	65	650
...	...	...	...	...

As students mature, you can extend the measurement chart to the left of the meter to include larger metric units: decameters, hectometers, and kilometers. In the absence of meter sticks, similar partitions can easily be illustrated on the number line, a common decimal model.

2-D models: 100-circles and 100-squares. Two very useful models to represent tenths and hundredths are the 100-circle and the 100-square (Figure 7.5).

- The 100-circle is graduated in 100 equal intervals, grouped into sections of 10, delineated by rays. These pie-like sections, each comprising one-tenth of the entire disc, are reminiscent of fraction discs.

FIGURE 7.5
100-Circle and 100-Square

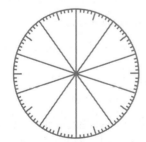
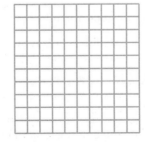

- The 100-square is a 10-by-10 grid; it is a common representation used in 6th and 7th grade. Earlier, we saw Denis use it with his 4th graders.

The 100-square lends itself well to examining thousandths and ten-thousandths. Partitioning the smallest squares of the 100-square (originally worth one-hundredth each) into 10 slivers each yields thousandths (100 × 10 slivers), and into 100 tiny squares each yields ten-thousandths (100 × 100 tiny squares) (Figure 7.6).

FIGURE 7.6
100-Square, 1,000-Square, and 10,000-Square

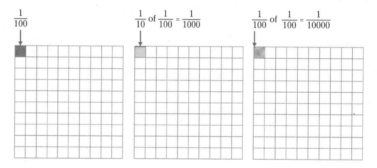

There is another option, but it is less correct: making a large rectangle with 10 copies of the 10-by-10 grid also generates thousandths. The problem with this representation is that hundredths and thousandths are the same size.

3-D models: Base-10 blocks. Base-10 blocks are concrete and powerful place-value representations. Their versatility helps convey the parallel structure between large whole numbers and small fractional numbers. Have your students practice (1) varying the block that denotes the unit, and (2) going back and forth between naming and constructing a decimal. Insist that they use different but equivalent verbal expressions.

Comparing Decimals Meaningfully

Well before students embark on decimal computation, they should develop a good sense of decimal magnitude. This allows them to figure out which among two or more decimals is the biggest or the smallest, which ultimately helps students estimate the outcome of operations on decimals.

Source of confusion. Whole numbers increase in size as their digits move leftward into larger and larger place values. The same is also true for decimals (0.078 increases as digits 7 and 8 move progressively leftward to give 0.78, or even 7.8). However, the reversal of the root words *ten*, *hundred*, *thousand*, and the whole-number meanings they connote, confuse students into thinking that decimals get larger as their digits move progressively rightward.

Comparison strategy. Here again there is consistency between the ways we compare whole numbers and decimals. In both cases, we line up place values and begin by comparing the leftmost non-zero digits; then, moving rightward, column by column, we compare subsequent place values. Just like with whole numbers, the higher digits imply greater numerical values. So, for instance, comparing 0.25 and 0.0888 is tricky if the whole numbers 25 and 888 catch the eye. But if we think about place value, then we see that 0.25 has two tenths, whereas 0.0888 has none. And even *one* tenth (0.1) is greater than 0.0999!

Balancing lengths with zeros. A helpful strategy when two decimals are of unequal length is to add zeros to equalize the lengths. Some school systems, such as the French school system I was educated in, encourages students to use this strategy because it makes the place-by-place comparison crystal clear. Consider comparing decimals 0.6 and 0.607. By adding two zeros to the first decimal, we obtain two decimals to the thousandths. They both have 6 tenths and 0 hundredths, but it's now clear that the second decimal also has 7 additional thousandths and therefore is greater.

Ones	.	Tenths	Hundredths	Thousandths
0	.	6	0	0
0	.	6	0	7

Decimal benchmarks. Just as students compared fractions to benchmarks, such as 0, $\frac{1}{2}$, and 1, so too should they compare decimals to the equivalent benchmarks. Once they learn the decimal expressions for the unit fractions $\left(\text{e.g., } 0.5 \text{ for } \frac{1}{2}, 0.333 \text{ for } \frac{1}{3}, 0.25 \text{ for } \frac{1}{4}, \text{ and } 0.2 \text{ for } \frac{1}{5}\right)$, they can find any multiples of them. For instance, if $\frac{1}{5}$ is 0.2, then $\frac{2}{5}, \frac{3}{5}, \frac{4}{5}$, and $\frac{5}{5}$ are simply integer multiples of 0.2—that is, 0.4, 0.6, 0.8, and 1.0.

FRACTIONS				DECIMALS			
$\frac{1}{2} \rightarrow$	$\frac{2}{2}$			$0.5 \rightarrow$	1		
$\frac{1}{3} \rightarrow$	$\frac{2}{3}$	$\frac{3}{3}$		$0.33 \rightarrow$	0.66	1	
$\frac{1}{4} \rightarrow$	$\frac{2}{4}$	$\frac{3}{4}$	$\frac{4}{4}$	$0.25 \rightarrow$	0.50	0.75	1
$\frac{1}{5} \rightarrow$	$\frac{2}{5}$	$\frac{3}{5}$	$\frac{4}{5}$ $\frac{5}{5}$	$0.2 \rightarrow$	0.4	0.6	0.8 1

Density of rational numbers. In middle school, students learn about the density property—a strategy for finding a fraction between any two given fractions. For example, $\frac{3}{5}$ clearly lives between $\frac{2}{5}$ and $\frac{4}{5}$, but finding a fraction between $\frac{3}{5}$ and $\frac{4}{5}$ is trickier. Writing the two fractions as equivalent fractions with greater denominators $\left(\frac{6}{10} \text{ and } \frac{8}{10}\right)$ gives us a solution: 7_10 . We can continue this process indefinitely to find a fraction between any two given fractions.

This density property of rational numbers is perhaps more accessible to students when viewed in decimal form. Consider the decimals 7.3 and 7.4.

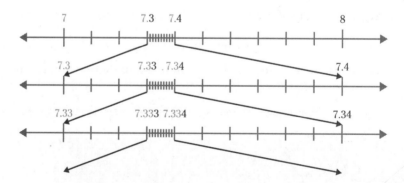

Partitioning the tenth interval between them into 10 smaller segments and then zooming in enables us to find nine obvious decimals in between: 7.31 to 7.39. Let's arbitrarily select 7.33 and 7.34. Repeating the process of subdividing and zooming in again enables us to find another nine decimals in between: 7.331 to 7.339. By continuing in this way, we show that between *any* two decimals, no matter how "close" on the number line, there are an infinite number of decimals—a mind-boggling fact for many!

 ## Teaching Tip: Create Tasks with Misconceptions in Mind

It's important to think about student misconceptions when creating or choosing assessment tasks about decimals, so you can be sure that the answers you receive reflect student understanding of the notation. Let's look, for instance, at the process of selecting decimals for an ordering task:

- List I: (a) .75, (b) 0.781, (c) 0, (d) .7

- List II: (a) .54, (b) .761, (c) .01, (d) .801. (e) .21

Creating a list of decimals for comparison seems like it should be a simple matter. However, these two lists, because they were created without considering common student errors in understanding, could result in the right answers for the wrong reasons. If students were asked to rewrite List I in ascending order, they could correctly order them while applying the misconception that "longer is greater." Similarly, if students completely disregard the decimal points, they could correctly rewrite List II in ascending order by treating the numbers as if they were whole.

Importance of the Unit

Throughout this book, the importance of fostering students' awareness of the unit when teaching fractions has been emphasized—and it is no less important when teaching decimals.

Consider comparing 0.59 and 0.54. We saw that many students reason that 0.59 > 0.54 because 59 > 54 (whole-number reasoning). But if this were the correct logic, then similarly 0.50 would be greater than 0.5 because 50 is greater than 5. The important and ever-present question of "What's the unit?" provides the answer: 0.59 and 0.54 are $\frac{59}{100}$ and $\frac{54}{100}$, respectively. The common unit fraction is $\frac{1}{100}$, so we can correctly conclude that 59 *one-hundredths* is greater than 54 *one-hundredths*.

Next, let's reconsider 0.50 and 0.5. The decimal 0.50 means 50 *one-hundredths*, but the decimal 0.5 means 5 *one-tenths*. Since the units (unit fractions) are not equal, we can't compare 5 and 50. If, however, we convert 5 *one-tenths* to 50 *one-hundredths* $\left(\frac{5}{10} = \frac{50}{100}\right)$, using our knowledge of equivalent fractions, we see that both 0.5 and 0.50 represent the same number of common units, so they are equal.

Whenever students are in doubt, remind them to reason with the fractional equivalents of decimals.

Sensing Approximate Values

Estimating. Cultivate in your students the habit of mind of estimating answers before computing exact answers. It's empowering and helpful in everyday life, especially when figuring out costs or measurements. For example, the sum $32.89 + $7.05 is *about* $40, because 32.89 is close to 33, 7.05 is close to 7, and 33 + 7 = 40. Or, the product of 0.49 × 10.08 is approximately 5, because 0.49 is close to 0.5 $\left(\text{or } \frac{1}{2}\right)$, 10.08 is close to 10, and half of 10 is 5. Estimation builds both strong decimal number sense and strong operation sense across all types of numbers, whole and rational.

Rounding. Estimation presupposes a good sense of rounding—to the next whole number, tenth, or even hundredth. When rounding to the nearest whole number, we must consider the digit in the tenths place only; when rounding to the nearest tenth, we must consider the digit in the hundredths place only; and so forth. If the digit is less than 5, we round down; if it's 5 or greater, we round up. That's the convention.

When the answer is not obvious, one effective technique is to draw a number line interval, decide on the pertinent endpoints, and place the decimal in question within the interval. The following example demonstrates how this method helps to resolve the rounding of 7.48 to the nearest whole (7) and to the nearest tenth (7.5).

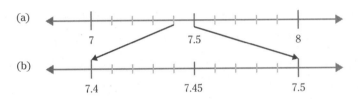

7.48 is on the left of 7.5, so it rounds to 7.

(a) ... 7 ... 7.5 ... 8

(b) ... 7.4 ... 7.45 ... 7.5

7.48 is on the right of 7.45, so it rounds to 7.5.

 ## A Bridge to Algebra: Cultivating Relational Thinking

Consider these equivalent expressions:

- $0.27 = \dfrac{2}{10} + \dfrac{7}{100} = \dfrac{20}{100} + \dfrac{7}{100} = \dfrac{27}{100}; 0.27 = 0.2 + 0.07$

- $0.27 = \dfrac{100}{100} - \dfrac{73}{100} = 1 - \dfrac{73}{100}; 0.27 = 1 - 0.73; 0.27 = 0.30 - 0.03$

- $0.27 = \dfrac{27}{100} = 27 \times \dfrac{1}{100}; 0.27 = 27 \times 0.01$

- $2.7 = \dfrac{27}{10} = 27 \times \dfrac{1}{10} = 27 \times 0.1$

Composing and decomposing in general—be it with numbers, algorithms, patterns, lengths, areas, volumes, and so forth—is a sign of deep mathematical understanding and a staple of algebraic insight. Being able to decompose decimals as sums, differences, products, and quotients helps students better understand the properties of operations, another foundation of algebraic thinking. For instance, understanding that $\frac{27}{100} = 27 \times \frac{1}{100}$, or that $\frac{27}{10} = 27 \times \frac{1}{10}$, helps students see that a division by 10 or 100 is equivalent to a product by the reciprocal of 10 or 100, respectively.

Making Sense of Operations

Some traditional math textbooks continue to teach "decimal computation rules," but this distinction is unnecessary; operating on decimals builds on place-value understanding and a seamless transition between fractions and decimals. Moreover, the meanings of operations remain the same no matter what numbers we work with. In this section, we focus on adding and subtracting with meaning.

Addition and subtraction. The additive nature of the base-10 place-value system is consistent for whole and rational numbers alike, and this understanding facilitates students' reasoning with operations. If students know the rule "Line up the decimal points," then help them demystify it. Since the decimal point is the conventional symbol indicating the ones digit to its left, the rule's objective is not new: when stacking numbers to add or subtract them, we align digits vertically so that place values correspond. This enables us to combine the digits that have the same place value, be they ones, tens, hundreds, tenths, hundredths, or thousandths.

To make this clear, continually go back and forth between decimal notation and fraction decomposition notation. For example, the 8 in 32.89 and the 0 in 7.045 both represent *tenths* because 32.89 equals $32 + \frac{8}{10} + \frac{9}{100}$, and 7.045 equals $7 + \frac{0}{10} + \frac{4}{100} + \frac{5}{1000}$.

Using models. If you use a variety of models to give meaning to addition and subtraction, eventually students won't need to rely on any one model as they move from concrete to abstract. The 100-square works nicely, as it can simultaneously model tenths and hundredths. Using different colors to model the addends (say, 0.3 and 0.57) and then representing their sum (0.87) with a third color on a third square is also effective.

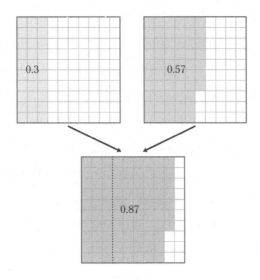

For subtraction, we saw that a powerful way to model a difference between two numbers, no matter their nature, is to consider their distance on the number line. This model supports decimal decomposition, relative magnitude, and the inverse relationship between subtraction and addition. For instance, computing 32.1 – 17.4 is equivalent to adding up from 17.4 to 32.1. The difference is the sum of 10, 4, 0.6, and 0.1, which is 14 + 0.7, or 14.7.

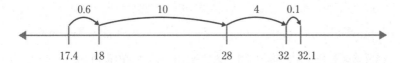

Note: Not drawn to scale.

Using decomposition and recomposition. Consider the sum 0.27 + 0.78. Decomposing the addends, mentally or by using a model, into (0.25 + 0.02) and (0.75 + 0.03), respectively, and then regrouping the four new addends as

(0.25 + 0.75) and (0.02 + 0.03) is a sign of strong number sense. The answer, 1 + 0.05 or 1.05, becomes obvious. We could name this method "making wholes."

Algebraic thinking: opposite change or same change. Consider the sum 3.77 + 5.18. Adding 2 (or another constant, such as 0.02) to one addend and subtracting 2 from the other does not change the sum, since + 2 – 2 makes 0, and 0 is the additive identity (the element that when added to any element x in the set yields x). Thinking of 3.77 + 5.18 as (3.77 – 0.02) + (5.18 + 0.02) transforms the sum to the equivalent sum 3.75 + 5.20, which is easier to add mentally from left to right: 8.95. We can name this algebraic approach "opposite change."

For subtraction, the approach would be "same change." To demonstrate, let's revisit 32.1 – 17.4. We could add 2.6 to both numbers, transforming the difference to the equivalent difference 34.7 – 20. The answer of 14.7 is now easily obtained by simply subtracting the whole numbers (34 – 20) and preserving the decimal fraction $\frac{7}{10}$ or 0.7. Viewing the difference as a "distance rod" on the number line, this is tantamount to shifting the distance rod *to the right* by 2.6 units.

 Teaching Tip: Think Mathematically About the Phrases You Use

We often make comparison statements between whole numbers and decimals that perpetuate a digit approach to decimal operations rather than foster decimal operation sense. Consider the following warning, which students internalize as a rule: "Adding zero (one, two, three, or more) to a whole number makes it bigger (10, 100, 1,000 times so), but adding a zero to decimals leaves them unchanged." We often support this statement with examples (e.g., 340 ≠ 34, but 0.340 = 0.34).

Why is this problematic?

First, because the wording is unclear. Rather than *add* a zero, we actually *append* the digit 0 at the right of the numeral. *Adding* a zero should be reserved for 34 + 0 and 0.34 + 0. We know that the addition of 0 leaves any number unchanged because 0 is the identity element of addition.

Second, for many students, "adding zeros" to a number is synonymous to multiplying by powers of 10, an unfortunate abuse of language that gets generalized and leads to misconceptions.

Let's examine *mathematically* what really happens to whole numbers and decimals when we multiply by a power of 10. For these examples, we'll use $10^1 = 10$:

$$10 \times 34 = 10(30 + 4) = (10 \times 30) + (10 \times 4) = 300 + 40 = 340.$$

Notice that the digits shifted leftward to the next place value: 3 shifted from the tens column to the hundreds column, and 4 shifted from the ones column to the tens column (Figure 7.7).

FIGURE 7.7
The Effect of Multiplying by Consecutive Powers of 10

Multiplying by 10: The numbers increase by a factor of 10 as they move downward from row to row.							
Thousands	Hundreds	Tens	ONES	.	Tenths	Hundredths	Thousandths
			0	.	0	3	4
			0	.	3	4	
			3	.	4		
		3	4	.			
	3	4	0	.			
3	4	0	0	.			

When working with students, our focus should be on these place-value shifts, not on "moving the decimal point to the right," as is so often taught.

$$10 \times 0.34 = 10 \times \left(\frac{3}{10} + \frac{4}{100}\right) = \left(10 \times \frac{3}{10}\right) + \left(10 \times \frac{4}{100}\right) = \left(\frac{10}{10} \times 3\right) + \left(\frac{10}{100} \times 4\right) = (1 \times 3) +$$

$$\left(\frac{1}{10} \times 4\right) = 3 + \frac{4}{10} = 3 + 0.4 = 3.4$$

Here we notice the same leftward shift of the digits to the next place value: 3 shifted from the tenths to the ones, and 4 shifted from the hundredths to the tenths. Again, the place-value shifts are more significant than simply moving decimal points. In other words, multiplication by 10 (or any 10^n) has the same effect on decimals as on whole numbers!

Targeting Misconceptions with Challenging Problems

Students need a variety of opportunities to make sense of decimals. Varying the context and models, relating back to fractions, developing a good sense of place value, and gradually moving away from dependence on any one model are all key. The following seven problems are designed for these purposes.

🔅 **Problem 1. Modeling multidigit whole numbers and decimals.** The following problems allow students to review whole numbers:

- Build the number 234 if the "long" base-10 block is the unit.
- Build a rod measuring 127 cm with Cuisenaire Rods. The small cube's length is 1 cm.

These problems give students practice with representing decimals:

- Build the number 7.05 using base-10 blocks, and specify the block representing the unit. Fill in the blanks: 7.05 has: ____ tens, ____ ones, ____ tenths, and ____ hundredths.

- Show a length of 492 millimeters (mm) on a meter stick. Fill in the blanks: 492 mm is equivalent to ____ centimeters (cm), ____ decimeters (dm), and ____ meters (m).

These problems give students practice with extending to thousandths:

- On a large 100-square, represent the decimal fractions $\frac{4}{10}$, $\frac{5}{100}$, and $\frac{6}{1,000}$ using three different colors. (Hint: There are 100 squares; how can you represent *thousandths*?)

- On another large 100-square, represent the decimal 0.456. Make an observation.

💡 **Problem 2. Whole numbers, fractions, and decimals cohabitate on the number line.** On each of the following number line intervals, name the number represented by the question mark.

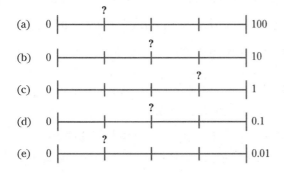

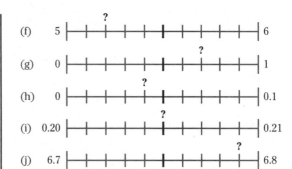

Now, on each of the following number line intervals, place the numbers *approximately* where they live.

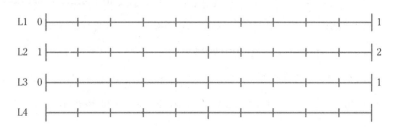

- On line L1, place 0.2, $\frac{1}{2}$, 0.5, and $\frac{1}{5}$. What do you notice?
- On line L2, place 1.2, 1.5, 1.25, and $\frac{3}{2}$.
- On line L3, place .6, 0.06, $\frac{1}{6}$, and $\frac{3}{5}$.
- On line L4, write the endpoints that help you place 1.05, 1.50, $\frac{9}{4}$, and 11.

💡 **Problem 3. Developing a sense of magnitude about decimals.** Use your decimal number sense to solve the problems that follow.

- Group these seven decimals into three groups such that each group contains numbers that are either *equal* or *very close* in size:

    0.5   0.05   0.50   0.55   0.005   0.505   0.055

- Fill in the blanks with digits of your choice and then group the seven numbers you created such that each group contains decimals that are either *equal* or *very close* in size:

    23._   2.3_ _   0._23   0._2   0.2_3   2._ 3   23.0_

- Match each decimal to a fraction or mixed number that is either *equal* or *very close* to it in size. Use your decimal number sense, not your calculator.

Decimal	Fraction	Decimal	Mixed Number
0.672	$\frac{2}{3}$	5.49	$5\frac{3}{10}$
0.501	$\frac{4}{5}$	5.028	$5\frac{28}{100}$
0.75	$\frac{1}{2}$	5.290	$5\frac{1}{2}$
0.79	$\frac{3}{4}$	5.30	$5\frac{29}{1000}$

- Consider these 10 numbers: $0.5, \frac{4}{5}, 0.9, 2.4, \frac{1}{2}, 2, 1.6, 0.05, 0, 1.5.$

  o Which number is greatest? Least? Closest to 0? Closest to 1? Equal to 0.5? Twice the value of $\frac{4}{5}$? Three times the value of 0.5? 0.5 greater than 1.5? 0.1 less than 1?

  o Which numbers are equal? Closest together? Farthest apart?

💡 **Problem 4. Comparing decimals, fractions, and whole numbers.** Use your number sense to solve the problems below.

- Circle each true statement, and use a place-value chart to justify your choice:

  a. $0 > .2$ or $0 < .2$?

  b. $0.7 > 0.65$ or $0.7 < 0.65$?

  c. $2.092 > 2.07$ or $2.092 < 2.07$?

- Circle each true statement, and use the fraction form of decimals to justify your choice:

  a. $5 > 5.01$ or $5 < 5.01$?

  b. $0.4 > 0.39$ or $0.4 < .39$?

  c. $0.78 > 0.709$ or $0.78 < 0.709$?

- Circle each true statement, and use a number line to justify your choice:

    a. 2.6 is closer to 2, or 2.6 is closer to 3?

    b. 3.49 is closer to 3.4, or 3.49 is closer to 3.5?

- Fill in the blanks with numbers of your choice that make the statements true:

    a. ___ > 2.5 and ___ < 2.5

    b. 4 > ___ and 4 < ___

    c. 4.___ > 4.___ and 4.___ < 3.___

Problem 5. Developing relational thinking. Use your number sense to fill in the blanks so that both sides of the equations are equivalent.

$3.5 = \underline{\quad} + 3$	$3.5 = \underline{\quad} - \frac{5}{10}$	$3.5 = 35 \times \underline{\quad}$
$4.25 = 4 + \underline{\quad} + \frac{5}{100}$	$4.25 = 4 + 0.2 + \underline{\quad}$	$4.25 = \underline{\quad} \times 0.01$
$4.25 = 42.5 \times \underline{\quad}$	$4.25 = \frac{425}{\underline{\quad}}$	$4.25 = \frac{\underline{\quad}}{10}$
$2.3 + 2.7 = \underline{\quad} + 2.5$	$2.3 - 1.9 = \underline{\quad} - 2$	$6.3 + 4.9 = 6.2 + \underline{\quad}$
$6.3 - 0.8 = 6.5 - \underline{\quad}$	$7.5 \times \frac{1}{10} = 75 \times \underline{\quad}$	$\frac{\underline{\quad}}{100} = 7.5$

Problem 6. Resolving dilemmas. Use your decimal operation sense to solve the problems below.

1. Brian and Jen need a wooden platform at least 7 feet long for a toy train. They found three boards in their garage measuring 1.4 feet, 2.8 feet, and 3 feet, respectively. Before carrying the boards inside, Brian and Jen computed the total length of the boards: Brian says it's 4.5 feet, but Jen says it's 7.2 feet.

    - Draw a tape or bar model that represents the sum of the three boards' lengths.

- Decide whether Brian or Jen is correct.

- Figure out the error the other person made. How might you help Brian or Jen avoid that error next time?

2. Erin says that $5 \times 0.8 = 4$ can't be right because "multiplication makes things bigger, but 4 is smaller than 5." Aaron uses base-10 blocks to show Erin that 4 *is* the correct answer.

- Use base-10 blocks and select your unit. Show how Aaron might have modeled the multiplication to get 4.

- How might you help Erin clarify her misconception?

- Describe a real-life situation that would give meaning to this multiplication problem.

3. Josh says that 3.49 rounds to 4 because ".49 rounds to .5, and .5 *rounds up* to the next whole number." Amal shows him on the number line that 3.49 rounds to 3. Who is correct? Use a number line model to justify the correct answer.

Problem 7. The effects of operations on decimals. To solve the following problems, don't carry out the computations with a calculator or paper and pencil. Use your decimal number sense and your knowledge of the meanings of operations.

1. Give a close decimal estimate for the result of each operation. For example, $0.52 + \frac{8}{17}$ is close to 1, because 0.52 is slightly greater than $\frac{1}{2}$ and $\frac{8}{17}$ is slightly less than $\frac{1}{2}$.

- $249.75 + 51.435$

- $6\frac{4}{10} - 3.22$

- $24.8 \times .101$

- $527.6 \div 9.97$

2. Figure out the approximate or exact answer to each problem, using your number sense:

- Jon lined up, end to end, several wooden slabs, each 0.2 yards long, to create a wooden foundation for a doghouse 1.2 yards long. How many slabs did he line up?

- There are 4.6 gallons of water remaining in a 10-gallon filtered water container that had been full. How many gallons of the water have already been consumed?

- By what decimal should you multiply 16 to get 4? What about to get 8? What about to get 1.6?

- Karima bought 1.6 pounds of mixed nuts to make small bags of equal weight. She could make 8 small bags. What was the common weight, in pounds, of each bag?

 What's the App for That? *Easy Decimals*

The **Easy Decimals** app (www.apps4math.com) does exactly what its title suggests—namely, it makes decimals easy to visualize and understand. Using models that make sense, students will grasp the meaning of decimal notation and learn how to represent decimals using the basic square grid.

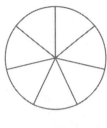

CONCLUSION

Moving from Rote to Reason

Instructional practices that tend toward premature abstraction and extensive symbolic manipulation lead students to have severe difficulty in representing rational numbers with standard written symbols and using the symbols appropriately.

National Research Council (2001, p. 234)

Foster These Seven Habits of Mind

The seven habits of mind described in this book and summarized in this conclusion are essential components of fraction sense—and indeed of good number sense as a whole.

Decompose and (re)compose. The habit of mind of decomposing and then recomposing fractions and operations on fractions in multiple ways to suit our purposes is foundational to a strong fraction sense and a deep understanding of fraction algorithms. The following examples are meant to exhibit *ways of thinking* that students can acquire:

- A fraction as a sum: $\frac{4}{5} = \frac{1}{5} + \frac{1}{5} + \frac{1}{5} + \frac{1}{5}$ or $\frac{1}{5} + \frac{3}{5}$ or $\frac{2}{5} + \frac{2}{5}$ or . . .

- A fraction as a difference: $\frac{4}{5} = \frac{5}{5} - \frac{1}{5}$ or $\frac{10}{5} - \frac{6}{5}$ or . . .

- A fraction as a product: $\frac{4}{5} = 4 \times \frac{1}{5}$ $\left(4 \text{ copies of } \frac{1}{5}, \text{ or a quantity 4 times greater than } \frac{1}{5} \right)$

- A fraction as a quotient: $\frac{4}{5} = 4 \div 5$ or $8 \div 10$ or . . .

- Addition: $\frac{6}{7} + \frac{5}{7} = \frac{6}{7} + \left(\frac{1}{7} + \frac{4}{7} \right) = \left(\frac{6}{7} + \frac{1}{7} \right) + \frac{4}{7} = \frac{7}{7} + \frac{4}{7} = 1 \text{ and } \frac{4}{7}$

- Subtraction: $\frac{3}{2} - \frac{3}{4} = \left(1 + \frac{1}{2} \right) - \left(\frac{1}{2} + \frac{1}{4} \right) = 1 + \left(\frac{1}{2} - \frac{1}{2} \right) - \frac{1}{4} = 1 + 0 - \frac{1}{4} = 1 - \frac{1}{4} = \frac{3}{4}$

Encourage and use estimation. Students depend on written computation and focus on exact answers because fraction instruction leans heavily on the side of procedures and neglects fostering estimation strategies. An often-cited example is this NAEP problem given to 13-year-olds: "Estimate the answer to $\frac{12}{13} + \frac{7}{8}$." Fewer than 75 percent selected the answer 2. An awareness of the "bigness" of fractions is essential in fraction computation.

Ali, a 4th grader, exhibited this awareness in explaining her answer: "Half of a bar and $\frac{3}{8}$ of another bar is a little less than a whole." When I prompted her to explain how she knew this, Ali said, "I know that another half would have to be $\frac{4}{8}$, so $\frac{3}{8}$ is a little less than a half." Ali didn't calculate the exact sum of the fractions; instead, she used her sense of the "bigness" of fractions $\frac{1}{2}$ and $\frac{3}{8}$ to determine that their sum is "a little less than a whole." For our students to think like Ali, we must regularly have them compare fractions to benchmarks and predict reasonable answers, long before teaching algorithms.

Articulate equivalence. Fraction addition and subtraction concepts are dependent on fraction equivalence. In Chapter 4, we stressed the importance of flexibly moving back and forth between the equivalent names of a fraction. In standard fraction algorithms for addition and subtraction, when finding common denominators, we move from fewer and larger fractional parts toward more numerous and smaller ones. Then, when interpreting answers to fraction problems, we are often asked to give answers in the lowest or simplest terms.

(a)   (b)

The critical piece of equivalence instruction is connecting the different ways of showing and explaining equivalence: with drawings, objects (Jai exchanged 1 rhombus for 2 triangles), symbols $\left(\text{Ian found 3 groups of } \frac{6}{3} \text{ and recognized that it was the same as 3 groups of } \frac{2}{1}, \text{ or 3 groups of 2}\right)$, oral explanations, and actions.

Employ multiple representations. Students need to be competent in using a variety of computational tools, and they need to know how and when to select the appropriate one for a given problem situation. In the problems described in this book, many different tools have been used to make sense of fraction magnitude, comparison, or computation, including length models, area models, volume models, commercial math manipulatives, discrete sets of objects, and clocks. Along with language, writings, and gestures, students use representational tools in close concert with their strategies; these representations are the outward means of expressing their thinking in solving problems.

The key to successfully using multiple representations is ensuring that students see the connections among the different ways of visualizing or talking about fractions in context, or any other mathematical object or process (Figure 8.1).

FIGURE 8.1
Connect the Multiple Ways of Representing Fractions in Context

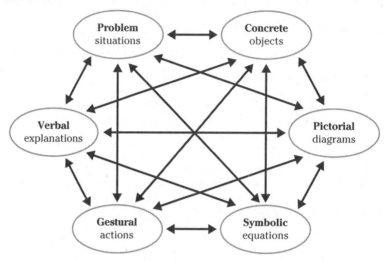

For example, you might have students circle two-thirds of a sandwich portions (pictorial), select the same color for every two cubes of a collection (concrete), and make two-third hops on the number line (symbolic), all of which represent the fraction $\frac{2}{3}$.

Deemphasize the distinction between *proper* and *improper*. As noted in this book, I've always recommended avoiding the term *improper*, as I believe it suggests something negative or difficult, and I was pleased to see that the CCSSM has deemphasized the distinction. The terms *proper* and *improper*, along with mixed-number notation, are particular to U.S. and UK curricula. Using them causes several problems:

- They are not universal.
- Students think that a multiplication binds the whole number and fraction in $2\frac{1}{3}$, as in $2x$.

- The proper/improper duality causes students to favor fractions between 0 and 1.

- Time spent on such distinctions is time away from focusing on the structure of *all* fractions.

- The mixed-number notation is a wall to algebra: there is *no* algebraic equivalent.

I suggest using the terms *less than 1* and *greater than 1*, as they are meaningful, connected, and mathematical. Given the CCSSM definition of $\frac{a}{b}$, conceptualizing $\frac{12}{5}$ is no more difficult than $\frac{3}{5}$. Once the unit fraction $\frac{1}{5}$ is determined, $\frac{3}{5}$ counts 3 copies and $\frac{12}{5}$ counts 12 copies—nothing improper there!

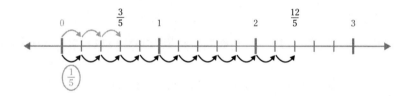

You might also foster the habit of naming the whole numbers as fractions, as in "Five-fifths is one, ten-fifths is two, fifteen-fifths is three," and so on.

Reiterate fractions and numbers. Problem situations introduce students to fraction computation. In 3rd–5th grade, fractions in problems are fractional quantities: amounts of food, money, time, length, and so on. Fractions as quantities are the first step toward fractions as numbers, though the transition is not obvious. Regularly using the number line representation, and having students locate fractions as points on the line, helps them move away from a seeing a fraction as two numbers and eases the transition to the concepts of fractions as rational numbers, further developed in middle school, and fractions as rational functions in high school.

Attend to the unit. Comparing fractions is only possible if the unit is common. We must ask students, again and again, "What's the whole?" or "What's the unit?" The same is true for fraction algorithms: we can't combine two fractions with addition or subtraction if they are not fractions of a common unit; or we can only make sense of multiplication and division of fractions if we realize that different units are at play. For instance, if we interpret the equation $3 \div \frac{1}{2} = 6$ as modeling the sentence "There are 6 half-dollars in 3 dollars," then we must understand that the dividend, 3, refers to *whole* dollars, whereas the divisor and quotient refer to *half*-dollars. Making students aware of the different units in a single fraction problem helps them make sense of the algorithmic procedures and numerical answers they produce.

Teach Meanings First, Algorithms Last

I have learned important lessons from practice and research about the long-standing rule-based approach to teaching fractions. I recall them in this closing chapter.

- Students need time to understand fractions, and teachers must be patient and give them this time. In particular, students need ample experience with constructing new meanings for fractional symbols, working with concrete and visual representations of fractions, connecting these representations, and developing a good sense of the kinds of quantitates the symbols may denote.

- Teachers should delay teaching formal operations with fractions at the symbolic level until 6th grade. If instructional time in grades 3–5 is used to cultivate key concepts—including the ideas of unit, a sense of fraction magnitude, and fraction equivalence—then students will be more successful with fraction computation, will have a stronger quantitative understanding, and will be better able to judge the reasonableness of their answers. Remember that operations are actions performed on numbers. Students need years to conceptualize fractions as numbers before operating on them with meaning.

- Fraction computation algorithms should not be taught in isolation. Students should have multiple experiences with problem situations where combining fractions (with any operation) has purpose and makes sense. Ideally, computational algorithms should emerge naturally through these problem-solving contexts. It is imperative that students develop meanings of the operations on fractions by building on the meanings they already know of operations on whole numbers. Teachers must guide the gradual evolution from student-invented algorithms to standard ones.

- When mathematical reasoning is replaced by rote learning, we use tricks, phrases, or songs to remember what to *do*, such as "To divide fractions, just invert and multiply." But rote learning eventually leads to errors when students apply rules mechanically and indiscriminately without considering what the symbols mean. For example, a typical error is forgetting which fraction to "invert" when dividing fractions. So, new adages come to the rescue, such as, "Flip the fellow that follows." Such practices are ludicrous and distance students from the beauty of mathematical reasoning.

- Finally, memorizing a disparate set of fraction rules without understanding does not contribute to students' meaning making of mathematics but rather contributes to a widespread belief that mathematics is a set of unrelated facts and senseless procedures given to us, which we shouldn't attempt to understand but should simply commit to memory.

Look Ahead to Ratios, Proportions, Proportional Relations, and Linear Functions

Attention to developing flexibility in working with rational numbers contributes to students' understanding of, and facility with, proportionality. . . . Proportionality is an important integrative thread that connects many of the mathematics topics studied in grades 6–8.

National Council of Teachers of Mathematics (2000, p. 217)

To get a glimpse of what lies ahead, I end this book by taking readers on a brief walk from fractions to linear functions, the math journey students travel from 3rd to 9th grade.

Fractions → Ratios → Proportions → Proportional Relations → Linear Functions

From Fractions to Ratios

There is much overlap between fractions and ratios; they possess the same mathematical properties since they are both interpretations of rational numbers. Nevertheless, their meanings are not interchangeable. This section addresses general differences that are important to know when working with elementary and middle school students.

General curricular distinctions. In the following distinctions, ES designates grades 3–5, and MS designates grades 6–8:

- Fractions are mainly investigated in ES and are understood as non-negative rational numbers. Ratios are mainly investigated in MS and can be non-negative rational numbers or non-negative irrational numbers. For example, the golden ratio is $\frac{\sqrt{5}+1}{2}$.

- The focus in constructing a fraction in ES is on dividing a number or partitioning a quantity into some number of equal-sized parts and understanding the relationships between the parts and the whole. The focus on ratios in MS is on their multiplicative nature and on reasoning with them to cultivate proportional thinking. This is not to say that students' multiplicative thinking and proportional reasoning do not begin earlier with the study of equivalent fractions; they do.

- Fractions, as used in ES, refer to part-whole comparisons. Ratios can refer either to part-part comparisons or to part-whole relationships.

Subtle distinctions. In middle and high school, students gradually learn to distinguish fractions and ratios in more subtle ways:

- Some ratios are not fractions, and some fractions are not ratios. For instance, a ratio that involves three or more numbers or quantities ($a : b : g$) can designate the ratio of the number of adults to the number of girls to the number of boys at an event. This ratio contains three multiplicative comparisons, so it is not a fraction. On the other hand, a fraction interpreted as a measure is not viewed as a multiplicative comparison and therefore is not a ratio.

- When representing equivalent fractions of $\frac{1}{3}$, for example, on a rectangular strip called the *unit* (using a tape diagram or bar model), as the numerator and denominator increase, the number of partitions also increases but the size of the pieces decreases. We shade *one* $\frac{1}{3}$, then *two* $\frac{1}{6}$, then *three* $\frac{1}{9}$, and so on. When representing equivalent ratios, on the other hand—such as $\frac{1}{3}$ for 1 part vinegar (V) out of 3 total parts (T) of a vinaigrette—the number of parts increases but the size of the parts remains the same. We commonly do this when multiplying recipes to make larger quantities (see Figure 8.2).

FIGURE 8.2
Equivalent Fractions Versus Equivalent Ratios

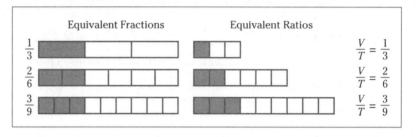

- When representing fractions and ratios as points, the fraction $\frac{3}{2}$ plots as a *single* point on a number line. In middle school, we call the number line the *x*-axis, and it defines a one-dimensional space. On the other hand, a ratio of 3:2, or $\frac{3}{2}$, could express the multiplicative relationship of length to width in a rectangle. In this case, it tells us that the length is $\frac{3}{2}$ of the width or the width is $\frac{2}{3}$ of the length. Since the ratio $\frac{3}{2}$ compares two quantities (width and length) in one context (rectangle), we represent it as a point in a two-dimensional space—also called the *xy*-plane—where the width is measured on one axis and the length on the other. Depending on one's choice of axes, the ordered pair (2, 3) or (3, 2) denotes a point in that plane.

- Finally, the trickiest distinction: we can add ratios in a way that we *cannot* add fractions. Let's create a ratio table for the infinite set of similar rectangles with a length-to-width ratio of three-halves: $\frac{L}{W} = \frac{3}{2}$. To find the width of a similar rectangle with length 12 (Column 4 in the table), we can multiply $\frac{6}{4}$ by $\frac{2}{2}$ to get $\frac{12}{8}$, using the multiplicative relationship between equivalent ratios. But we can also can add the values in Column 1 and the values in Column 3 to yield the values of the ratio in Column 4, yielding an $\frac{L}{W}$ ratio of $\frac{12}{8}$. Yet another way would be to iterate the ratio $\frac{3}{2}$ four times to get $\frac{12}{8}$. As another example, to find the length of a similar rectangle of width 9 (Column 5), we can partition $\frac{3}{2}$ into $\frac{1.5}{1}$ and then add it to $\frac{12}{8}$ (Column 4) to obtain $\frac{13.5}{9}$ (Column 5). The lesson here is that we can create equivalent ratios to $\frac{a}{b}$ by iterating or partitioning the composed unit $\frac{a}{b}$ or by multiplying *or* dividing the two quantities *a* and *b* by the same factor. When working with fractions, however, we cannot add fractions $\frac{3}{2}$ and $\frac{9}{6}$ to obtain the fraction $\frac{12}{8}$, nor can we add $\frac{3}{2} + \frac{3}{2} + \frac{3}{2} + \frac{3}{2}$ to obtain $\frac{12}{8}$!

	1	2	3	4	5	6	7	...
Length	3	6	9	12	?	17	?	...
Width	2	4	6	?	9	?	21	...

From Ratios to Proportions

A proportion is a relationship of equality between two ratios—for example, $\frac{3}{2} = \frac{6}{4}$ or $\frac{6}{4} = \frac{21}{14}$. As the numerical *values* of the compared quantities vary, the *ratio* remains invariant. Ratios are the building blocks for proportions. Understanding proportionality is one of the greatest challenges of middle school mathematics. Just as fractional thinking is much more than knowing how to add or multiply fractions, proportional thinking is much more than being able to solve proportions such as $\frac{7}{9} = \frac{21}{y}$ or $\frac{6}{4} = \frac{x}{14}$. It involves both qualitative and quantitative reasoning. Qualitatively, proportional reasoning involves a sense of reasonableness, as in asking oneself, "If there are four quarters to a dollar, does it make sense that there would be 20 quarters to five dollars? Should it be more? Should it be less?"

Quantitatively, proportional reasoning builds on a solid understanding of fractions, ratios, and the properties of multiplicative structures. Comparing two ratios is complex because one ratio is already a multiplicative comparison, but comparing two ratios, such as $\frac{1}{4}$ and $\frac{5}{20}$, actually means comparing two comparisons: downward, *within* each ratio (times 4) and across, *between* the two ratios (times 5). Ratios, proportions, and proportional thinking are useful in solving a wide variety of problems that affect our daily lives.

From Proportions to Proportional Relationships

Let's revisit our similar rectangles.

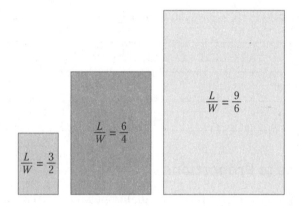

First, consider the three similar rectangles of dimensions 3-by-2, 6-by-4, and 9-by-6. The ratio of length to width, $\frac{L}{W}$, is constant for all three rectangles since $\frac{3}{2} = \frac{6}{4} = \frac{9}{6}$. As discussed previously, we can plot the three corresponding points (2, 3), (4, 6), and (6, 9) in a two-dimensional plane. (I chose to plot W on the x-axis and L on the y-axis, but the reverse is equally possible.) We notice that the three points line up.

Moreover, since there exists an infinite number of different size rectangles with the same length-to-width ratio of $\frac{3}{2}$, "plotting the ratio $\frac{3}{2}$" really means plotting an infinite number of points. This infinite number of points $\left(\text{symbolizing the infinite number of ratios equivalent to } \frac{3}{2}\right)$ constitute the graph of a proportional relationship between L and W. Algebraically, we write $L = \frac{3}{2} W$ (or $W = \frac{2}{3} L$ if we had made the other choice of axes). Geometrically, in a 2-D space, this relationship is graphed as a straight line that passes through the origin. Why must it pass through the origin?

Because the two quantities (here, L and W) are proportional. As one stretches, so does the other; as one shrinks, so does the other—and both always vary by the same factor. So, if $W = 0$, then $L = \frac{3}{2} W = 0$.

I graphed three sample rectangles onto the xy-plane only to show the connection between the similarity of rectangles and the proportionality of their numerical dimensions. But remove the rectangles, change the quantities in the story, and you have the graph of any two variables related by the proportional relationship $y = \frac{3}{2} x$. The different real-world situations that can be modeled by this equation are also infinite. An example: "In a Labor Day sale, two power bars are selling for \$3."

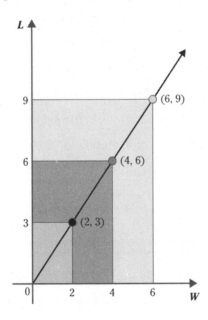

From Proportional Relationships to Linear Functions

In middle school, students study relationships between quantities that change; in high school, these relationships are formalized and called *functions*. Length as a function of width in the geometry of similar rectangles; cost as a function of the number of power bars purchased in economics; or temperature as a function of the time of day in meteorology. All are examples of functional relationships between two variables (multivariable functions are studied mostly in college). A special property of a function is that it assigns to every x-value (the independent variable) in a given set of possible values a unique y-value (the dependent variable). The x-y pairs are denoted by ordered pairs (x, y) and can be plotted in a 2-D plane. The set of all points in the plane form the graph of the function. In the middle grades, students explore multiple representations of functions: verbal descriptions, algebraic equations, tables of numbers containing the (x, y) values, and geometric graphs.

Linear functions. The first and simplest functions students explore are linear functions. The root of *linear* is *line*. Indeed, the graph of a linear function is a straight line. A general algebraic equation for all linear functions that gives y in terms of x is $y = mx + b$, or $f(x) = mx + b$. This is known as the slope-intercept form of a linear function. A special subset of linear functions are those in which the value b is zero, leaving $y = mx$ or $f(x) = mx$. The rectangle example we explored is of this form: $y = \frac{3}{2}x$, where $m = \frac{3}{2}$. This special subset of linear functions is the set of all proportional functions. The letter m in the equation stands for the slope of the line. While space does not permit an in-depth study of linear functions and their graphs, I do wish to leave you with the fundamental connections between slope, ratio, and proportionality.

Intuitively, the slope of a line can be thought of in terms of the amount of slant, measured by the angle the line makes with the horizontal. Numerically, the slope of a line can be thought of as the embodiment of a ratio (think: the infinite set of equivalent ratios). We can confirm this algebraically: if $y = mx$, then $\frac{y}{x} = m$. This equation translates into algebra the sentence: "x and y vary proportionally if their ratio remains constant."

In summary:

- A proportional relationship between two variables x and y has the form $y = mx$.

- $y = mx$ is a subset of the family of linear functions of the form $y = mx + b$.

- All linear function graphs are straight lines.

- The graphs of functions $y = mx$ all pass through the origin [the point $(0, 0)$].

- If two quantities vary proportionally, their ratio is constant.

- The embodiment of this ratio is the slope of the straight line graph.

Concluding Thoughts

The road to teaching and learning fractions, from the basics of partitioning wholes to the complexities of proportional functions, is a long one. The journey of unpacking fractions, from senseless memorization of rules to understanding and sense making for all, is a challenging one. My sincere hope is that teachers, coaches, teacher educators, math specialists, and other educators who are undertaking this journey will find in this book—through the classroom vignettes, revealed misconceptions, detailed mathematics, pedagogical insights, bridges to algebra, and challenging problems—new and exciting ways of thinking about, discoursing on, and working with fractions.

May they inspire you to cultivate in your students a strong sense of fractions, their meanings and their uses, that will serve them throughout their lifetimes. In the process, enjoy yourselves, for mathematics *can be* enjoyable! And don't forget those apps! They will help your students find joy in fractions!

References

Barnett-Clarke, C., Fisher, W., Marks, R., & Ross, S. (2010). *Developing essential understanding of rational numbers for teaching mathematics in grades 3–5.* Reston, VA: NCTM.

Bassarear, T. (1997). *Mathematics for elementary school teachers.* Boston: Houghton Mifflin.

Behr, M., Harel, G., Post, T., & Lesh, R. (1992). Rational number, ratio and proportion. In D. Grouws (Ed.), *Handbook of research on mathematics teaching and learning* (pp. 296–333). New York: Macmillan.

Behr, M., Harel, G., Post, T., & Lesh, R. (1994). Units of quantity: A conceptual basis common to additive and multiplicative structures. In G. Harel & J. Confrey (Eds.), *The development of multiplicative reasoning in the learning of mathematics* (pp. 123–180). Albany, NY: SUNY Press.

Behr, M., Lesh, R., Post, T., & Silver, E. A. (1983). Rational number concepts. In R. Lesh and M. Landau (Eds.), *Acquisition of mathematical concepts and processes* (pp. 91–126). New York: Academic Press.

Behr, M., & Post, T. (1992). Teaching rational number and decimal concepts. In T. Post (Ed.), *Teaching mathematics in grades K–8: Research-based methods* (2nd ed.) (pp. 201–248). Boston: Allyn and Bacon.

Bezuk, N., & Cramer, K. (1989). Teaching about fractions: What, when, and how? In P. Trafton (Ed.), *National Council of Teachers of Mathematics 1989 yearbook: New directions for elementary school mathematics* (pp. 156–167). Reston, VA: National Council of Teachers of Mathematics.

Blanton, M. L. (2008). *Algebra in the elementary classroom: Transforming thinking, transforming practice.* Portsmouth, NH: Heinemann.

Carpenter, T. P., Franke, M. L., & Levi, L. (2003). *Thinking mathematically: Integrating arithmetic & algebra in elementary school.* Portsmouth, NH: Heinemann.

Clements, D. H. (1999). Concrete manipulatives, concrete ideas. *Contemporary Issues in Early Childhood, 1*(1), 45–60.

Collins, A., & Dacey, L. (2010). *Zeroing in on number and operations: Key ideas and common misconceptions, Grades 5–6*. Portland, ME. Stenhouse.

Common Core State Standards Initiative. (2010). *Common Core State Standards for mathematics*. Washington, DC: CCSSO & National Governors Association. Retrieved from www.corestandards.org/math

Cramer, K., & Whitney, S. (2010). Learning rational number concepts and skills in elementary school classrooms. In D. V. Lambdin & F. K. Lester (Eds.), *Teaching and learning mathematics: Translating research for elementary school teachers* (pp. 15–22). Reston, VA: National Council of Teachers of Mathematics.

Cuoco, A., Goldenberg, E. P., & Mark, J. (1996). Habits of mind: An organizing principle for a mathematics curriculum. *Journal of Mathematical Behavior, 14*(4), 375–402.

Empson, S. B., & Levi, L. (2011). *Extending children's mathematics: Fractions and decimals*. Portsmouth, NH: Heinemann.

Enyedy, N., Rubel, L., Castellón, V., Mukhopadhyay, S., Esmonde, I., & Secada, W. (2008). Revoicing in a multilingual classroom. *Mathematical Thinking and Learning, 10*(2), 134–162.

Falkner, K. P., Levi, L., & Carpenter, T. P. (1999). Children's understanding of equality: A foundation for algebra. *Teaching Children Mathematics, 6*(4), 232–236.

Fosnot, C. T., & Dolk, M. (2002). *Young mathematicians at work: Constructing fractions, decimals, and percents*. Portsmouth, NH: Heinemann.

Freudenthal, H. (1983). *Didactical phenomenology of mathematical structures*. Boston: D. Reidel.

Huinker, D. (2002). Examining dimensions of fraction operation sense. In B. Litwiller & G. Bright (Eds.), *Making sense of fractions, ratios, and proportions: 2002 yearbook of the National Council of Teachers of Mathematics* (pp. 72–78). Reston, VA: National Council of Teachers of Mathematics.

Kamii, C., & Dominick, A. (1998). The harmful effects of algorithms in grades 1–4. In L. J. Morrow & M. J. Kenney (Eds.), *The teaching and learning of algorithms in school mathematics* (pp. 130–140). Reston, VA: National Council of Teachers of Mathematics.

Kieren, T. (1976). On the mathematical, cognitive, and instructional foundations of rational numbers. In R. Lesh (Ed.), *Number and measurement: papers from a research workshop* (pp. 101–144). Columbus, OH: ERIC/SMEAC.

Lamon, S. J. (1996). The development of unitizing: Its role in children's partitioning strategies. *Journal for Research in Mathematics Education, 27*(2), 170–193.

Lamon, S. J. (1999). *Teaching fractions and ratios for understanding: Essential content knowledge and instructional strategies for teachers*. Mahwah, NJ: Lawrence Erlbaum.

Lamon, S. J. (2005). *Teaching fractions and ratios for understanding: Essential content knowledge and instructional strategies for teachers* (2nd ed.). Mahwah, NJ: Lawrence Erlbaum.

Lamon, S. J. (2012). *Teaching fractions and ratios for understanding: Essential content knowledge and instructional strategies for teachers*. New York: Routledge.

National Council of Teachers of Mathematics. (2000). *Principles and standards for school mathematics*. Reston, VA: Author.

National Mathematics Advisory Panel. (2008). *Foundations for success: The final report of the National Mathematics Advisory Panel*. Washington, DC: U.S. Department of Education.

National Research Council. (2001). *Adding it up: Helping children learn mathematics.* Washington, DC: National Academy Press.

Neagoy, M. (2012). *Planting the seeds of algebra, PreK–2: Explorations for the early grades.* Thousand Oaks, CA: Corwin.

Neagoy, M. (2014). *Planting the seeds of algebra, 3–5: Explorations for the upper elementary grades.* Thousand Oaks, CA: Corwin.

O'Connor, M. C., & Michaels, S. (1996). Shifting participant frameworks: Orchestrating thinking practices in group discussion. In D. Hicks (Ed.), *Discourse, learning, and schooling* (pp. 63–103). New York: Cambridge University Press.

Otto, A. D., Caldwell, J. H., Hancock, S. W., & Zbiek, R. M. (2011). *Developing essential understanding of multiplication and division for teaching mathematics in grades 3–5.* Reston, VA: National Council of Teachers of Mathematics.

Seeley, C. L. (2015). *Faster isn't smarter* (2nd ed.). Sausalito, CA: Math Solutions.

Smith III, J. P. (2002). The development of students' knowledge of fractions and ratios. In B. Litwiller & G. Bright (Eds.), *Making sense of fractions, ratios, and proportions: 2002 yearbook of the National Council of Teachers of Mathematics* (pp. 3–17). Reston, VA: National Council of Teachers of Mathematics.

Sowder, J. (2002). Place value as the key to teaching decimal operations. In D. L. Chambers & National Council of Teachers of Mathematics, *Putting research into practice in the elementary grades: Readings from journals of the National Council of Teachers of Mathematics* (pp. 113–118). Madison: Wisconsin Center for Education Research, University of Wisconsin-Madison.

Tirosh, D., & Graeber, A. O. (1989). Preservice elementary teachers' explicit beliefs about multiplication and division. *Educational Studies in Mathematics, 20*(1), 79–96.

Van de Walle, J. A., Karp, K. S., & Bay-Williams, J. M. (2010). *Elementary and middle school mathematics: Teaching developmentally* (8th ed.). Boston: Pearson.

Van de Walle, J. A., & Lovin, L. A. H. (2006). *Teaching student-centered mathematics: Grades 3–5.* Boston: Pearson.

Van de Walle, J. A., & Lovin, L.A.H. (2006). *Teaching student-centered mathematics: Grades K–2.* Boston: Pearson.

Vergnaud, G. (1979). The acquisition of arithmetic concepts. *Educational Studies in Mathematics, 10*, 263–274.

Index

The letter *f* following a page number denotes a figure.

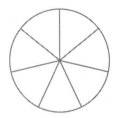

About the Author

Monica Neagoy is an author, international consultant, and popular keynote speaker with a passion for mathematics. In addition to writing books, her 25-year mathematics career has included teacher professional development, math specialist training, live television courses, video creation, math app conception, and live math shows, such as *MathMagic*. Whether in the United States, Europe, or elsewhere; whether presenting in English, French, or Spanish; whether working with teachers, parents, or students, Dr. Neagoy's lifelong goal has been to cultivate and inspire a fascination for the beauty, power, and wonder of mathematics.

Dr. Neagoy's mathematical expertise spans grades preK through 12. After creating more than 50 videos for high school–level mathematics—including video series for Discovery Education and The Annenberg Channel—over the past decade, she has focused on grades preK–8. She's convinced that if a child enters middle school disenchanted with mathematics, the probability of rekindling a love for mathematics is slim.

Having begun her teaching career in the Georgetown University Mathematics Department and then serving as program director at the National Science Foundation, Dr. Neagoy's knowledge of higher mathematics enables her to empower teachers and parents to appreciate the bridges from early concrete mathematics to advanced mathematics. She is the author of *Planting the Seeds of Algebra, PreK–2* (2012) and *Planting the Seeds of Algebra, 3–5* (2014), both published by Corwin Press.

Presently living in Paris, France, giving talks and offering professional development in Europe and the United States, she is the director and lead author of the elementary mathematics series *Maths, Méthode de Singapour*, a brand new adaptation of Singapore Mathematics to the latest French math standards (www.lalibrairiedesecoles.com). Finally, she collaborates with two Israeli math colleagues, Zvi Shalem and Gali Shimoni, in the conception and creation of original and exciting math apps (www.apps4math.com).

Read more about Dr. Neagoy's work on her website: www.monicaneagoy.com.

Related ASCD Resources

At the time of publication, the following ASCD resources were available (ASCD stock numbers in parentheses). For up-to-date information about ASCD resources, go to www .ascd.org. This book relates to the **engaged** and **challenged** tenets of ASCD's Whole Child Initiative; to learn more about this initiative, go to www.ascd.org/wholechild. Search the complete archives of *Educational Leadership* at www.ascd.org/el.

ASCD EDge®

Exchange ideas and connect with other educators on the social networking site ASCD EDge at http://ascdedge.ascd.org.

Print Products

Building a Math-Positive Culture: How to Support Great Math Teaching in Your School (ASCD Arias) by Cathy L. Seeley (#SF116068)

Common Core Standards for Middle School Mathematics: A Quick-Start Guide by Amita Schwols and Kathleen Dempsey; edited by John Kendall (#113013)

Concept-Rich Mathematics Instruction: Building a Strong Foundation for Reasoning and Problem Solving by Meir Ben-Hur (#106008)

Engaging Minds in Science and Math Classrooms: The Surprising Power of Joy by Eric Brunsell and Michelle A. Fleming (#113023)

Learning to Love Math: Teaching Strategies That Change Student Attitudes and Get Results by Judy Willis (#108073)

Making Sense of Math: How to Help Every Student Become a Mathematical Thinker and Problem Solver (ASCD Arias) by Cathy L. Seeley (#SF116067)

The Mathematics Program Improvement Review: A Comprehensive Evaluation Process for K–12 Schools by Ron Pelfrey (#105126)

Priorities in Practice: The Essentials of Mathematics, Grades K–6: Effective Curriculum, Instruction, and Assessment by Kathy Checkley (#106032)

Priorities in Practice: The Essentials of Mathematics, Grades 7–12: Effective Curriculum, Instruction, and Assessment by Kathy Checkley (#106129)

For more information: send e-mail to member@ascd.org; call 1-800-933-2723 or 703-578-9600, press 2; send a fax to 703-575-5400; or write to Information Services, ASCD, 1703 N. Beauregard St., Alexandria, VA 22311-1714 USA.